"Thoughtful, balanced, and deeply informed, this book brings clarity to one of the most complex areas of clinical work. The authors skillfully weave research, theory, and therapeutic wisdom into a guide that is both practical and humane. It is a timely and essential contribution to the field."

Rachael C. Marshall, PhD, *associate professor of counseling, California State University, Sacramento*

"Blending compassion, creativity, and clinical wisdom, this book brings a refreshing perspective to counseling clients who share paranormal or anomalous experiences. It's an inspiring and much-needed resource for those committed to meeting clients where they are—with curiosity, respect, and care."

Sarah Danielle Irvin, PhD, LPC, NCC, *assistant professor of counseling, Stephens College*

"Opening up thoughtful and timely conversations about how counsellors can engage with experiences that sit outside conventional therapeutic frameworks, this book offers valuable insights for practitioners working with clients in diverse and sometimes challenging contexts."

Sarah-Anne Munoz, PhD, MSc, MA (Hons), *FRGS, National Centre for Remote and Rural Health and Care, NHS Education for Scotland*

PARANORMAL AND ANOMALOUS EXPERIENCES IN THERAPY

A PRACTITIONER'S GUIDE

Steve F. Bain and Kristopher K. Garza

Routledge
Taylor & Francis Group
NEW YORK AND LONDON

Designed cover image: Getty Images

First published 2027
by Routledge
605 Third Avenue, New York, NY 10158

and by Routledge
4 Park Square, Milton Park, Abingdon, Oxon, OX14 4RN

Routledge is an imprint of the Taylor & Francis Group, an informa business

ISBN: 9781032868356 (hbk)
ISBN: 9781032868349 (pbk)
ISBN: 9781003529477 (ebk)

DOI: 10.4324/9781003529477

Typeset in Baskerville
by KnowledgeWorks Global Ltd.

Dedicated to every counselor, client, practitioner, and seeker who dares to explore the mysterious with courage, humility, and compassion; those who question, listen, and encounter the unexplained, and in doing so find meaning, growth, and healing.

Contents

Preface

There was a time, not so long ago, when even quietly admitting to a paranormal or anomalous experience could result in immediate dismissal—socially, professionally, and clinically. For generations, individuals who reported seeing, hearing, or sensing something beyond conventional explanation were often labeled unstable, delusional, or superstitious. Within many mental health settings, these experiences were viewed almost exclusively through a diagnostic lens. To speak openly was to risk being misunderstood, marginalized, or pathologized. Yet the reality is unmistakable. Surveys consistently show that more than half of all people report at least one anomalous experience in their lifetime. These events are often emotionally intense, sometimes frightening, and frequently life-altering. Still, most mental health professionals receive little to no formal training on how to respond when clients disclose such experiences. As a result, many clients carry not only the confusion of what occurred, but also the fear of whether they will be believed or judged.

This book was born out of that gap. As clinicians, educators, and supervisors, we—Steve F. Bain and Kristopher K. Garza—have spent decades working with individuals whose stories did not fit neatly into diagnostic categories. We have heard countless accounts of unexplained lights, sensed presences, voices without sources, visitations during sleep, and physical sensations without clear explanation. What became clear is that regardless of how these experiences are interpreted, their psychological and emotional impact is undeniably real. Our motivation for writing this book emerged from three intersecting realities: the frequency of these experiences in clinical practice, the lack of training available to address them, and the quiet anxiety many professionals feel about responding "correctly." Too often, clinicians admit feeling unprepared when a client asks, with visible fear, "Am I crazy for telling you this?" This book is written for those moments.

The journey of writing has mirrored the very themes explored within these pages—uncertainty, humility, and meaning-making. We intentionally resisted the pressure to either explain everything away or sensationalize what cannot be easily explained. This is not a book for proving or disproving the paranormal. Instead, it rests on a simple clinical premise: what matters most is not whether an experience can be verified, but whether it affected the client.

Our professional backgrounds inform this work. Steve F. Bain is a professor of counseling with over four decades of pastoral and professional experience, with research spanning rural mental health, trauma, and anomalous phenomena. Kristopher K. Garza is a professor, licensed counselor, and clinical supervisor specializing in trauma, crisis intervention, and counselor education. Together, we bridge theory, practice, and the deeply human stories that unfold in counseling spaces every day. Ultimately, this book exists to give clinicians permission to do what they already do best: listen, remain present, and walk alongside clients without rushing to judgment or forcing meaning. Whether or not an anomalous event can ever be fully explained, the client's emotional reality is real—and it deserves safety, curiosity, and care.

Acknowledgments

To my family and friends, thank you for reminding me why these stories matter and why compassion must always lead the way. And to my love, Angela Flores, thank you for your steady love, encouragement, and thoughtful feedback that sustains me throughout this journey and the future to come.

–Steve F. Bain

To God, who has given me life each day and the strength to pursue my dreams and goals. To my wife Mari, whose love, patience, and unwavering belief in me have made this journey possible. To my family, for their constant support and encouragement to dream beyond limits. And to my friends, who have always believed in my vision and reminded me why this work matters.

–Kristopher K. Garza

Chapter **1**

Are You Serious?
Uh, Yeah!

INTRODUCTION

In July 2010, my family and I (Bain) were enjoying a relaxing vacation at Disney World when I received a phone call that changed everything. My sister told me that our 85-year-old mother was being rushed by ambulance to the emergency room. Just the day before, she had been driving and in good health, but she suddenly collapsed with severe abdominal pain. My sister and middle brother hurried to her house, and as they helped her into the ambulance, she looked at them and said, "I will not be coming back. I am dying." Assuming it was her usual melodramatic flair, they tried to reassure her, but she calmly and firmly repeated, "I will never come back to my house again." That evening, I was able to speak briefly with her by phone and was assured she was stable. But when I called the next morning, I heard the unmistakable alarm of a cardiac monitor in crisis. As my sister-in-law answered, the hospital staff were clearing the room for a code blue. All I could say through the phone was, "Tell Mother I love her." Later that day, she passed away.

I made emergency flight arrangements, but even with the two-hour drive back to my hometown in rural Tennessee, I arrived too late. I arrived with my family, including our 8-year-old son, and we reached the church just two hours before the funeral. I felt robbed of a proper goodbye—the chance to hold her hand, look into her eyes, and kiss goodbye the woman who had given me life. From that moment, my grief seemed frozen in place. My mother was more than a parent; she was my best friend. As the youngest child, I spent much of my early life alone with her while my father worked construction away from home. Though small in stature, just five-foot-two and 115 pounds, she was fiercely protective and strong. Losing

DOI: 10.4324/9781003529477-1

her left an unfillable void in my soul. Two years later, when I went through a divorce and became a single father, that grief deepened into something even heavier. It was during this difficult time that something extraordinary happened. One morning, as I was waking, I heard my mother's voice. A mother can say your name in a way no one else can, and she had a way of saying "Steve" that carried instant meaning—sometimes discipline, sometimes encouragement. But this morning it was unmistakably her loving, reassuring voice: "Steve…Steve." I was awake enough to know I was not dreaming. Standing in that liminal space between sleep and waking, I found myself at a strange crossroads, surrounded by massive, treeless hills. Her voice came from just over the rise to my right. "I'm coming, Mother—where are you?" I called. But she answered firmly: "No, don't come after me. I am all right. You keep going…I'm okay."

I shared the experience with my counselor, but she could not understand. She dismissed it as stress or anxiety. Even as a licensed professional counselor myself, I struggled with how to interpret it. Still, I knew it was real. Nearly five years later, I traveled to Scotland for the first time. On a private tour of the Highlands, our guide drove us north, stopping near the ancestral lands of the McKay clan. As I walked toward an ancient monument, I froze. The landscape was the very crossroads I had seen years earlier, the same treeless hills, covered in heather, exactly as in my vision. Overwhelmed, I told my guide, "I've been here before." A deep peace flooded my soul. In that moment, I knew my mother was safe, and my grief—held captive for years—was finally released. That experience has never repeated itself. I have never again heard her voice. Yet the peace I felt in those Highlands convinced me that life is more than what we see or touch. Existence is layered, meaningful, multi-dimensional, and eternal. Carl Jung would have called it synchronicity, but to me it was a final gift from my mother—a reminder that love endures, and that our souls continue beyond this life.

When Shakespeare penned Hamlet's words spoken to Horatio in Act 1, Scene 5, he made a remarkably profound statement about the paranormal world. At its core, this book grapples with a timeless struggle—finding meaning in experiences that defy conventional explanation yet leave lasting imprints on our hearts, minds, and relationships. The main point being conveyed is that our understanding of the world around us is inherently inadequate and restricted. Despite our efforts to gain knowledge and grasp the complexities of our environment, our perception remains partial and imperfect. As a result, the things we confidently believe to be true might only represent a fraction of the broader reality that eludes our comprehension. In essence, what we think we know for certain about this world in which we live is incomplete and limited at best. We are reminded daily of the thresholds of science, theology, psychology, philosophy, and a host of other sources that attempt to explain and inform our human existentialism. As human beings, we are often compelled to explain life from a neat and tidy practical perspective, longing for a clean and rational explanation for things that are not easily understood or explained. Perhaps the proper view should not be trying to explain the experience as much as trying to identify the meanings and purposes of the experience. So, in light of this realization, uh, yeah…we are serious about this topic!

As authors, we want to thank you for choosing this book as a potential resource for you as a professional. It really is a cutting-edge approach to working with clients who are trying to make sense of experiences that are connected to the fparanormal, high strangeness, and anomalous events. As you begin the journey of this read, we want to make some things clear about our purposes in writing this volume. This book will not delve into the various pathological explanations for individuals experiencing phenomena that fall under the category of high strangeness. Instead, our focus will be on assisting those who work with people whose experiences cannot be attributed to psychotropic drugs or underlying pathological conditions. This specific approach might be unexpected for many practitioners who encounter clients dealing with such extraordinary experiences. Clients often feel isolated due to their unique experiences, and similarly, counselors may struggle to find adequate methods to address these issues during their sessions. Our goal as authors will be to present the material in a manner that is accessible and beneficial to all practitioners who provide support across different fields, whether it be mental, emotional, religious, spiritual, psychological, or medical. We believe that additional specialized training beyond the existing requirements for a licensed or certified therapist, medical professional, or similar practitioner is unnecessary for effectively utilizing this resource. Our hope is that this book will serve as a consistent and valuable tool for you, the reader, throughout your journey. By the end of this chapter, we hope you will come to a practical, professional, and personal realization that paranormal experiences are becoming the norm rather than the exception and that you are not alone in encountering or addressing them.

Regardless of whether you are a mental health professional, a religious leader, life coach, or someone whose calling in life is to encourage others, helping others make sense of life is at the core of what we do. And that includes helping people work through their life events which clash with what we try to identify as "the norm." The fact that you are reading our book tells us that you are likely working with people (probably in a therapeutic capacity) and you are interested in, dealing with, or coming to grips with, one or more paranormal or anomalous experiences that have directly impacted you or the people you work with. It also suggests that you or the people you serve have had some type of unexplained experience yourself. So, before you launch into a full read of this book with any preconceived notions as to its content, context, purpose, or passion, allow us to make some things clear. *First*, this is not a book designed solely for entertainment, though we hope it will be a fun and informative read and resource for you. This will not be an in-depth quantitative and qualitative treatise of the subject which would undoubtedly serve as both a complete bore and a defeat of the purpose to provide you as a service professional with a quick and person-centered approach to serving a unique population of people who are struggling to make sense of a paranormal experience. However, some important (and very general) statistics will be shared in this chapter to provide the foundation of how serious this issue is. *Second*, we want to be clear about what we mean when we say "paranormal!" We are not attempting to emphasize ghosts, demons, spirits, devils, or spiritual entities as much as we are the lived experiences of people who are trying to make sense of whatever happened to them. The working definition of paranormal for us is "the perceived personal experiences of people that are beyond a logical, scientific, or empirical definition or explanation." The word "paranormal" is made up of two words—*para* and *normal*. The Greek word "para" literally means "next to," "side by side," "beyond," or "contrary." The word "normal" is an old 17th-century Latin word (normalis) that refers to a carpenter's square. So, we could accurately say, for our book's purposes, that whatever does not "square up" with conventional thought, experience, philosophy, or spiritualism can be considered *paranormal*. *Third*, this book is not written to prove or disprove the things that go bump in the night. Rather, our mission is to encourage those who serve others to validate people's experiences and feelings associated with the things they cannot identify apart from the paranormal context. By embracing this perspective, we allow both ourselves and our clients to shift the focus from trying to explain these experiences in a strictly rational or empirical manner to exploring the potential meanings and purposes. This approach both honors the subjective reality of the individual and can provide a richer, more supportive understanding of their life experiences. We will touch upon the impact of stigma often associated with making these experiences public, but it would suffice to say that such an approach would be welcomed with open arms by those who sense they are in constant danger of being labeled, ostracized, dismissed, or (in some very real cases such as the military) relieved of their jobs. Our hope is that as you journey deeper into this book, you'll begin to see not just how these experiences happen, but why they echo so powerfully within the human mind—and why they stay with us long after they are over.

This chapter seeks to bring you, the reader, fully into the intensions and focus of the book by attesting to the full validity of what mental health professionals and their clients are experiencing. Those who are looking for a sensational and lurid book on ghostly encounters and scary stories are going to be disappointed. This is not our purpose. It is true we are going to discuss very real stories from people who are, in our estimation, very genuine, credible, and believable. At times, their accounts may be a little unsettling. But our intentions are not to sensationalize or dramatize. Rather, we are seeking to advocate for those whose anomalous life events have been suppressed, repressed, or oppressed. Our hope is that we will provide a resource that encourages readers to tell their stories without fear of ridicule, mockery, and disbelief. Additionally, we want this book to support professional helpers as they offer their services as a haven for those who have far too long felt the devastation of the rejections of their feelings and fears.

AND THUS IT BEGAN

For us as authors, this idea of a book designed to help professionals has been a smoldering passion for the past ten years or so. But it was not until the National Board of Certified Counselors' "Law and Ethics" Conference in 2024 that the doors of opportunity were flung wide open to us. The NBCC conference is a rigorously peer-reviewed and prestigious venue for professional counselors, counselor educators, and counselors-in-training across the nation to have an opportunity to submit proposals and make in-person or virtual presentations on important research topics related to the professional counseling field. Over the past two decades, we have been passionate about helping those in our field of professional counseling to explore new and innovative ways to work with those clients who believe they have experienced some level of paranormal or anomalous experience. This could involve what some would consider hauntings, ghosts, demons, spiritual manifestations, unexplained sounds, voices, smells, and sights, as well as potential unidentified flying objects (UFOs) or unidentified anomalous phenomena (UAPs). We chose a theme and entitled it "An ethical haunting: Counseling clients who present paranormal and anomalous experiences." We were certainly not convinced the subject would be given earnest consideration, even though the conference city was to be held, of all places, in New Orleans, Louisiana!

Our main purpose was summarized in our proposal abstract which stated: "Participants will examine the emotional impact of these paranormal experiences on their clients and review key clinical intervention strategies." Our learning objectives were listed as follows:

1. Participants will review the frequency, impact, and fears associated with clients who present with anomalous or paranormal experiences within the counseling sessions.
2. Participants will address the importance of creating a trusting and safe environment within which clients are able to discuss their experiences.

3. Participants will examine the significance of helping their clients interpret and/or assimilate their paranormal experiences rather than immediately assuming a psycho-pathological stance which can lead clients to feel dismissed, not believed, and judged.
4. Participants will review potential areas of professional development that may produce efficacious clinical experiences with these clients.

Imagine how excited we were to learn that our proposal had been accepted! We were very pleased, but also immediately began to weigh the implications of this presentation. Obviously, the conference leadership took our topic very seriously. On the morning of the first full day of the conference, we arrived early to discover that our session had been reassigned to the larger ballroom because of the number of people who had decided to attend. Over 70 conference attendees decided to join our session both in person and in the synchronous virtual setting. We conducted a very informal and brief survey which simply asked: "How many of you as professionals and/or your clients have experienced something that might be characterized as paranormal or anomalous in nature?" We were stunned when approximately 90% of those attending indicated they had! At this point, it was game on. We led the one-hour, in-person formal presentation and focused on those four learning objectives and themes. We also reminded the mental health professionals, counselors, and counselor educators that we are NOT ghost investigators. Our job is not to prove or disprove what our clients are presenting. Instead, our job is to affirm the feelings, frustrations, and fears that are so often associated with these phenomena. We allowed the participants some 15–20 minutes to come to the microphone and briefly describe their experiences. It was like a surreal moment of emotional-driven discussions which seemed to affirm what these professionals and their clients had experienced. Here is one of those stories:

> Sue is a Licensed Professional Counselor with a thriving private practice in northern Louisiana. Her acceptance and belief in the paranormal would be classified as skeptical at best. Sue had been seeing a 10-year-old female who was brought in to see the counselor by her mother. The mother reported that her daughter had been seeing a dark shadow in her room and particularly at night as she was preparing to go to bed. As the first session (an evaluative session) began, Sue noticed there was an unusual pressure upon the top of her head. But sitting behind her desk, she continued to ask the same essential questions most professionals ask of their clients. Sue noticed that the young lady was pre-occupied and focused on something directly behind the therapist's chair. "Are you okay?" asked Sue to the 10-year-old, who by now had become transfixed on whatever it was that caught her attention. "He's here…and he is standing directly over you and behind you" said

> the girl with a chilling calmness that sent cold shivers down Sue's spine. As she stood before the microphone and recounted her disturbing experience, it was clear that moment was not far from her thoughts. She was, even then, experiencing fear and trepidation to even speak of this anomaly. The girl would later tell Sue that this dark figure often invades her bedroom feels like an ominous and dark presence who tends to follow her...even to her counseling session. Sue told the audience "I tried to keep a brave face, but immediately after the session I got out of there as quickly as I could! I've never been so afraid. It was as if I physically felt this entity touch me, even though I am very skeptical of these types of reports." Once Sue shared her account, others felt more comfortable coming forward and speaking of their own experiences, both professionally and personally.

Consider how much courage it took for Sue to stand before a huge crowd of her professional peers and colleagues and relate that story. What thoughts do you have about her experience? How do they resonate with you and your own experiences?

A WHISP OF RESEARCH

We want to provide you with a whisp of research that will both illustrate the seriousness of true investigators and encourage the reader to search for truth in both empirical and experiential circles. A vast number of articles and wide array of research activity has been employed to make sense of these anomalous phenomena, and the one key takeaway is that a sizable number of people believe in some aspect of the paranormal. Depending on which research paper you read, it is safe to surmise that between half and three-quarters of the population believe in or have ghostly and unexplained experiences. The sheer numbers themselves demand a more serious, open, and accepting approach to working with this population. Throughout the course of mankind's time on earth, these strange experiences have been credited to a host of causes such as demons, angels, aliens, star people, witchcraft, biblical experiences, mental illness, and untold other explanatory suspects. But the world we live in is driven by scientific observation; if you can't quantify it, it isn't real. Consider a person who believes they have had a paranormal encounter, such as seeing a ghost or feeling a presence. From the strictly empirical or scientific viewpoint, these experiences might be dismissed as hallucinations, illusions, or misunderstandings. But these sterile explanations do little to help the experiencer of these events.

Those who have encounters related to high strangeness often ask: *What does this mean in my life? What is the significance for me? What can I learn from this? What will this mean to my interpretation of the world in which I exist?* For the person who has experienced it, such an encounter can be profoundly real and meaningful. They may interpret it as a sign or message, something that impacts their life and worldview. Instead of dismissing or overly rationalizing these experiences, practitioners have an opportunity to explore what these events mean to the individual, how they affect their emotional and psychological state, and what broader implications they might have on their life and beliefs. This is particularly true for those practitioners who work with people to help make their lives better.

Remember our four learning objectives for our presentation? We selected those because they best articulated re-occurring themes that we were seeing in our literature reviews. We suggest, as you navigate the growing research literature, that you consider these four themes as guides to help you flesh out your own theoretical, practical, and personal stand on this highly controversial topic. Here are just some that we, the authors, have found both interesting and compelling.

Not Everyone Who Has a Paranormal Experience Has a Mental Health Issue or Mental Illness

If our conference assembly was any indication of the mental well-being of those who openly admitted to having paranormal or anomalous experiences, it should firmly establish that these individuals were not suffering from delusions, mass hallucination, or schizophrenic episodes. On the contrary, the participants exhibited a wide range of psychological resilience, self-awareness, and groundedness, challenging long-held misconceptions about the mental state of those who report such phenomena. Far too often, there is an erroneous notion that only individuals grappling with mental health conditions—such as psychosis or schizophrenia—report experiences of high strangeness. This stereotype has perpetuated a stigma, discouraging open discussion and further alienating those who encounter unexplained phenomena. However, contemporary research has increasingly debunked this idea, demonstrating that such experiences are not necessarily indicative of psychological instability.

A notable study by Dagnall et al. (2022) has been instrumental in reshaping this narrative. Their research, which examined over 4,500 British citizens, directly challenged the assumption that frequent paranormal experiences correlate with poor mental health. Instead, their findings highlighted the commonality of these experiences across diverse populations, emphasizing that they are not as rare or as pathological as once believed. The study also explored how paranormal belief systems, far from being detrimental, can offer psychological benefits, such as providing comfort, fostering resilience, and offering a framework for understanding life's mysteries. Furthermore, the research addressed the social stigma and stereotyping often directed at individuals who report paranormal or anomalous experiences. By shedding light on the prevalence and potential positive effects of these phenomena, it called for greater acceptance and open-mindedness, urging society to reconsider how we understand and support those who encounter the unexplained. This perspective aligns with the observations at our conference assembly, reinforcing the notion that these experiences are far more nuanced and normalized than the prevailing stereotypes suggest.

Our Role as Counselors is to First Listen and, Second, to Support

Our role as counselors, therapists, consultants, life-coaches, professionals, and helpers is to first and foremost take the time to listen. How can anyone fix a problem if you don't know what the problem is? There must be a clear identification of the issue at hand which only comes after careful and attentive listening skills are employed. One of the most repeated concerns of clients, patients, and experiencers is that they do not feel heard or taken seriously. A study conducted by Roxburgh and Evenden (2021) concluded that even therapists admitted those clients who had an anomalous or paranormal experience felt very apprehensive about disclosing their experiences, even in a therapeutic setting, for fear of how those experiences might be judged.

As scholars and practitioners, we must also understand the fact that much empirical research tends to debunk or cast doubt on paranormal belief and phenomena which may further exacerbate the reluctance of paranormal experiencers to fully disclose. Betsch et al. (2020) focused their research on personal beliefs and the individual differences of those who experience the paranormal. One of their main conclusions stated "believers in the paranormal appear to have lower cognitive ability, motivation, and formal skills to review conceptions in a reasoned fashion" (p. 5). They do, however, confess the limitations of their study include not having a formally validated scale, not being able to identify 80% of the variance in paranormal belief, and a need to understand the motivation and adaptive qualities of paranormal beliefs and experience.

Paranormal and/or Anomalous Experiences May Be Considered Culturally Normal and Non-Harmful

Paranormal and anomalous experiences, often associated with supernatural or unexplained phenomena, can be seen as culturally normal and nonharmful in various societies and contexts. The perception of these experiences is deeply rooted in cultural, spiritual, and historical narratives, shaping how individuals and communities interpret and integrate them into their lives. In many cultures, paranormal experiences—such as encounters with spirits, prophetic dreams, or interactions with mysterious energies—are considered a natural part of human existence. For example, in Indigenous cultures around the world, communication with ancestors or spirits is often regarded as a sacred and meaningful experience. These encounters are not only accepted but are often celebrated as a vital connection to the spiritual realm and a source of guidance or wisdom. Similarly, in societies with strong religious traditions, visions of saints, angels, or divine entities are frequently viewed as affirmations of faith and are met with reverence rather than skepticism.

What is considered anomalous or paranormal in one culture might be entirely normal in another. For instance, belief in reincarnation, energy healing, or telepathy is widely accepted in certain spiritual traditions like Hinduism, Buddhism, or various New Age practices. In these contexts, such phenomena are not classified as "anomalies" but as integral aspects of reality, woven into the worldview of practitioners. This cultural normalization often alleviates any potential fear or stigma associated with these experiences, making them psychologically and socially nonharmful.

From a psychological perspective, whether paranormal experiences are harmful often depends on how they are interpreted and supported within a cultural framework. In societies that accept such phenomena, individuals who report these experiences are more likely to receive validation rather than dismissal. This acceptance can prevent feelings of isolation or alienation and even provide comfort or a sense of purpose. For example, someone who experiences a near-death experience might interpret it as a transformative spiritual event, leading to personal growth and a renewed appreciation for life.

In your role as a professional, you may find that type of acceptance rare, particularly in the United States. In cultures where skepticism prevails, such experiences might be labeled as delusions or dismissed as purely psychological phenomena. This dissonance between personal experience and societal belief can create distress or feelings of invalidation. The key difference lies in the cultural context: whether the society acknowledges and validates the experience as meaningful and acceptable or stigmatizes it as irrational or pathological. Ultimately, the impact of paranormal and anomalous experiences depends on the cultural lens through which they are viewed. When these phenomena are regarded as natural and integrated into cultural norms, they are less likely to be perceived as harmful. Instead, they can serve as sources of meaning, connection, and even healing, enriching the lives of individuals and communities alike.

Those Who Experience These Anomalous Phenomena Often Need to Process Them for Meaning

People who experience anomalous phenomena, such as paranormal encounters, near-death experiences, or unexplained events, often feel a deep need to process these occurrences in order to make sense of them. These experiences can challenge an individual's understanding of reality, prompting them to seek meaning, validation, and integration into their personal worldview. Processing anomalous phenomena can involve reflecting on the event's emotional, spiritual, or psychological impact. For some, the experience may be life-affirming or transformative, offering profound insights about existence, mortality, or the interconnectedness of life. For others, it may be unsettling or confusing, raising questions about what is real, their place in the universe, or whether their experience will be understood by others.

This search for meaning often leads individuals to explore various frameworks, including religious or spiritual traditions, scientific inquiry, or philosophical reflection. In cultures or communities that embrace the idea of the paranormal, individuals may find supportive networks where their experiences are validated and contextualized. This can help them feel less isolated and more empowered to understand the significance of their experiences. Conversely, in societies or environments that dismiss or stigmatize such phenomena, individuals may struggle to reconcile their experiences with dominant cultural narratives. This can lead to feelings of alienation or self-doubt. Regardless of the context, the act of processing anomalous phenomena is a crucial step in integrating the experience into one's identity and worldview, ultimately allowing for personal growth, healing, and a sense of clarity.

A 2009 study by Pew Research Center found nearly 20% of Americans believe they have seen or been in contact with a ghost and 29% felt they had been in touch with someone who had died (Lipka, 2015). Valid research concludes that over one-half of the American population report having at least one paranormal or anomalous experience while a 2022 YouGov research poll found that 67% of Americans are convinced they have had some type of paranormal or anomalous experience they cannot rationally explain (Orth, 2022). Research also indicates the importance of acknowledging and treating paranormal experiences as real. Dagnall et al. (2022) concluded in their study that having an elevated level of paranormal belief does not equate to poor psychological functioning or mental illness. Thus, it is important to understand how this type of maladaptive reasoning may lead to increases in stigma and social ostracization, phenomena we will address throughout the book. In a recent survey conducted by a company related to the housing industry, over 80% of homeowners report they have had paranormal experiences in their own home. Over one-third of those experiences involved hearing sounds, lights turning off and on, and hearing voices that cannot be explained. How can so many families be wrong about what they have seen, felt, and heard?

ROUNDING UP THE USUAL CULPRIT—STIGMA

Individuals who report paranormal experiences, whether ghostly encounters or UFO/UAP sightings, often choose not to share them openly. The primary reason for this silence is the enduring stigma that continues to surround such experiences. Stigma is a term derived from ancient Greek and has historically referred to a mark or brand of shame. In the contemporary context, it signifies a form of social condemnation that marginalizes and ostracizes individuals or groups. This phenomenon is particularly corrosive when applied to those who report paranormal experiences, and it significantly hampers both the willingness of individuals to come forward and the advancement of fundamental research in the field. Stigma is a damnable and destructive social condemnation that is forced on an individual or individuals that is typically societally based and fueled by negativity, prejudicial perspectives, and certain myth-ridden belief systems. Indeed, stigma has been (and continues to be) one of the main reasons there has been so little advancement in the research of the paranormal. For the empirical evidence gurus, if it is not quantifiable, it is not qualified as truth. Paranormal experiences, including ghostly encounters and UFO/UAP sightings, have long been subjects of fascination and intrigue. And even with the widespread public interest and legitimate reports, those who have had these experiences often feel a reluctance to share their stories, especially those who are in the military or work in a public arena. Society tends to categorize and evaluate the validity of experiences based on a combination of empirical evidence and prevailing cultural narratives. Paranormal experiences, by their very nature, often lack empirical substantiation and are thus relegated to the fringes of accepted reality. This relegation is not benign; it actively contributes to the stigmatization of individuals who report such experiences. They are frequently dismissed as delusional, attention-seeking, or mentally unstable, despite the potential validity and significance of their encounters.

The societal disdain for the paranormal is rooted in a complex web of factors, including scientific skepticism, religious doctrine, and media portrayal. Scientific communities often dismiss paranormal phenomena due to their inability to be substantiated through conventional experimental methods. This dismissal is compounded by a cultural emphasis on rationalism and materialism, leading to a prejudicial perspective that views paranormal experiences as antithetical to established scientific understanding. Additionally, many religious doctrines cast paranormal phenomena in a negative light, framing them as demonic or heretical when, in fact, religion itself is the epitome of paranormality. We will address the issues of spirituality, religion, and the paranormal in Chapter Six. The media also plays a crucial role in perpetuating stigma, with sensationalized and often mocking portrayals of paranormal enthusiasts and witnesses further discrediting their accounts.

The impact of stigma on individuals who have experienced the paranormal is profound. Many of the people whom you serve are individuals who suffer in silence, reluctant to share their stories for fear of ridicule and ostracism. This internalized stigma can lead to significant psychological distress, including feelings of isolation, shame, and self-doubt. Furthermore, the social consequences can be severe, with individuals potentially facing rejection from family, friends, and professional communities. To reemphasize the points made earlier, this marginalization not only affects individual well-being but also stifles collective progress in understanding paranormal phenomena. The detrimental effects of stigma extend beyond the individual to the broader field of paranormal research. The academic study of paranormal phenomena suffers from a lack of credible data and empirical research, largely because potential participants are deterred by the negative consequences of coming forward. Stigma acts as a barrier to open dialogue and honest disclosure, leading to a dearth of comprehensive and systematic investigations. As a result, the field remains underdeveloped and often dismissed as pseudoscientific. As mental health professionals, this is where advocacy can be brought to bear.

The helping professions can do much to change collective mindsets and address the stigma associated with paranormal experiences through multifaceted approaches. First, there must be a shift in societal attitudes toward a more open and inclusive understanding of human experiences. Educational initiatives can play a pivotal role in deconstructing prejudicial beliefs and fostering a culture of empathy and respect. By highlighting the historical and cultural prevalence of paranormal experiences, educators can normalize these phenomena and reduce the stigma associated with them. Second, the academic community must engage with paranormal research in a more rigorous and open-minded manner. This involves developing interdisciplinary methodologies that bridge the gap between empirical skepticism and experiential validity. Embracing qualitative research methods, such as in-depth interviews and ethnographic studies, can provide richer insights into the personal and cultural significance of paranormal experiences. Additionally, fostering collaborative research initiatives with organizations dedicated to the study of anomalies can enhance the credibility and visibility of the field. Third, the media has a responsibility to portray paranormal experiences and those who report them with greater sensitivity and accuracy.

Moving away from sensationalist depictions toward more nuanced and respectful representations can help to destigmatize these experiences. Media narratives that validate the lived experiences of individuals and emphasize their psychological and social realities can contribute to a more informed and empathetic public discourse. Many watched with both appreciation and sadness as the UAP hearings were conducted in early 2024. Appreciation as finally the issue of UAP/UFO sightings and experiences were finally being validated. Sadness because of the stigma and shame that is still attached to those who report paranormal experiences of this nature. By addressing stigma through education, rigorous research, and responsible media portrayal, society can create an environment where individuals feel safe to share their paranormal experiences without fear of condemnation. This, in turn, will facilitate a deeper and more comprehensive understanding of paranormal phenomena, enriching both individual lives and collective knowledge.

As the reader, please keep in mind this is a book about the paranormal and anomalous experiences that people have had who are similar to the people you work with. Not all of these experiences are directly related to ghosts. There are other forms of unexplained phenomena that are not easily tucked away into neat and tidy packages within the recesses of one's perceived collective consciousness. An example of this might be the person who has seen, heard, or felt presence that cannot be explained through normal avenues and so society has judged that person as being crazy or afflicted with a mental health malady. Another example might include the vast number of military personnel who have seen and encountered something in the skies about which they have no logical explanation–a true UFO or UAP. Among the harmful byproducts of stigmatization is the sense that one believes their own government seeks to discredit and denounce what they know they have seen and experienced. This leaves witnesses feeling confused, rejected, disbelieved, and fearful. They often become disillusioned, cynical, and angry when the governmental entities whom they have served for so long are now turning against them, ignoring them, or calling into question their character. There is an overwhelming sense that certain governmental and social entities are trying to hide information at all costs.

CONCLUSION

As we have seen in this chapter, the accounts of paranormal and anomalous experiences are both widespread and diverse, defying easy categorization. While these narratives provide a compelling glimpse into the human encounter with the unexplained, they also raise profound questions about the nature of reality, perception, and the limits of our understanding. Chapter 2 delves into the theoretical frameworks that seek to explain these experiences, drawing on insights from psychology, neuroscience, sociology, and quantum physics. By exploring how cognitive processes, cultural influences, and even cutting-edge scientific theories intersect with paranormal phenomena, we aim to uncover the mechanisms that might underpin these extraordinary events. So, let's talk about some theory, dearie!

Personal Reflection Questions for Chapter 1

How do your personal beliefs and professional training shape the way you view paranormal or anomalous experiences shared by clients?

In what ways might normalizing and validating these experiences—without attributing them to pathology—strengthen the therapeutic alliance between counselor and client?

Considering the high percentage of individuals reporting paranormal experiences, how prepared do you feel to engage with such narratives in your own professional practice, and what additional insights or skills might you need to cultivate?

REFERENCES

Betsch, T., Aßmann, L., & Glöckner, A. (2020). Paranormal beliefs and individual differences: Story seeking without reasoned review. *Heliyon, 6*(6), e04259. https://doi.org/10.1016/j.heliyon.2020.e04259

Dagnall, N., Denovan, A., & Drinkwater, K. G. (2022). Variations in well-being as a function of paranormal belief and psychopathological symptoms: A latent profile analysis. *Frontiers in Psychology*. https://doi.org/10.3389/fpsyg.2022.886369

Lipka, M. (2015, October 30). *18% of Americans say they've seen a ghost.* Pew Research Center. https://www.pewresearch.org/short-reads/2015/10/30/18-of-americans-say-they've-seen-a-ghost/

Orth, T. (2022, October 20). *Two-thirds of Americans say they've had a paranormal encounter.* YouGov. https://today.yougov.com/society/articles/44143-americans-describe-paranormal-encounters-poll

Roxburgh, E. C., & Evenden, R. E. (2021). They daren't tell people': Therapists' experiences of working with clients who report anomalous experiences. In Loewenthal, Del (ed.), *What is paranormal?* (pp. 26–44). Routledge.

Chapter 2

How About Some Theory, Deary?

INTRODUCTION

Counseling theories serve as the foundation of professional practice, offering structured and evidence-based approaches for understanding behavior, emotion, and the human experience (Sue & Sue, 2021). These frameworks become particularly meaningful when working with clients who describe experiences that fall outside conventional psychological understanding. Such experiences, often referred to as anomalous or paranormal, may challenge traditional models of thought, yet they also open opportunities for empathy, creativity, and depth within the therapeutic relationship. Through the integrated use of counseling theories, practitioners can help clients interpret these experiences, assign meaning, and promote psychological and emotional healing. Person Centered, Humanistic, and Gestalt approaches emphasize empathy, authenticity, and present moment awareness qualities that create an atmosphere of trust and growth. Carl Jung's concept of synchronicity further expands this lens by suggesting that meaningful coincidences reflect inner psychological patterns that connect to larger realities of human consciousness (Jung, 2010; Taylor, 2020). Alongside these perspectives, Narrative Therapy, Existential Therapy, and Mindfulness Based Counseling offer tools for enhancing awareness, acceptance, and resilience (Palsson, 2025; Rabeyron, 2022). Together, these perspectives provide a holistic way to approach the unusual, often transformative experiences clients bring to therapy.

At the center of all these frameworks is the therapeutic relationship itself. This relationship is grounded in respect and authenticity, allowing clients to explore even the most unconventional experiences without fear of judgment. Validation does not require uncritical acceptance but rather

DOI: 10.4324/9781003529477-2

a willingness to honor a client's lived reality as an important part of their story. When clients feel understood, they are more likely to examine their thoughts, sensations, and emotions in ways that foster personal growth and integration. Working with paranormal or anomalous content presents complexity because it asks the counselor to hold scientific reasoning and spiritual meaning in the same space. The task is not to prove or disprove what happened but to support the client in understanding what it means for them. By drawing from Humanistic, Existential, Narrative, and Mindfulness principles, counselors can meet these experiences with sensitivity, competence, and openness. This approach both acknowledges the potential distress they may cause and recognizes the personal transformation they can inspire (Escolà Gascón, 2021; Rabeyron, 2022).

Counselors must also recognize that these experiences are often deeply intertwined with culture, spirituality, and personal identity. For some clients, paranormal or extraordinary events reinforce faith traditions or family narratives that have been passed down through generations. For others, such experiences may challenge previously held beliefs and create tension between what they once understood and what they have now encountered. A counselor's sensitivity to cultural context, language, and worldview is essential in preventing the pathologizing of beliefs that hold profound symbolic or spiritual meaning (Sue & Sue, 2021). Maintaining this awareness promotes inclusion and ensures that the counseling relationship remains rooted in cultural humility and respect for individual differences. Integrating counseling theory with clients' lived experiences reminds practitioners that meaning is not always discovered through certainty, but through thoughtful exploration. When counselors approach the unknown with compassion, openness, and curiosity, they embody the true spirit of therapeutic presence, which exemplifies the capacity to sit with mystery and still nurture understanding. Within this relational space, counseling becomes both a mirror that reflects the client's inner world and a bridge that connects confusion to clarity, and isolation to a renewed sense of connection and peace.

UNDERSTANDING THE CLIENT'S BELIEF SYSTEM

Before selecting or combining theoretical approaches, it is vital to first understand the client's worldview and belief system. This understanding determines which framework or combination of strategies will best support the client's needs and worldview. For many individuals, beliefs about spiritual or supernatural phenomena form a central part of their identity. If these beliefs are dismissed or minimized, it can create barriers that hinder trust and the depth of therapeutic work (Rabeyron, 2022). Clients may interpret their experiences as signs from deceased loved ones, contact with spiritual beings, or other extraordinary encounters. These interpretations often carry significant emotional or cultural meaning. The counselor's role is not to challenge or confirm such experiences, but to meet the client with curiosity and respect. This posture allows clients to speak freely and to begin integrating their experiences into a broader understanding of self.

Establishing a safe, nonjudgmental space encourages openness and reflection. Through active listening, paraphrasing, and gentle inquiry, counselors can help clients explore their emotions and perceptions. Asking questions such as "What does this experience mean to you?" or "How has this shaped your understanding of yourself or your relationships?" invites deeper reflection. Such dialogue enables clients to discover how their experiences relate to identity, coping, and spiritual connection. When clients sense that their perspectives are genuinely valued, they often experience relief and begin moving toward healing and insight (Rabeyron, 2022). An additional consideration involves the influence of culture, religion, and family in shaping beliefs about the supernatural. What one culture describes as communication with ancestors may be labeled intuition or symbolism in another. Counselors who approach these differences with cultural humility and openness demonstrate respect for the diverse ways human beings interpret the unknown (Sue & Sue, 2021). Exploring these contextual factors can help the counselor understand whether the client's experience aligns with long held traditions, community norms, or personal spirituality. This exploration is not about endorsement or skepticism but about recognizing meaning within the client's frame of reference. Finally, understanding belief systems allows counselors to differentiate between experiences that may be distressing and those that are comforting or identity affirming. Some clients may find great peace in their experiences, while others may feel confusion or fear. Counselors who remain grounded, open-minded, and empathic help clients explore both possibilities safely. By meeting clients where they are, within their unique belief systems, counselors honor the individuality and humanity at the center of every therapeutic relationship.

INTEGRATING THE PARANORMAL WITH PSYCHOLOGICAL FRAMEWORKS

Validation is an essential part of counseling clients who report paranormal or extraordinary experiences. However, validation must be balanced with grounded psychological understanding. Effective integration involves exploring both the subjective meaning of the event and its possible symbolic or emotional dimensions. For instance, a client who believes they are haunted may be processing grief, trauma, or guilt. Within therapy, this can be reframed as the psyche's effort to express unresolved emotion in symbolic form (Rabeyron, 2022).

Jungian theory offers a particularly rich framework for this process. Jung's writings on archetypes and the collective unconscious suggest that symbols and imagery serve as bridges between the conscious and unconscious mind (Jung, 1968; Taylor, 2020). Through this lens, paranormal experiences can be understood as expressions of deeper psychological truths or as encounters with archetypal patterns that represent personal or collective transformation. Counselors using a Jungian approach can guide clients to explore the underlying emotional significance of their experiences rather than focusing solely on external explanations.

Narrative Therapy provides another effective pathway for integration. It invites clients to reframe their stories and assign meaning in ways that foster empowerment and understanding (Shumaker & DeStefano, 2023; White & Epston, 1990). Through the act of storytelling, clients can examine how their experiences shape identity, values, and worldview. By reframing fear or confusion into themes of resilience and meaning, they begin to see their experiences not as evidence of instability but as opportunities for personal growth and transformation.

In some cases, clients may hold beliefs that appear to conflict with scientific or clinical explanations. Rather than engaging in debate, counselors can approach these moments as opportunities for collaborative meaning making. Asking questions such as, "What does this experience reveal about what matters most to you?" allows exploration that honors the client's belief system while maintaining psychological grounding. This process promotes self-reflection and emotional regulation while avoiding polarization between faith and science.

Integrating the paranormal within counseling also requires an awareness of potential trauma. Some clients experience their encounters as distressing or disruptive, particularly when they challenge prior assumptions about reality. Counselors can use mindfulness and grounding techniques to help clients remain present while processing these experiences. Others may describe positive or transformative encounters that deepen spirituality or resilience. In both cases, integration focuses on the personal meaning of the event, the client's emotional response, and the ways the experience contributes to growth and self-understanding. Ultimately, the counselor's goal is not to explain or validate the phenomenon itself but to guide clients toward coherence and wholeness. Counselors use empathy, theory, and clinical skills to help clients gain psychological balance and spiritual understanding.

Person-Centered Therapy

Person-Centered Therapy, developed by Carl Rogers, centers the counseling process on the client's inner world and capacity for self-growth. The foundation of this approach is the belief that individuals are naturally oriented toward health and self-actualization when provided with an atmosphere of acceptance and understanding. Rogers (1961) identified three essential conditions for personal change: empathy, unconditional positive regard, and genuineness. These qualities form the basis for a trusting relationship in which clients can explore their experiences without fear of judgment. For clients describing paranormal or anomalous events, these core conditions take on added importance. Such experiences often carry emotional weight and can provoke confusion or social isolation. When a counselor responds with genuine empathy and curiosity, clients begin to feel safe enough to share what they may have concealed from others (Cooper, 2021). The counselor's role is not to interpret or challenge the client's worldview but to remain present and supportive as the client discovers personal meaning in the experience.

Unconditional positive regard communicates deep respect for the client's reality, even when it diverges from conventional explanations. A counselor might say, "It sounds like that event was meaningful to you," allowing the client to remain the expert on their own story. Genuineness, or congruence, reinforces trust by showing that the counselor is authentic and transparent in interaction (Yao & Kabir, 2022). This honest presence helps reduce defensiveness and deepens the therapeutic alliance. Person-Centered Therapy does not label or pathologize unusual experiences. Instead, it supports the client's self-understanding and sense of coherence. A client who reports perceiving synchronicities or spiritual guidance can be encouraged to explore how these experiences affect identity, purpose, and connection with others. In this way, the approach honors subjective truth while promoting psychological balance and self-acceptance. The emphasis remains on helping clients grow toward greater self-awareness and authenticity rather than analyzing the paranormal event itself (Cooper, 2021).

Humanistic Therapy

Humanistic Therapy shares many values with the person-centered approach but expands its scope to include existential and creative exploration. It encourages clients to examine who they are, what they value, and what gives their lives meaning (Maslow, 2022; May, 2020). For clients reporting paranormal experiences, this orientation can be particularly affirming.

Such encounters often provoke questions about existence, spirituality, and purpose—precisely the kinds of inquiries that humanistic counselors welcome in the therapeutic space. Maslow's hierarchy of needs positions self-actualization as the highest level of psychological development, representing a state of authenticity and inner fulfillment. When clients describe extraordinary experiences—such as near death events, perceived messages from loved ones, or meaningful coincidences—the humanistic framework invites them to explore what these events might reveal about their growth and identity. Rather than dismissing the experience as irrational, the counselor supports reflection on its potential to foster insight or transformation (MacDonald & Pribram, 2023). Humanistic Therapy also emphasizes creativity and authenticity. Clients who have felt dismissed or ridiculed for their experiences often regain confidence when they can express themselves openly in a supportive environment. This approach encourages curiosity and imagination as pathways to healing. A counselor might help a client reflect through art, journaling, or dialogue about what the event symbolizes in their life (Green & Taylor, 2024).

Another vital element of this perspective is the search for personal meaning. Humanistic counselors help clients examine how their experiences influence their values, goals, and relationships. For example, a client who frequently dreams of symbolic images might discover that these dreams reinforce core beliefs about perseverance or love. In exploring such meaning, clients often report a renewed sense of clarity and inner peace. Rather than viewing paranormal experiences as disruptions, the humanistic approach treats them as opportunities to deepen understanding of the self and the human condition (Green & Taylor, 2024).

Gestalt Therapy

Gestalt Therapy, originally developed by Fritz Perls, emphasizes awareness of the present moment and personal responsibility for one's own feelings and behavior. The approach encourages clients to focus on immediate experience rather than intellectualizing the past or projecting into the future (Smith & Malloy, 2023). Through this awareness, clients learn how their thoughts, emotions, and bodily sensations interact in shaping their perception of reality.

For individuals reporting paranormal experiences, Gestalt Therapy offers a grounding and integrative framework. Extraordinary encounters can evoke fear, fascination, or confusion, sometimes leaving clients unsure of what is real or safe. The Gestalt method helps them anchor attention in the here and now, connecting with bodily sensations and emotions that accompany the experience (Kaisler et al., 2023). This grounding fosters stability and allows the counselor to guide exploration without invalidating the client's perceptions.

Techniques such as role playing or the empty chair exercise can be particularly effective. A client who believes they have seen an apparition, for instance, might be invited to engage in a dialogue with that image to uncover underlying emotions or unfinished grief. This process can reveal themes of loss, guilt, or longing that manifest symbolically through the paranormal narrative. The emphasis remains on awareness and integration, not explanation (Ramu et al., 2023). Gestalt Therapy also encourages clients to take ownership of how they respond to their experiences. Rather than positioning themselves as passive recipients of mysterious forces, clients are guided to explore what choices they can make in processing or finding meaning in the event. This shift from passivity to agency helps reduce fear and supports empowerment. Ultimately, the goal is for clients to reconnect with their authentic selves and to integrate even the most unusual experiences into a coherent sense of identity and purpose (Smith & Malloy, 2023).

Carl Jung's Theory of Synchronicity

Carl Jung's theory of synchronicity offers a framework for understanding experiences that appear to link internal states with external events. Jung proposed that such meaningful coincidences reveal patterns within the unconscious that correspond to events in the outer world (Jung, 1968; Taylor, 2020). For clients who report repeated signs, dreams, or spiritual symbols, this concept provides language for discussing experiences that defy linear logic yet feel deeply significant. In counseling, synchronicity can be used to explore meaning rather than to verify supernatural claims. A client who continually encounters a symbol during a period of transition, for example, might examine what that image represents emotionally or spiritually. This reflection often leads to valuable insight into unresolved grief, emerging purpose, or identity development (Taylor, 2020). The process helps clients interpret rather than explain, empowering them to connect inner experience with personal growth. Jung's idea of individuation, the lifelong journey toward integration of the conscious and unconscious, aligns closely with this work. Paranormal experiences can serve as catalysts for individuation, pushing clients to reconcile rational and intuitive aspects of themselves. Counselors can help clients view these moments not as disruptions but as invitations to self-awareness. Through such exploration, clients often experience renewed balance and acceptance of mystery as part of life's complexity (Jung, 1968).

Narrative Therapy

Narrative Therapy, created by Michael White and David Epston, empowers clients to reconstruct their personal stories and separate themselves from problems that have dominated their identity (White & Epston, 1990). The central idea is that people make sense of their lives through the stories they tell. When clients experience events that challenge their sense of normalcy—such as paranormal encounters-these stories may become fragmented or filled with fear. Narrative Therapy helps restore coherence and control. In this process, clients externalize the problem. Rather than seeing themselves as "strange" or "unstable," they begin to recognize the experience as one part of a larger life narrative. By renaming the story, clients reclaim authorship and agency (Shumaker & DeStefano, 2023). A counselor might guide a client to identify strengths that emerged from the experience, such as courage, intuition, or openness to change. This shift from victimhood to authorship promotes resilience and personal empowerment. Narrative Therapy also invites connection with community. Sharing one's story in trusted space support groups, cultural settings, or therapy sessions—can reduce isolation and normalize the experience. When clients see that others have faced similar questions or transformations, they often feel less alone and more grounded in meaning. In this way, the counselor supports healing through story, helping clients integrate their experiences into a larger framework of purpose, identity, and belonging.

An additional benefit of Narrative Therapy lies in its ability to integrate multiple perspectives. Clients are encouraged to examine how social, cultural, or spiritual factors shape the way they understand their experiences. For example, a person raised in a community that embraces spirituality may see their encounter as a sacred message, while another raised in a more skeptical environment might frame it as intuition or coincidence. Exploring these perspectives helps clients move from confusion toward clarity and agency, recognizing that their interpretation is both personal and evolving. Counselors can further support clients by encouraging alternative storylines that highlight strength and hope. Instead of viewing themselves as powerless recipients of an inexplicable event, clients can begin to see themselves as active participants in the process of discovery. This re-authoring of experience often restores dignity and self-trust. Over time, the story becomes not only a record of something extraordinary but also a testament to the client's ability to adapt, grow, and find meaning in the unknown. Narrative Therapy, therefore, becomes a bridge between confusion and understanding, allowing clients to reclaim their narrative voice and continue their journey toward wholeness.

Existential Therapy

Existential Therapy encourages clients to face the realities of human existence directly, freedom, isolation, mortality, and meaning—and to use these realities as opportunities for self-discovery and growth (Frankl, 2020; Watkins & Wang, 2021). This approach invites deep reflection rather than avoidance. Clients are encouraged to explore how they respond to life's uncertainties and to take responsibility for shaping their own path. Paranormal or anomalous experiences often trigger profound existential questions. Clients who report contact with deceased loved ones, meaningful coincidences, or vivid premonitions may struggle to understand what these events reveal about life, death, and purpose. Rather than reducing such experiences to pathology or superstition, the existential counselor creates a space for reflection. The focus remains on personal meaning: What does this experience reveal about the client's values, relationships, or sense of being? (Menzies, 2024).

An essential theme in existential work is responsibility. Clients are invited to consider how they choose to respond to their experiences rather than being defined by them. A person who feels frightened or disoriented after a perceived supernatural event, for example, can examine whether that fear restricts or motivates growth. This process empowers clients to make decisions that align with authenticity and purpose (Watkins & Wang, 2021). For some, these experiences may reinforce spiritual beliefs; for others, they may challenge them. The counselor's role is not to impose interpretation but to accompany the client in exploring the significance of these moments. By approaching uncertainty with curiosity and courage, clients often discover renewed appreciation for life and connection. Existential Therapy transforms anxiety into inquiry and mystery into meaning, helping clients find stability and strength in their ongoing search for understanding (Menzies, 2024). This approach also emphasizes the importance of choice and self-determination. Clients learn that even in the face of the unknown, they possess the freedom to choose their response. This awareness can reduce helplessness and foster empowerment. When a client experiences something inexplicable, such as a vision or synchronistic event, the counselor can help them explore how this encounter informs their sense of direction or purpose. Through dialogue and reflection, clients may uncover values that have remained hidden beneath fear or uncertainty. Furthermore, Existential Therapy encourages acceptance of life's impermanence and the mystery of existence. Confronting death, uncertainty, and isolation can paradoxically awaken gratitude and purpose. For many clients, facing existential questions born from paranormal experiences leads to a deeper appreciation of the present and a more compassionate engagement with others. The process does not aim to resolve mystery but to help clients live meaningfully within it. In doing so, the therapeutic encounter becomes an act of courage that allows clients to embrace both the known and the unknowable as integral parts of being human.

Mindfulness-Based Counseling

Mindfulness Based Counseling offers practical techniques to help clients remain grounded and aware of the present moment while developing a calm, accepting attitude toward their inner experiences (Harris & Lee, 2022; Hyland, 2021). By cultivating awareness without judgment, mindfulness enables individuals to respond to thoughts and sensations with clarity rather than fear or avoidance. For clients who experience anxiety, confusion, or distress related to paranormal events, mindfulness can be profoundly stabilizing. Paranormal encounters (whether perceived visions, sensations, or vivid dreams) often provoke uncertainty. Mindfulness teaches clients to observe these reactions without attaching labels such as "good" or "bad." For example, a person who feels fear after hearing unexplained sounds might learn to focus on breathing, notice the sensations of tension in the body, and allow them to settle naturally. This process creates emotional distance from the event and allows greater regulation of anxiety (Harris & Lee, 2022). Mindfulness also encourages acceptance and compassion toward oneself. Many clients feel ashamed or fearful of judgment when sharing paranormal experiences. Counselors who model nonjudgmental awareness demonstrate that acceptance of experience does not mean agreement with its literal interpretation. Instead, it reflects respect for the client's perception and emotional reality (Hyland, 2021). This fosters trust and safety, allowing for honest exploration. Over time, mindfulness can transform fear into insight. As clients become more attuned to their inner states, they begin to recognize patterns of thought and emotion connected to their experiences. They may find that certain encounters occur during periods of stress or transition, linking the extraordinary with underlying psychological or spiritual themes. Through this process, mindfulness promotes self-awareness and emotional resilience, helping clients navigate the unknown with calm and curiosity (Harris & Lee, 2022; Hyland, 2021).

An additional benefit of mindfulness practice is its emphasis on nonattachment and perspective taking. Clients learn that thoughts and sensations can arise without needing immediate interpretation or reaction. This skill helps reduce reactivity, allowing clients to witness their own inner experience rather than becoming consumed by it. For example, when a client reports feeling a presence or an unexplained energy, mindfulness allows them to acknowledge the experience without judgment, breathe through the moment, and reflect on what emotions or memories it might symbolize. Counselors can also incorporate mindfulness exercises into sessions to help clients stay grounded during moments of emotional intensity. Simple practices such as body scans, guided imagery, or mindful breathing help clients return to the present, fostering a sense of safety and control. These interventions can be particularly effective for clients whose paranormal experiences have triggered trauma responses or heightened sensitivity to environmental stimuli. By teaching clients how to center themselves, counselors empower them to meet these experiences with stability and openness rather than fear. Mindfulness Based Counseling therefore provides an integrative approach that bridges the gap between grounding and meaning making. It equips clients with the ability to regulate emotion, maintain presence, and cultivate compassion, all of which are vital for integrating experiences that challenge ordinary perceptions. Through consistent mindfulness practice, clients learn that peace is not found in avoiding the unknown but in meeting it with awareness, balance, and acceptance.

CONCLUSION

Integrating counseling theories with the lived experiences of clients who report paranormal or anomalous events requires both openness and skill. Each theoretical model—Person Centered, Humanistic, Gestalt, Jungian, Narrative, Existential, and Mindfulness Based—offers a unique framework for exploring the complex emotional, psychological, and spiritual dimensions of these experiences. Together, they remind counselors that such narratives are not deviations from normal human functioning but expressions of deep personal meaning deserving of empathy and understanding. At its core, this work is about presence. When clients share experiences that defy conventional explanation, the counselor's task is not to determine what is real but to understand what the experience represents to the individual. This requires humility, patience, and genuine curiosity. The Person Centered and Humanistic approaches emphasize the healing power of authentic connection and unconditional respect. Gestalt Therapy adds grounding and awareness, helping clients process what they feel in the present moment. Jung's notion of synchronicity provides language for exploring experiences that link inner and outer worlds. Narrative Therapy empowers clients to reshape their stories in ways that affirm strength and coherence. Existential Therapy encourages reflection on the mysteries of life, death, and purpose, while Mindfulness Based Counseling fosters calm and self-compassion in the face of uncertainty.

Across these perspectives, a consistent message emerges:healing begins in relationship. When counselors provide safety and acceptance, clients find permission to explore even the most mysterious experiences without shame. This openness often becomes the catalyst for transformation. The counseling space thus becomes more than a setting for interpretation; it becomes a place where meaning unfolds through trust, empathy, and reflection. As the counseling profession evolves, practitioners are called to expand their understanding of human experience. Integrating the paranormal into counseling practice does not compromise scientific integrity; it enriches it. These experiences often intersect with grief, trauma, spirituality, and identity, and addressing them with sensitivity enhances the counselor's ability to meet diverse human needs. Combining evidence-based approaches with cultural and existential awareness enables practitioners to serve clients more fully, honoring both the psychological and the transcendent dimensions of experience. This integration also encourages counselors to examine their own comfort with uncertainty. Working with clients who describe extraordinary events requires the ability to tolerate ambiguity and to remain grounded in professional ethics while allowing room for mystery. Counselors who model openness teach clients that questions about meaning do not always have definitive answers, and that wisdom can emerge from reflection rather than explanation. In doing so, the counselor becomes both guide and companion in the shared journey toward understanding. Ultimately, this integration reaffirms counseling's most enduring values: empathy, authenticity, and the belief in every individual's capacity for growth. When counselors meet clients where they are, with openness and respect, even the most inexplicable experiences can lead to insight, balance, and healing. Within that shared space of trust, the unknown ceases to be something to fear and becomes instead a path toward self-discovery, peace, and wholeness.

Personal Reflection Questions for Chapter 2

How might traditional counseling theories such as Person Centered, Humanistic, or Gestalt Therapy need to be adapted when working with clients who describe paranormal or anomalous experiences?

In what ways can integrating approaches like Narrative Therapy, Existential Therapy, or Mindfulness Based Counseling help clients find meaning and coherence in their experiences?

What ethical and cultural considerations should counselors keep in mind when building a therapeutic relationship with clients who report unconventional experiences?

REFERENCES

Cooper, M. (2021). *Recent developments in person centered therapy.* Counselling Tutor. https://counsellingtutor.com/recent-developments-person-centred-therapy/

Escolà Gascón, A. (2021). Integrating transpersonal and anomalous experiences into psychological work. *Journal of Transpersonal Psychology, 53*(2), 123–139.

Frankl, V. (2020). *Man's search for meaning* (Reissue ed.). Beacon Press.

Green, J., & Taylor, L. (2024). Humanistic approaches to spiritual and anomalous experience in counseling. *Journal of Humanistic Psychology, 64*(1), 88–105.

Harris, S., & Lee, M. (2022). Mindful presence in trauma informed counseling. *Mindfulness in Clinical Practice, 7*(3), 201–216.

Hyland, P. (2021). Mindfulness and self-compassion in clients reporting extraordinary experiences. *Counselling Psychology Quarterly, 34*(4), 345–360.

Jung, C. G. (1968). *The archetypes and the collective unconscious* (R. F. C. Hull, Trans.). Princeton University Press. (Original work published 1959)

Jung, C. G. (2010). *Synchronicity: An acausal connecting principle* (R. F. C. Hull, Trans.). Princeton University Press. (Original work published 1973)

Kaisler, R. E., Fede, M., Diltsch, U., Probst, T., & Schaffler, Y. (2023). Common mental disorders in Gestalt therapy treatment: A multiple case study comparing patients with moderate and low integrated personality structures. *Frontiers in Psychology, 14,* 1304726. https://doi.org/10.3389/fpsyg.2023.1304726

MacDonald, Z., & Pribram, H. (2023). Self-actualization, meaning making, and anomalous phenomena: A humanistic approach. *Journal of Humanistic Psychology, 63*(4), 415–432.

Maslow, A. H. (2022). *Toward a psychology of being* (Reprint ed.). Wiley.

May, R. (2020). *Existence: A new dimension in psychology and politics* (Reprint ed.). Routledge.

Menzies, R. G. (2024). Existential therapies and emerging research trends. *Journal of Existential Psychology and Psychotherapy, 15*(2), 77–96.

Palsson, O. S. (2025). Anomalous experiences are associated with high subconscious connectedness. *Psychology of Consciousness: Theory, Research, and Practice.* 12(3), 430–451.

Rabeyron, T. (2022). When the truth is out there: Counseling people who report anomalous experiences. *Frontiers in Psychology, 12,* 693707. https://doi.org/10.3389/fpsyg.2021.693707.

Ramu, A., McNamara, S., Gunturu, S., (2023). *Gestalt Therapy.* StatPearls [Internet]. https://www.ncbi.nlm.nih.gov/books/NBK613291/

Rogers, C. R. (1961). *On becoming a person: A therapist's view of psychotherapy.* Houghton Mifflin.

Shumaker, S., & DeStefano, L. (2023). Re storying experiences of the extraordinary: Narrative therapy with anomalous events. *Journal of Narrative Therapy, 12*(1), 34–52.

Smith, P., & Malloy, J. (2023). Gestalt therapy in context: Contemporary practice and applications. *Gestalt Review, 27*(2), 56–72.

Sue, D. W., & Sue, D. (2021). *Counseling the culturally diverse: Theory and practice* (9th ed.). Wiley.

Taylor, M. (2020). *Exploring synchronicity: Symbols, meaning, and transformation.* Routledge.

Watkins, C., & Wang, J. (2021). Existential therapy: Concepts and application. *Journal of Contemporary Psychotherapy, 51*(3), 217–229.

White, M., & Epston, D. (1990). *Narrative means to therapeutic ends.* Norton and Company.

Yao, L., & Kabir, R. (2022). *Person Centered Therapy (Rogerian Therapy).* StatPearls [Internet]. https://www.ncbi.nlm.nih.gov/books/NBK589708/

Chapter 3

An Ethical Haunting

INTRODUCTION

Working with clients who have experienced paranormal-related events presents unique challenges for mental health professionals, particularly those who lack ethics-based training in this area. Counselors and other helping professionals often encounter clients who report encounters with phenomena that fall outside traditional psychological explanations—experiences such as sensing presences, seeing apparitions, having precognitive dreams, or feeling guided by synchronicities. Though these experiences may be viewed by some as supernatural, for clients they often hold deep personal and spiritual meaning. Whether they evoke awe, fear, confusion, or transformation, such experiences can become integral to a client's worldview and emotional life.

Unfortunately, most counselor education programs offer little to no formal training on addressing paranormal phenomena ethically and clinically. This gap in preparation can lead to significant challenges, such as unintentionally dismissing or pathologizing a client's experience, misinterpreting the meaning behind it, or alienating clients who already fear being misunderstood. As counseling continues to expand toward multicultural and spiritually integrated models, it becomes increasingly important to address this gap. Developing an ethical framework for understanding and supporting clients who report paranormal experiences is essential for promoting trust, healing, and professional integrity. Ethical considerations play a central role in cultivating a respectful and culturally competent therapeutic environment. Supporting clients who encounter unexplained phenomena requires counselors to rely on the five moral principles of ethical practice: autonomy, justice, nonmaleficence, beneficence, and

DOI: 10.4324/9781003529477-3

fidelity. These principles serve as the compass that guides the counselor's decision-making, ensuring that client welfare remains at the forefront. By practicing these principles consistently, counselors and helping professionals can provide compassionate and ethically sound care while also safeguarding professional boundaries and maintaining public trust.

AUTONOMY

Autonomy emphasizes a client's right to self-determination—the ability to make their own choices and interpret their experiences according to their beliefs and values (Gladding, 2018). When working with clients who report paranormal encounters, honoring autonomy requires sensitivity, humility, and a genuine respect for diverse worldviews (Vilhauer, 2021; Zur, 2020). Counselors must support the client's freedom to explore and assign meaning to their experiences without fear of coercion, judgment, or disbelief. The first step in supporting autonomy is validation. Counselors demonstrate respect for a client's autonomy when they listen without imposing their own interpretations. For example, if a client reports seeing a deceased loved one, an ethical counselor avoids framing the experience as either "hallucinatory" or "spiritual truth." Instead, the counselor's focus remains on the *meaning* the experience holds for the client and how it affects their life, relationships, and emotional well-being. By taking this stance, the counselor empowers the client to engage in reflection and meaning-making that aligns with their personal and cultural framework.

Autonomy also involves informed consent and transparency. Counselors should clearly communicate their professional role, scope of practice, and therapeutic intentions when exploring these topics. For example, clients must understand that the counselor's purpose is not to confirm or debunk paranormal phenomena, but to help them process and integrate the emotional and psychological impact of the experience. This transparency prevents misunderstandings and helps build trust. Moreover, ethical autonomy involves providing clients with accurate information and a balanced perspective on their experiences. Counselors should refrain from imposing personal beliefs or skepticism, instead encouraging clients to critically examine their experiences and consider various interpretations or explanations that align with their own values and understanding (Vilhauer, 2021).

Additionally, counselors safeguard autonomy by avoiding suggestion or influence. Ethical counselors never attempt to shape a client's belief system, even when their own personal views differ. Instead, they facilitate exploration by asking open-ended, reflective questions such as, "What does this experience mean to you?" or "How has it affected your sense of peace or purpose?" Such questions invite clients to direct their own process of self-discovery. Furthermore, ethical autonomy requires counselors to remain vigilant against any attempts to influence or coerce the client's beliefs or interpretations regarding paranormal phenomena. Instead, they support the client in developing resilience and coping with strategies that align with their values and promote their overall well-being. Below you will find key principles and considerations when counseling clients who are dealing with paranormal experiences, ensuring ethical autonomy.

Respect for Client Autonomy: Ethical practice in counseling requires respecting the client's right to self-determination and decision-making. This includes respecting their beliefs, interpretations, and choices regarding their paranormal experiences. Counselors should avoid imposing their own beliefs or interpretations on clients and instead support them in exploring their experiences in a way that aligns with their values and autonomy.

Informed Consent: It's essential to ensure that clients have informed consent regarding the therapeutic process, including how paranormal experiences may be discussed or integrated into therapy. Clients should understand the goals, methods, potential benefits, and risks involved in addressing these experiences within counseling sessions.

Non-judgmental Attitude: Maintaining a non-judgmental attitude is crucial when working with clients experiencing paranormal phenomena. Clients may fear stigma or judgment related to their beliefs or experiences. Counselors should create a safe and accepting environment where clients feel comfortable sharing openly without fear of criticism or disbelief.

Cultural Sensitivity: Many paranormal experiences are deeply rooted in cultural, spiritual, or religious beliefs. Counselors should be sensitive to the cultural context of these experiences and recognize that interpretations may vary widely across different cultural backgrounds. Understanding and respecting these cultural perspectives is essential in supporting clients effectively.

Avoiding Influence or Suggestion: Counselors should refrain from influencing or suggesting interpretations of clients' paranormal experiences. Instead, they should facilitate exploration and reflection, allowing clients to arrive at their own understanding and meaning. This approach supports ethical autonomy by empowering clients to make their own decisions and interpretations based on their personal experiences and beliefs.

Boundary Setting: Boundaries are crucial in maintaining ethical autonomy. Counselors should establish clear boundaries regarding the scope of their role in addressing paranormal experiences. This may include clarifying that counseling aims to support clients' emotional well-being and personal growth rather than proving or disproving the existence of paranormal phenomena.

Referral and Collaboration: If clients' experiences extend beyond the counselor's expertise or scope of practice, ethical practice may involve referring clients to other professionals or specialists who can provide appropriate support. Collaboration with other professionals, such as psychologists specializing in trauma or psychiatrists, may be necessary if clients' experiences are causing significant distress or impairment.

Overall, ethical autonomy in counseling clients dealing with paranormal experiences involves honoring clients' beliefs, ensuring informed consent, maintaining cultural sensitivity, avoiding undue influence, setting clear boundaries, and collaborating as needed to provide comprehensive support while respecting the client's autonomy throughout the therapeutic process.

Ethical justice in counseling is fundamental to maintaining the integrity of the therapeutic relationship and ensuring the well-being of clients. This principle requires counselors to uphold ethical standards that prioritize respect, autonomy, beneficence, and nonmaleficence. When working with clients who have experienced the paranormal, ethical considerations become particularly nuanced. It is essential to approach these clients with openness and respect for their beliefs, refraining from imposing personal judgments or skepticism. Counselors should validate clients' experiences as real and significant to them, acknowledging the potential cultural and personal context that shapes their interpretations. At the same time, it is crucial to avoid diagnosing paranormal experiences as revealing of mental illness without clear evidence and to focus instead on supporting clients in processing their emotions and understanding the impact of these experiences on their lives. Ethical justice also involves recognizing one's limitations and seeking appropriate referrals or consultation, when necessary, especially if the counselor lacks expertise in addressing paranormal phenomena. By adhering to ethical principles, counselors can create a safe and supportive environment where clients feel validated and empowered to explore and integrate their experiences into their personal growth and healing journey.

ETHICAL JUSTICE

Justice in counseling is grounded in fairness, respect, and the equitable treatment of all clients, regardless of belief or background. When working with individuals who report paranormal or anomalous experiences, justice extends beyond equal access to services; it also involves ensuring that clients are not marginalized or dismissed because their experiences fall outside conventional frameworks of reality. Ethical justice calls on counselors to uphold professional integrity by offering the same level of care and respect to these clients as they would to any other.

Justice requires counselors to be mindful of the social and cultural factors that influence how paranormal experiences are understood. For instance, in many cultures, communication with ancestors, dreams of departed loved ones, or sensing presences are not considered abnormal but part of spiritual life. A counselor unfamiliar with these perspectives risks misinterpreting such experiences as symptoms of pathology. Practicing ethical justice means expanding one's cultural competence to include an understanding of spiritual and anomalous experiences within the client's worldview.

A just counselor avoids bias—neither trivializing nor sensationalizing paranormal accounts. Instead, they assess the impact of these experiences on the client's mental health, relationships, and functioning. Justice also requires the counselor to advocate for clients who have been stigmatized because of their beliefs, helping them reclaim a sense of agency and dignity. In practice, this might mean using inclusive language in intake forms, avoiding dismissive terminology, and promoting awareness among colleagues about the psychological importance of these experiences. Finally, ethical justice includes professional accountability. Counselors must remain aware of their own cultural blind spots and the potential for implicit bias. Engaging in consultation or supervision ensures that personal beliefs do not interfere with professional responsibilities. Justice, in this context, becomes an act of ethical awareness, a reminder that fairness includes respecting the unseen dimensions of human experience as much as the visible ones.

NONMALEFICENCE

Nonmaleficence, or "do no harm," is a cornerstone of ethical counseling and particularly vital when addressing paranormal experiences. The potential for unintentional harm arises when counselors dismiss or minimize clients' accounts, leading to alienation, shame, or emotional distress. Ethical practice requires the counselor to create a safe space where clients can speak freely without fear of ridicule. To prevent harm, counselors should approach paranormal disclosures with an open, curious stance, balancing empathy with clinical discernment. This involves neither accepting every experience as literal truth nor categorically rejecting it as delusion. Instead, the counselor's goal is to understand the *meaning* of the experience in the client's life. For example, a client who feels haunted may not need the counselor to prove or disprove the haunting, but rather to explore how the experience impacts their emotions, sense of safety, and relationships.

Nonmaleficence also involves recognizing professional limits. Counselors should not attempt to interpret paranormal phenomena beyond their expertise. When the client's needs surpass the counselor's scope of practice, perhaps requiring spiritual guidance, trauma therapy, or medical evaluation, ethical care includes referring the client to the appropriate resources. Collaboration with other professionals, including spiritual leaders or parapsychology-informed clinicians, may support holistic healing and reduce harm. Self-awareness plays a critical role here. Counselors must continuously monitor their own reactions, whether fear, fascination, disbelief, or over-identification, to prevent countertransference. Reflective supervision and consultation are essential for maintaining professional balance and ensuring that the counselor's personal worldview does not interfere with the client's growth. Ethical counseling in this area demands humility: recognizing that the counselor's role is not to define reality but to promote the client's psychological safety and well-being.

BENEFICENCE

Beneficence goes beyond avoiding harm; it asks counselors to actively promote the client's well-being and support growth. In cases involving paranormal experiences, this means providing compassionate, tailored care that acknowledges the emotional, spiritual, and psychological dimensions of the experience. Clients usually seek therapy to understand how paranormal experiences impact their lives, rather than seeking validation of those events. A beneficent counselor works to strengthen the client's coping skills and resilience. This might include mindfulness strategies, journaling, or relaxation techniques to manage fear and anxiety related to their experiences. By focusing on emotional regulation and self-understanding, the counselor helps the client regain control over their internal world. In some cases, integrating culturally or spiritually appropriate coping methods, such as prayer, meditation, or rituals, can also enhance well-being, as long as they align with the client's belief system.

Beneficence also includes educating clients about the range of possible interpretations for their experiences without invalidating them. For example, a counselor might discuss how grief, trauma, or heightened emotional states can make one more open to unusual perceptions, while still acknowledging the profound comfort or meaning those experiences may hold. Such balanced dialogue encourages insight and helps clients process experiences constructively.

Importantly, beneficence calls counselors to advocate for inclusion and understanding within the profession. Promoting research, training, and dialogue about paranormal experiences in counseling education contributes to the broader goal of client welfare. The more informed the profession becomes, the more effectively it can meet the needs of clients who bring these experiences into the therapy room. At its heart, beneficence is about promoting healing, helping clients integrate extraordinary experiences into their life story in a way that strengthens identity, purpose, and psychological health. When practiced with empathy and ethical mindfulness, beneficence transforms the counseling relationship into a bridge between the unknown and the understood, where clients find both validation and empowerment.

FIDELITY

Ethical fidelity in counseling emphasizes the importance of establishing trust, maintaining confidentiality, and fostering a professional relationship grounded in honesty and respect (American Counseling Association, 2014). When counseling clients who have experienced paranormal phenomena, this ethical principle becomes especially significant in several essential aspects. First, counselors uphold ethical fidelity by creating a safe and confidential space where clients feel comfortable sharing their paranormal encounters without fear of judgment or disclosure. Respecting client confidentiality is paramount, as these experiences can be deeply personal and sensitive, potentially impacting various aspects of their lives. Second, maintaining fidelity begins with consistency and reliability. Counselors demonstrate fidelity when they follow through on promises, uphold confidentiality, and remain emotionally present for clients. In cases involving paranormal phenomena, where the client may already feel misunderstood or marginalized, the counselor's dependability becomes a source of safety and stability. Even subtle signs of disbelief or discomfort can weaken the therapeutic alliance. Therefore, the counselor's commitment to honesty and compassion must remain unwavering. Third, ethical fidelity also involves clarifying roles and limitations. Counselors should be upfront about what counseling can and cannot provide in relation to paranormal events. For example, they might explain that while they cannot confirm supernatural causes, they can help the client process the experience's emotional and psychological impact. This transparency fosters mutual understanding and helps prevent false expectations. It also reminds the client that the counselor's role is to support, not to validate or refute, the experience's objective reality. Moreover, fidelity demands self-awareness and accountability. Counselors must regularly examine their own beliefs, biases, and emotional responses to ensure these do not distort their professional conduct. When working with clients who report experiences outside the norm, curiosity and humility serve as the counselor's best allies. Upholding fidelity means remaining faithful not only to the client but also to the ethical standards and values that define the profession.

RESPECT FOR CLIENT BELIEFS

A cornerstone of ethical practice in therapy is the therapist's respect for the client's worldview, including beliefs in the paranormal. Mental health professionals are tasked with creating an environment where clients feel safe to express themselves fully, without fear of judgment or invalidation. When clients share their experiences of paranormal events, they may be doing so in a vulnerable way, especially if they have encountered skepticism or disbelief from others in their personal lives. Therefore, therapists must adopt a nonjudgmental stance that recognizes and validates the client's experiences, regardless of whether they are perceived as paranormal by mainstream standards. In this context, it is important to recognize that paranormal experiences are often tied to the client's cultural, spiritual, or personal framework. For example, belief in ancestral spirits is common in many Indigenous cultures, and such experiences may have deep spiritual significance. Similarly, synchronicities, or the meaningful coincidence of events, may be seen as a form of divine communication or guidance in some belief systems, such as those influenced by Carl Jung's psychological theories. Given the diverse cultural and spiritual backgrounds of clients, mental health professionals must take the time to understand the context in which paranormal experiences are situated, recognizing that they may be integral to the client's sense of meaning, identity, and personal narrative.

Key Strategies

***Cultural Competence*:** It is essential for therapists to familiarize themselves with the cultural and spiritual frameworks in which paranormal beliefs may be situated. This understanding allows for a deeper appreciation of the client's experience and provides a more accurate context for exploring these phenomena. For instance, if a client reports experiencing the presence of a deceased loved one, the therapist should consider the cultural practices surrounding death, grieving, and afterlife beliefs within the client's tradition.

***Empathy and Validation*:** An empathetic response is essential when clients discuss their paranormal experiences. Rather than dismissing the experience as delusional or fantastical, the therapist should strive to validate the emotional impact of the experience. A simple reflection such as, "That sounds like it was a profound experience for you," can go a long way in affirming the client's feelings and fostering trust.

INFORMED CONSENT AND BOUNDARIES

Informed consent and professional boundaries are essential pillars of ethical counseling practice. These principles protect both the client and counselor while promoting transparency and safety in the therapeutic process. When working with clients who report paranormal experiences, informed consent ensures that expectations are realistic and clearly defined. At the outset, counselors should communicate their role and the scope of therapy. Clients may come to counseling seeking validation of a paranormal event or assistance in interpreting its meaning. Ethical practice requires that counselors clarify they are not investigators or spiritual authorities, but professionals trained to address the emotional and psychological effects of such experiences. This discussion helps prevent misunderstanding and reinforces the collaborative nature of therapy. Establishing boundaries is also crucial when clients request interventions that fall outside the therapist's training or professional competence. Some clients may seek spiritual or metaphysical guidance, such as rituals, energy healing, or mediumship. While these practices may be meaningful to the client, it is important for the therapist to communicate the limits of their expertise and offer referrals when appropriate.

Key Strategies

Clarify the Therapist's Role: Therapists should be explicit about their role in therapy and make it clear that they are not there to validate or dismiss the paranormal nature of the client's experiences. The therapeutic process should focus on the psychological and emotional impact of the experiences, rather than verifying their objective reality.

Transparent Communication: If a client requests spiritual or metaphysical interventions that are outside the therapist's training, it is important to communicate the limitations of professional expertise. For example, a therapist might say, "I am not trained in spiritual practices, but I can refer you to a trusted professional who specializes in that area." Clear communication of professional boundaries fosters trust and ensures that the client's needs are addressed in an ethical manner.

AVOIDING PATHOLOGIZATION

Perhaps one of the most delicate ethical challenges in working with paranormal experiences is the risk of pathologization—interpreting a client's report as a symptom of mental illness rather than a meaningful personal event. While it is vital for counselors to assess potential psychological disorders, premature labeling can cause significant harm, invalidating the client's experience and eroding trust. Avoiding pathologization does not mean abandoning clinical judgment. Instead, it involves balancing careful assessment with empathy and curiosity. A counselor might ask: *Does this experience impair the client's functioning or cause significant distress? Does it align with the client's cultural or spiritual background?* These questions help distinguish between a clinical symptom and a non-pathological experience that may still carry emotional weight.

Key Strategies

Holistic Assessment: It is critical to differentiate between paranormal experiences and symptoms of mental health conditions, such as psychosis or dissociative disorders. This requires a comprehensive evaluation of the client's history, context, and functioning. The therapist should explore the emotional, psychological, and social impact of the experience, and assess whether it is impairing the client's ability to function in daily life.

Strength-Based Approach: Rather than automatically labeling paranormal experiences as problematic or pathological, therapists should adopt a strength-based approach. This means viewing the experience as potentially meaningful, transformative, or integrative for the client, rather than something to be "cured" or eliminated. By exploring the positive aspects of the experience, such as personal growth or insight, therapists can help clients find meaning and purpose in their experiences. Counselors can also adopt a strength-based perspective, viewing the experience as an opportunity for growth rather than an indicator of pathology. For instance, a client who reports seeing apparitions during grief might be encouraged to explore the symbolic or comforting aspects of those encounters. This approach affirms the client's emotional reality while maintaining ethical responsibility.

Pathologization can be avoided through collaboration as well. Consulting with colleagues, supervisors, or culturally informed practitioners provides additional perspectives and safeguards against bias. In doing so, counselors honor both scientific integrity and cultural sensitivity. When clients feel heard rather than judged, they are more likely to engage openly and find healing through the process. Ultimately, avoiding pathologization reflects a deeper ethical stance: one that sees the client not as a collection of symptoms, but as a whole person whose experiences—ordinary or extraordinary—deserve empathy, respect, and understanding.

CONFIDENTIALITY AND CULTURAL SENSITIVITY

Confidentiality is one of the most sacred ethical obligations in counseling. When clients disclose paranormal experiences, they may already carry a heavy burden of secrecy, fearing disbelief or ridicule from others. The assurance of confidentiality allows them to speak freely, creating a foundation of trust that enables deeper exploration and healing. Counselors must protect these disclosures with the same diligence as any other sensitive information, maintaining clear ethical boundaries regarding privacy and professional integrity.

Cultural sensitivity adds to another essential layer. Paranormal experiences often intersect with cultural and spiritual traditions, shaping how individuals interpret and respond to them. A counselor unfamiliar with these traditions risks misunderstanding or inadvertently offending the client. Ethical sensitivity requires a willingness to learn from the client's worldview, to ask questions respectfully, and to remain open to perspectives that differ from one's own. This practice not only protects client dignity but also enhances the counselor's effectiveness in fostering meaningful dialogue. Cultural humility is an ongoing process, not a fixed achievement. It involves recognizing that clients are experts in their own experiences and that the counselor's role is to listen, learn, and provide support through a lens of empathy rather than authority. By maintaining confidentiality and approaching each session with cultural humility, counselors help ensure that clients feel valued, respected, and safe to explore even their most extraordinary experiences.

Key Strategies

Secure Communication: The therapist must maintain the same level of confidentiality when discussing paranormal experiences as with any other aspect of the client's personal history. Clients must feel assured that their experiences will be respected and protected within the therapeutic relationship.

Cultural Awareness: Recognizing that paranormal beliefs may be central to a client's cultural identity is essential for fostering an inclusive and respectful therapeutic environment. Therapists should avoid making assumptions about the validity of the client's beliefs and instead approach the discussion with curiosity and openness.

ETHICAL COMPETENCE THROUGH TRAINING AND SUPERVISION

Competence is not static; it evolves with continued learning, reflection, and engagement. For most mental health professionals, formal training rarely includes instruction on how to ethically address paranormal experiences in therapy. This lack of preparation can lead to uncertainty, discomfort, or missteps that compromise ethical care. Developing competence in this area is therefore an act of professional responsibility. Therapists can enhance competence by seeking continuing education, attending specialized workshops, and engaging with scholarly literature that explores the intersection of psychology, spirituality, and anomalous experience. This professional development strengthens a counselor's ability to respond with both curiosity and discernment. It also helps normalize conversations about experiences that, though uncommon, are deeply meaningful to many clients.

Supervision and peer consultation are equally valuable. Working with supervisors or colleagues who have experience in spiritual or transpersonal counseling can provide fresh perspectives and ethical guidance. Case consultations allow counselors to reflect on challenges such as countertransference, cultural misunderstanding, or boundary navigation. Through these discussions, counselors cultivate a deeper awareness of their own limitations and biases, ensuring they remain grounded and ethical in practice. Ultimately, competence in this area involves both knowledge and humility. It means being willing to admit when additional expertise is needed and to seek appropriate referrals when necessary. Ethical competence is not about having all the answers—it is about remaining teachable, reflective, and committed to the client's best interest.

Key Strategies

Continuing Education: Therapists should seek out resources, such as workshops or books, that address the ethical and psychological aspects of working with clients who report paranormal experiences. Staying informed about emerging research and practices in this area can enhance the therapist's ability to respond effectively.

Supervision and Peer Consultation: Given the complexities of working with paranormal phenomena, it is beneficial for therapists to seek guidance from supervisors or peers who have experience in this area. Supervision can help therapists process challenging cases, reflect on their approach, and maintain ethical standards in their practice.

BALANCING SKEPTICISM AND OPEN-MINDEDNESS

A central ethical challenge in counseling clients who report paranormal experiences is finding balance between professional skepticism and open-mindedness. Counselors are trained to ground their work in evidence-based practice, yet they must also remain open to experiences that defy conventional explanation. Ethical practice means respecting both the limits of science and the breadth of human experience. Skepticism, when applied ethically, protects clients from harm and ensures that interventions remain grounded in psychological understanding. Open-mindedness, on the other hand, allows for genuine empathy and connection. The goal is not to prove or disprove a client's account but to explore its meaning and impact. Maintaining this balance requires emotional maturity and self-awareness. A counselor who leans too heavily toward skepticism may alienate the client, while one who becomes overly affirming may blur professional boundaries or reinforce beliefs that increase distress. The most ethical approach lies in curiosity. Asking questions like "What was that experience like for you?" or "How has this changed your outlook?" keeps the focus on the client's interpretation rather than the counselor's. This stance also encourages critical reflection, helping clients develop insight and resilience. Balancing skepticism and openness models an ethical form of neutrality, a position that honors the client's truth while upholding professional responsibility. It reminds both counselor and client that the goal of therapy is not certainty but understanding, healing, and meaning.

Key Strategies

Non-Directive Exploration: The therapist should encourage clients to explore their own interpretations of their paranormal experiences, without imposing the therapist's own beliefs or skepticism. This approach allows the client to take ownership of their narrative and make sense of the experience in a way that is personally meaningful.

Focus on Impact: Rather than debating the objective reality of paranormal experience, therapists should focus on the emotional and psychological impact of the experience. By addressing the effects of the experience on the client's well-being, therapists can help clients integrate the experience into their broader life narrative.

CASE EXAMPLES

Case Study 1: Spiritual Encounter

A client reports seeing the spirit of a deceased loved one during a time of deep grief. The experience brings comfort but also confusion. Rather than challenging the experience, the counselor helps the client process its emotional significance. Through reflective listening and empathy, the client can explore how the encounter symbolizes love, memory, and unresolved grief. Together, they identify coping strategies and rituals for honoring the relationship, fostering healing without judgment.

Case Study 2: Synchronicities

A client describes a series of meaningful coincidences that seem to point toward a major life change. The counselor uses a person-centered and narrative approach, helping the client examine how these experiences align with their values and goals. Instead of validating or refuting the synchronicities, the counselor focuses on the client's decision-making process and sense of empowerment. By the end of therapy, the client feels more confident interpreting such events as symbolic guides for growth and self-understanding.

CONCLUSION

Working ethically with clients who report paranormal or anomalous experiences requires both compassion and courage. The counselor's task is not to interpret the unexplained but to provide a safe, structured space where clients can explore the personal and emotional meaning of their experiences. Through the application of the five moral principles—autonomy, justice, nonmaleficence, beneficence, and fidelity, counselors safeguard client welfare while promoting respect for diverse worldviews. This chapter emphasizes that ethical competence in this area is not achieved through certainty, but through humility and openness. Counselors must be willing to sit with ambiguity, to listen deeply, and to validate human experience in all its complexity. Whether a client's experience is viewed as spiritual, psychological, or symbolic, the counselor's role remains the same: to meet the client with empathy, ethical integrity, and professional care.

As the helping professions evolve, there is a growing recognition that human experience extends beyond the measurable. Counselors are called not to resolve the mystery of the paranormal, but to respond to it ethically with sensitivity, inclusiveness, and respect. Developing training, supervision, and dialogue around these topics strengthens not only clinical competence but also the professional's commitment to understanding the full range of human experience. Ultimately, ethical practice in this area is about honoring the client's story. When counselors uphold integrity, maintain compassion, and respect cultural and spiritual diversity, they help transform what might feel isolated into something deeply meaningful. In doing so, they affirm the counselor's most sacred ethical duty to do good, avoid harm, and hold space for the mystery that lives within the human spirit.

Personal Reflection Questions for Chapter 3

How can counselors maintain ethical neutrality when a client's paranormal experiences challenge their personal beliefs or worldview?

In what ways might cultural humility and collaboration with spiritual leaders enhance ethical care for clients reporting paranormal phenomena?

How can supervision and continued education strengthen a counselor's ability to balance skepticism with empathy when addressing anomalous experiences?

REFERENCES

American Counseling Association. (2014). *ACA Code of Ethics.* https://www.counseling.org/docs/default-source/default-document-library/ethics/2014-aca-code-of-ethics.pdf

Gladding, S. T. (2018). *Counseling: A comprehensive profession* (8th ed.). Pearson.

Vilhauer, R. P. (2021). *The power of belief: A therapeutic approach to unexplained experiences.* Routledge.

Zur, O. (2020). *Boundaries in psychotherapy: Ethical and clinical explorations.* American Psychological Association.

Chapter 4

The GHOST Method

This chapter will emphasize on the vital importance of equipping counselors with fundamental principles that guide their work with clients presenting anomalous or paranormal experiences. Working with individuals who have had unusual or unexplained encounters requires an approach that is nuanced, empathetic, and respectful of the client's perspective. As in all successful people-helping work, the foundation of effective therapeutic relationships is built upon trust, collaboration, and the ability of the counselor to create a safe space for the client. This chapter will explore how counselors can foster these elements specifically when working with clients who have experienced paranormal or anomalous phenomena—experiences that may be met with skepticism or disbelief from others.

INTRODUCING THE GHOST METHOD

At the core of this approach is Carl Rogers' person-centered therapy, a model of counseling that emphasizes the importance of the therapeutic relationship itself. According to Rogers, the therapist's role is not to provide all the answers, but to offer a space where the client feels heard, understood, and accepted without judgment. What approach could be better suited for those who are struggling to understand a paranormal experience or integrate that which their logical mind cannot seem to comprehend? This perspective creates a foundation of trust that allows for deep therapeutic work to occur. The authors have built upon Rogers' principles, drawing from their own clinical experiences working with clients struggling to make sense of paranormal events. As a result, they have developed a

DOI: 10.4324/9781003529477-4

specialized framework for counselors working with this unique population, encapsulated in the acronym GHOST. Each letter in GHOST represents a key principle that counselors can apply specifically to the therapeutic process when dealing with clients who report anomalous experiences. These principles, while rooted in basic counseling skills, are tailored to the particular challenges and nuances of working in this specialized area. The chapter will not only outline the GHOST method but will also support it with examples, case studies, and real-world applications to give counselors concrete tools for their practice. With that said, let's get started with the five basic principles of effective paranormal therapy as alliterated by the GHOST Method.

G: Genuine Graciousness

The first principle, Genuine Graciousness, serves as the cornerstone of any strong counseling relationship. It is not merely a superficial gesture of kindness; rather, it is the foundation upon which a therapeutic relationship is built. Genuine graciousness refers to the counselor's ability to establish a deep, authentic connection with the client, one that is rooted in trust, warmth, and empathy. This is a critical element in any counseling relationship, but it is especially vital when you are working with clients who present paranormal or anomalous experiences. Their experiences are often shrouded in mystery, skepticism, and, at times, fear, and clients may feel vulnerable or even isolated in sharing them. Therefore, it becomes even more important that you, the professional, foster an environment of acceptance and understanding.

For counselors, establishing genuine graciousness means creating an atmosphere where clients can feel safe, heard, and valued. This is more than just going through the motions of therapy—it requires the counselor to be present in the moment, engaging with the client in a way that conveys authenticity and respect. In a world where many individuals are quick to dismiss or minimize experiences they don't understand, especially paranormal ones, the counselor's ability to validate the client's reality without judgment is paramount. A client who feels heard and accepted is far more likely to open up to you about their experiences and trust the therapeutic process. Conversely, if you convey any form of insincerity or disinterest, clients can quickly pick up on this disconnect, and it can severely damage the therapeutic alliance. Clients who report paranormal or anomalous experiences often encounter skepticism not only from the general public but sometimes even from mental health professionals themselves. Paranormal experiences—such as encounters with ghosts, extraterrestrial beings, or other unexplained phenomena—are inherently difficult to discuss within mainstream social or cultural contexts. Roxburgh and Evenden (2016) reported that people who report such anomalous experiences (AE) may feel marginalized, doubted, or even ridiculed. Consequently, when a client seeks therapy to discuss an experience that may be considered outside the bounds of normal reality, they may already be feeling a heightened sense of vulnerability. They may fear that their therapist will dismiss their experience as a delusion, a misperception, or even a sign of mental illness. In this context, your ability to demonstrate genuine graciousness can make all the difference.

By offering unconditional positive regard—an essential aspect of Carl Rogers' person-centered therapy—the counselor affirms the client's experience as real and worthy of attention. This does not mean that you should believe in the paranormal yourself, but it does mean that you should respect your client's perception of reality. By approaching the session with the assumption that the client's experience is meaningful to them, regardless of whether you can personally validate or understand the experience, speaks volumes to the people you work with. This approach helps prevent the client from feeling judged or dismissed, which can be especially damaging in the context of discussing something as potentially stigmatized as paranormal phenomena. A counselor who demonstrates genuine graciousness also creates a space for the client to explore their emotions fully. Often, clients presenting paranormal experiences are not merely looking for someone to listen to the facts of their encounter; they are seeking emotional support and validation for the feelings that accompany those experiences. These emotions may include confusion, fear, awe, or even a sense of empowerment or transformation. A counselor who responds with phrases such as, "That must have been frightening," or "I can see why that would feel overwhelming," helps the client feel that their emotional reactions are valid and worthy of attention. Another response might be: "Can you articulate the feelings you were having during and after the experience such as sadness, joy, happiness, anxiousness, etc.?" By normalizing these feelings and acknowledging their significance, the counselor fosters a sense of emotional safety, which in turn encourages the client to explore their experience more deeply. This kind of empathetic response, built on genuine graciousness, is essential for building a trust-based therapeutic relationship.

Moreover, a therapist's genuine graciousness involves not only being receptive to the client's feelings but also actively engaging in the therapeutic process with compassion and humility. The counselor must be open to the idea that, even if they have never personally experienced paranormal phenomena, they do not have all the answers. They must approach the session with curiosity, compassion, and a willingness to be open-minded. This approach allows the counselor to provide emotional support while also maintaining a stance of professional integrity and objectivity. By setting aside their personal beliefs about the supernatural and instead focusing on the client's emotional and psychological experience, the counselor can more effectively help the client process their encounter and its significance in their life. Genuine graciousness is also about avoiding any form of dismissal or disbelief when clients present their experiences. While some counselors may feel uncomfortable or skeptical when clients share stories of paranormal events, it is crucial for the counselor to remain neutral and nonjudgmental. Any form of disbelief or premature dismissal can damage the therapeutic relationship and lead to feelings of shame, guilt, or embarrassment on the part of the client. When a counselor responds with comments like "That sounds impossible," or "I don't believe in ghosts," the client is likely to feel invalidated, and may even become reluctant to share further details or express their thoughts and feelings in future sessions.

The challenge for counselors in these situations is to remain nonjudgmental, even in the face of experiences that seem extraordinary or outside the realm of typical human experience. This is where the concept of *bracketing*—setting aside one's own personal beliefs and biases—becomes particularly important. The counselor must approach the client's experience from a place of neutrality, allowing the client to explore their feelings, fears, and interpretations without the counselor imposing their own worldview. The counselor might not share the client's belief in the paranormal, but they can still respect the significance of the experience for the client and help them explore it in a therapeutic context. Creating a space where the client feels accepted and valued involves more than just validating their emotions. It also means demonstrating active listening skills and empathic engagement. We will discuss active listening in more detail in the next section. Suffice it to say active listening is a key skill in any therapeutic relationship, and it involves not just hearing the words the client is saying but also paying attention to the underlying emotions, thoughts, and experiences that those words may represent. Empathy, on the other hand, takes active listening a step further. It involves understanding and sharing in the client's emotional experience. When a counselor listens with empathy, they strive to feel what the client is feeling, without judgment or analysis. In the case of paranormal experiences, this can mean understanding the fear or confusion that the client might feel when encountering something they don't fully understand or that challenges their sense of reality. An empathic counselor not only listens but also expresses understanding and emotional support in a way that encourages the client to explore their feelings and thoughts openly.

Ultimately, genuine graciousness is about creating a therapeutic environment where the client feels safe enough to explore their most vulnerable thoughts and feelings, including those related to paranormal experiences. It's about being fully present in the moment and providing the client with a sense of acceptance, respect, and understanding. This foundational quality not only strengthens the counselor-client relationship but also opens the door for deeper therapeutic work, allowing clients to explore, process, and ultimately integrate their paranormal experiences in a way that is healing and empowering. Whether or not you as the professional personally believe in the supernatural, your willingness to approach the people you are helping with genuine graciousness allows these individuals to feel that their experience is legitimate, their emotions are valid, and their journey of exploration is worthy of attention. In this way, the counselor can help guide the client toward a greater sense of self-understanding, empowerment, and acceptance.

H: Holistic Hearing

For these authors, Holistic Hearing is actually a more advanced form of Active Listening in that we are not just talking about sitting up, paying attention, and parroting back what is said. Rather it is a vital skill for effective communication, especially in contexts where individuals may feel misunderstood or dismissed. At its core, holistic hearing involves fully engaging with the speaker, demonstrating genuine interest, and providing responses that affirm their feelings and experiences. This practice includes giving the client space to express themselves, refraining from interrupting, and reflecting back key emotions and statements to ensure mutual understanding. While this level of listening and hearing is universally beneficial, it takes on unique importance when dealing with individuals sharing paranormal experiences, as these encounters are often accompanied by feelings of isolation, disbelief, or skepticism from others. Let's explore some key results from this level of listening:

Creating a Safe and Open Environment

One of the foundational aspects of holistic hearing is creating a safe environment where the client feels comfortable sharing their thoughts and emotions. This is particularly important for individuals recounting paranormal experiences, as they may already fear ridicule or rejection. Offering this space begins with maintaining nonverbal cues, such as steady eye contact, an open posture, and nodding at appropriate times. These signals demonstrate attentiveness and empathy, fostering trust between the listener and the speaker. Moreover, it is essential to approach the conversation with an open mind, suspending personal judgments or biases. Whether or not the listener believes in the paranormal, the priority should be validating the client's feelings and perceptions. Take a moment to try this out by reviewing a couple of options:

Option 1 (Dismissive): Your client has just told you about a paranormal experience and how it has visibly shaken them and created more questions and answers. Your initial response is: "Well, it may just be your imagination?" Or perhaps you might say, "You know these types of things are not real." What response from your client might you expect? Try to put yourself in their seat for a moment and ask yourself: "What if I had a paranormal experience and my counselor responded like that? What might I feel, what might I think? Would I feel validated?"

Option 2: (Accepting): In this option, the professional focuses on the emotional impact of the experience. A response like, "It sounds like that situation was really unsettling for you," or "How does this make you feel?" acknowledges their perspective without invalidating it. If you can imagine you are the one sharing this experience, how does this level of response resonate with you? Do you feel validated and heard? Does it encourage you to further divulge your thoughts and feelings?

Refraining From Interruptions

Allowing clients to fully express themselves without interruptions is another cornerstone of holistic hearing. This principle is crucial when dealing with paranormal experiences because such narratives are often complex and deeply personal. Interrupting a client mid-story, even with good intentions, can disrupt their thought process and make them feel unheard. It may also cause them to withdraw, particularly if they sense skepticism or impatience. Silence, in this context, becomes a powerful tool. Giving clients the space to pause, collect their thoughts, or process emotions without immediately jumping in with advice or questions shows respect for their narrative. This practice also helps the listener gather more context, allowing for a deeper understanding of the client's experience.

Reflecting Key Emotions and Statements

Reflection is also a critical aspect of holistic hearing, particularly when engaging with individuals who feel marginalized or dismissed. Reflecting involves paraphrasing or summarizing what the client has said and mirroring their emotional tone to ensure that their message is understood. For instance, if a client shares that they felt terrified after hearing strange noises in their home, you as an active listener might respond, "It sounds like that was a really frightening experience for you. Can you tell me more about what happened?" This technique serves several purposes. First, it demonstrates that the listener is fully present and attentive. Second, it allows the client to clarify or elaborate on their story if needed. Finally, it helps build rapport and trust, as the client sees that their emotions are being taken seriously.

The Power of Validation in Paranormal Contexts

For individuals sharing paranormal experiences, the act of being truly heard can be transformative. Ridicule, dismissal, mockery, and even ostracization are the effects of sharing a paranormal experience. People who believe they have seen or had an experience such as an unidentified flying object (UFO) or an unidentified anomalous phenomena (UAP) are consistent in their reports of being minimized, mocked, and even threatened. As an interesting note, the US government has significantly intensified its focus on UFOs, now referred to as Unidentified Anomalous Phenomena (UAPs). Congress has held multiple hearings, including testimony from military pilots and intelligence officials about encounters with unexplained objects. The Pentagon established the All-domain Anomaly Resolution Office (AARO) to investigate UAPs systematically. Lawmakers are also advocating for greater transparency through legislation requiring the declassification of UAP-related documents and protections for whistleblowers. These steps reflect growing acknowledgment of potential national security and safety implications. It also is a testament to the fact that people are taking these UAP/UFO experiences more seriously, especially with the testimony of those who have such stellar reputations and respect.

But the same can be said as much for those who experience other forms of paranormal...they often report being met with critical and condescending responses from those with whom they share their experience. It is our hope that such acceptance and credibility will be afforded to those who have experienced the paranormal at other levels. As discussed earlier, we were shocked that so many education professionals at the national conference reported they or their clients experienced paranormal and anomalous events. The paranormal will hopefully enjoy the same level of appreciation as the UAP/UFO witnesses. After all, too many people with impeccable backgrounds are opening up about these anomalous experiences. Within the professional context, these people can be traumatized if their professional counselor, minister, or life coach communicates any form of skepticism, which can lead to feelings of alienation or self-doubt. An active listener who validates their feelings—even without necessarily endorsing the supernatural explanation—provides a much-needed sense of acceptance. Validation does not mean agreeing with everything the client says. Instead, it involves recognizing and affirming the emotional reality of their experience. For example, if a client describes seeing an apparition and feeling overwhelmed with fear, the listener might respond, "That must have been so overwhelming for you. It's understandable to feel scared in that situation." This response focuses on the client's emotional experience rather than debating the factual basis of the event.

Building Trust Through Empathy

Empathy is at the heart of holistic hearing and is particularly crucial when working with clients, discussing sensitive topics like paranormal experiences. By stepping into the client's shoes and striving to understand their perspective, the listener can create a stronger connection. Empathy goes beyond simply hearing words, it involves tuning into the underlying emotions and responding in a way that conveys understanding. For instance, if a client shares that their family has dismissed their paranormal experiences, an empathetic listener might say, "It sounds like it's been really difficult not to feel supported by your family. That must be really painful." This acknowledgment of their emotional struggle helps the client feel seen and valued.

Encouraging Deeper Exploration

Holistic hearing also encourages clients to explore their experiences more deeply. By asking open-ended questions and reflecting on their responses, the listener creates an opportunity for the client to uncover insights or express thoughts they may not have previously articulated. For example, a listener might ask, "What do you think this experience means to you?" or "How has this event affected how you see the world?" These questions invite the client to engage in self-reflection, which can be especially meaningful in the context of paranormal experiences. Often, these encounters challenge individuals' existing belief systems or evoke profound existential questions. Providing a space for this exploration without imposing judgments or solutions is a hallmark of effective holistic hearing.

Practical Challenges and Considerations

While holistic hearing offers immense benefits, it also comes with challenges, particularly in the realm of paranormal experiences. Listeners may need to set aside their own biases or discomfort with the subject matter. It can also be difficult to balance empathy with maintaining professional boundaries, especially if the client's experiences are traumatic or evoke strong emotions. Additionally, listeners should be mindful of their own emotional reactions. If a client's story is particularly intense or unsettling, the listener must regulate their response to avoid projecting their feelings onto the client. Practicing self-awareness and seeking supervision or peer support when needed can help listeners navigate these challenges.

In summary, holistic hearing is a powerful tool that fosters connection, understanding, and healing. By giving clients the space to express themselves, refraining from interruptions, and reflecting key emotions and statements, listeners create an environment of trust and acceptance. This approach is particularly impactful for individuals sharing paranormal experiences, as it addresses their unique need for validation and support. In a world where such experiences are often met with skepticism, the gift of being truly heard can make all the difference, helping clients feel less isolated and more empowered in their journey.

O: Objective Observation

The third principle of effective counseling, objective observation, underscores the critical importance of maintaining objectivity within the therapeutic relationship. This principle ensures that counselors approach their work with impartiality, focusing entirely on the client's emotional and psychological well-being. While it is natural for counselors to experience personal reactions to a client's narrative—whether empathy, curiosity, or even skepticism—it is vital that these reactions do not interfere with the therapeutic process. This section explores practical strategies for cultivating objectivity, particularly when addressing emotionally charged or unconventional topics like paranormal experiences. Let's examine some proven strategies for cultivating objective observation.

Focus on the Client's Perspective

Objective observation begins with actively centering the client's perspective. This involves setting aside personal beliefs or biases to deeply engage with the client's narrative. For instance, if a client describes an extraordinary or paranormal event, the counselor's role is not to validate or debunk the occurrence but to understand its emotional and psychological impact. Questions like, "What does this experience mean to you?" or "How has it influenced your emotions or thoughts?" allow clients to reflect and share without judgment. Again, the session is not about you or your personal perspective…it's about the client and helping them process the event.

You as a helping professional must demonstrate that you are in observation of all the client is presenting. As we have already mentioned, reflective listening is a powerful tool for fostering objectivity. By summarizing or paraphrasing what the client has shared, counselors can confirm their understanding of the client's perspective and feelings. For example, if a client expresses fear and confusion after a paranormal event, the counselor might respond, "It sounds like this experience left you feeling both scared and unsure of what to think. Is that correct?" This approach not only validates the client's emotions but also ensures clarity in communication. The authors have also found that notetaking is an effective way to maintain objectivity. By recording key details of the client's story, emotional responses, and behaviors, counselors create a factual account that can be revisited later. This practice reduces the influence of memory distortions or emotional biases, ensuring that therapeutic decisions are based on an accurate understanding of the client's situation. Notes can also help identify patterns over time, such as recurring themes or changes in mood. You can also share these observations over time with your client to review their progress (or lack of) as time moves along.

Managing Personal Reactions

Those who help others in the area of psychology, counseling, ministry, etc. are human and, as such, may have strong emotional or cognitive responses to a client's story. These reactions can range from empathy to skepticism or even discomfort, especially when dealing with unfamiliar or extraordinary topics like paranormal encounters. While these responses are natural, they must be carefully managed to avoid influencing the therapeutic process. Self-awareness is key in this context. Counselors should regularly reflect on their emotional responses, seeking supervision or peer consultation if necessary. Techniques such as mindfulness or grounding exercises can also help counselors remain present and focused during sessions, reducing the risk of projecting their feelings onto the client. This is a great place to remind you of one of our core beliefs…every counselor needs a counselor! Make sure to address this with your personal counselor.

Emphasizing the Importance of Neutrality

Neutrality is a cornerstone of effective counseling, particularly when addressing sensitive or polarizing subjects. For clients discussing paranormal experiences, neutrality ensures that the focus remains on their emotional and psychological needs rather than the counselor's beliefs or opinions about the phenomenon. This approach fosters a safe and nonjudgmental environment, encouraging clients to share openly. For example, a client who believes they have encountered a ghost may be seeking validation of their fear or confusion rather than an explanation of the event itself. A neutral response might involve exploring how the experience has affected their daily life or relationships, rather than debating its reality. Questions like, "How has this experience impacted your sense of safety?" or "Have you talked to others about this? If so, how did they respond?" shift the focus to the client's emotional world.

Attending to Nonverbal Cues

Objective observation extends beyond the content of a client's story to include their nonverbal communication. Factors such as tone of voice, body language, facial expressions, and overall demeanor can provide valuable insights into the client's state of mind. For instance, a client recounting a paranormal event might exhibit anxiety through fidgeting, changes in speech patterns, or avoidance of eye contact. Recognizing these cues helps counselors better understand the client's emotional processing and tailor their responses accordingly. Counselors should also be attuned to inconsistencies between verbal and nonverbal communication. A client who verbally downplays the significance of an event but exhibits signs of distress may require deeper exploration of their emotions. Questions like, "I noticed you seem tense as you talk about this—can you tell me more about how you're feeling right now?" can open the door to greater emotional insight.

Bracing for Unique Challenges

When dealing with clients who report paranormal experiences, counselors face unique challenges related to objective observation. These narratives often evoke heightened emotions, including fear, confusion, or existential questioning. Additionally, clients may have encountered skepticism or dismissal from others, making it crucial for counselors to approach these topics with sensitivity and an open mind. Objective observation in this context involves understanding not only the content of the experience but also its broader implications for the client. For instance, does the reported event exacerbate existing mental health issues, such as anxiety or trauma? Does it affect the client's relationships or sense of self? By exploring these dimensions, counselors can provide holistic support while remaining grounded in objective observation.

While objectivity is essential, it must be balanced with empathy to ensure that clients feel heard and supported. Empathy involves understanding and validating the client's emotions, even if their experiences are unconventional or difficult to comprehend. This dual focus—on objective observation and empathetic connection—creates a therapeutic space where clients can explore their emotions and find meaning in their experiences.

In summary, objective observation is a critical principle that you can nurture and develop for maintaining professionalism and effectiveness as you work with this special population. By focusing on the client's perspective, using tools like note-taking and reflective listening, and managing personal reactions, counselors can navigate even the most challenging narratives with impartiality. This skill is particularly important when addressing paranormal experiences, which often carry intense emotional and psychological weight for clients. By remaining neutral, attentive, and empathetic, counselors ensure that their work supports the client's well-being above all else.

S: Sympathetic Searching

Sympathetic searching represents a novel application of a key principle in counseling that emphasizes the importance of exploring a client's experiences with openness and empathy, particularly in contexts where the experiences may defy conventional explanation. This approach seeks to foster a therapeutic environment where clients feel validated and supported in exploring their inner worlds without fear of judgment or dismissal. This principle is closely tied to Carl Jung's concept of synchronicity, which posits that certain events are meaningfully connected, even in the absence of a discernible causal relationship. Synchronicity challenges traditional notions of causality by suggesting that some events are linked by their symbolic or subjective significance, rather than by direct cause-and-effect mechanisms. In counseling, sympathetic searching adopts this framework by encouraging practitioners to focus on the subjective meaning of a client's experiences rather than attempting to fit those experiences into pre-existing theoretical or religious models. Jung's concepts on synchronicity have been validated in a variety of recent studies. Russo-Netzer and Icekson (2023) conducted an intense study designed to closely examine the correlations related to awareness, meaning-making, receptiveness, and well-being for those who have had anomalous experiences. Among its conclusions, this study concluded: "synchronicity awareness and meaning-detecting are positively associated with openness to experience and tolerance for ambiguity" (p. 13). That is, those people who were more willing to accept that concrete and specific answers may never be found for their experience, had an easier time of processing and finding some measure of meaning. Sacco (2020) conducted an extensive review of the extant literature related to Jung's theory of synchronicity. His meta-analysis emphasized synchronicity experiences are more widespread than first thought, there is a definite lack of a unifying conceptual framework to understand the phenomena, and that there is a consummate lack of research on this subject.

To be clear, the essence of sympathetic searching lies in its emphasis on bracketing the counselor's personal beliefs and biases, particularly regarding topics that might be considered paranormal, metaphysical, or anomalous. This practice of bracketing requires counselors to set aside their own assumptions and judgments in order to fully engage with the client's perspective. By doing so, counselors create a safe and open space for clients to explore their experiences authentically. This is particularly important in cases where clients present experiences that fall outside the realm of conventional understanding, such as encounters with the paranormal or other anomalous phenomena. Rather than attempting to rationalize, explain, or dismiss these experiences, the counselor's role is to inquire into what the experience means to the client on emotional, psychological, and spiritual levels. For example, if a client reports an experience of seeing an apparition or having a precognitive dream, a counselor operating from a sympathetic searching perspective would not immediately seek to classify or explain the experience through a psychological or scientific framework. Instead, the counselor would ask exploratory questions aimed at uncovering the deeper personal significance of the event. What emotions did the experience evoke? How has it influenced the client's sense of self or their worldview? Does the client perceive this experience as affirming, distressing, or transformative? By addressing these questions, the counselor helps the client engage with their experience in a reflective and meaningful way. The goal is not to determine whether the event "really" happened in a literal sense, but to understand its subjective impact and integrate it into the client's broader life narrative.

Sympathetic searching thus shifts the focus of counseling from external validation to internal exploration. This approach aligns with humanistic and existential traditions in psychology, which prioritize the client's subjective experience as the foundation for therapeutic work. From an existential perspective, the meaning of an experience is often more important than its objective reality. Anomalous or paranormal experiences can challenge clients to confront profound questions about the nature of reality, their place in the universe, and the boundaries of human understanding. By approaching these questions with curiosity and openness, sympathetic searching helps clients navigate existential and metaphysical themes in a way that is both therapeutic and empowering.

A key element of sympathetic searching is its potential to uncover layers of meaning that the client may not have consciously considered. Anomalous experiences often carry rich symbolic significance that can resonate with the client's psychological and spiritual concerns. For instance, a client who reports seeing an apparition might associate the experience with unresolved grief, a desire for closure, or a need to feel connected to a deceased loved one. By exploring these associations, the counselor can help the client articulate and process underlying emotions or conflicts. Similarly, a precognitive dream might reflect the client's anxieties about the future or their aspirations for personal growth. In both cases, sympathetic searching enables the counselor to guide the client toward a deeper understanding of their experience and its implications for their life.

Another important aspect of sympathetic searching is its emphasis on integration. Anomalous experiences can be disorienting or even traumatic, especially if they challenge the client's existing beliefs or sense of reality. Through the process of sympathetic searching, clients are encouraged to integrate these experiences into their sense of self in a way that is coherent and affirming. This process may involve reframing the experience as an opportunity for growth, transformation, or spiritual awakening. By doing so, clients can move from a place of confusion or distress to one of empowerment and clarity. The philosophical underpinning of sympathetic searching also invites counselors to adopt a broader perspective on human experience. By engaging with clients' anomalous experiences in a nonjudgmental and exploratory manner, counselors can expand their own understanding of the diverse ways in which people make sense of the world. This openness to the unknown fosters a more inclusive and holistic approach to counseling, one that recognizes the complexity and richness of human experience.

In conclusion, sympathetic searching is a powerful principle that encourages counselors to explore clients' experiences with empathy, openness, and a focus on meaning. Grounded in Jung's concept of synchronicity, this approach emphasizes the importance of understanding subjective significance rather than seeking objective explanations. By bracketing their own beliefs and biases, counselors create a safe space for clients to reflect on their experiences and integrate them into their personal narratives. Ultimately, sympathetic searching enables clients to engage with their anomalous encounters in a way that is therapeutic, reflective, and transformative, fostering greater self-awareness and personal growth.

T: Therapeutic Trust

The principle of therapeutic trust serves as a cornerstone for effective counseling and is intricately woven throughout the therapeutic process. Trust acts as the thread that binds the counselor and client, fostering a relationship in which meaningful dialogue and healing can occur. Without trust, the counseling process stagnates, particularly when clients discuss sensitive, controversial, or stigmatized experiences, such as encounters with the paranormal. The establishment and maintenance of trust are not merely desirable but essential, as they provide the foundation for an open, honest, and transformative therapeutic relationship. In this discussion, we will explore the multifaceted strategies for building, enhancing, and preserving trust in the therapeutic setting, with an emphasis on its critical role in working with clients who have experienced marginalization or misunderstanding. What can we learn about trust and its importance in working with clients who have experienced high strangeness?

To begin with, trust is cultivated through fundamental practices such as maintaining confidentiality, demonstrating reliability, and showing empathy. Confidentiality is a vital element of any therapeutic relationship, as clients must feel assured that their disclosures will remain private. This assurance is particularly important when clients are sharing experiences that they fear may be ridiculed or dismissed. By clearly explaining the limits of confidentiality at the outset of therapy and consistently adhering to these boundaries, counselors lay the groundwork for a trusting relationship. Reliability further strengthens this trust, as clients must be able to depend on their counselor to be consistent, punctual, and responsive. Actions such as keeping appointments, following through on commitments, and maintaining professional boundaries signal to the client that the counselor values the therapeutic relationship and respects the client's time and vulnerability.

Empathy and respect form another critical dimension of therapeutic trust. Empathy involves actively listening to the client and striving to understand their experiences from their perspective, without judgment. This is particularly important when working with clients who recount paranormal experiences, as these narratives often challenge conventional understandings of reality. Respecting the client's feelings and beliefs, even if they differ from the counselor's own views, creates a safe space where clients feel validated and understood. By communicating this respect, counselors affirm the client's worth and foster a sense of psychological safety, which is essential for therapeutic progress.

Verbal and non-verbal communication play a significant role in nurturing trust. Verbal communication that is clear, compassionate, and attuned to the client's needs can help establish a rapport that supports open dialogue. For instance, counselors can use affirming language to convey acceptance and understanding, such as saying, "It sounds like this experience was very meaningful for you," or, "I appreciate you sharing something so personal with me." Additionally, the use of reflective listening techniques, such as paraphrasing or summarizing the client's statements, signals to the client that the counselor is actively engaged and genuinely interested in their narrative. Non-verbal communication is equally important. Body language, facial expressions, and tone of voice can all convey empathy and attentiveness. Maintaining appropriate eye contact, adopting an open posture, and using gentle nods or encouraging smiles can help put the client at ease and demonstrate that the counselor is fully present. Conversely, non-verbal cues such as crossed arms, averted gaze, or a distracted tone can undermine trust, as they may be interpreted as disinterest or judgment.

Creating a safe and non-judgmental space is another essential strategy for fostering trust. Clients who discuss paranormal experiences may already feel marginalized or dismissed by friends, family, or society at large. In such cases, it is imperative for the counselor to provide an environment where the client feels free to express themselves without fear of ridicule or invalidation. This can be achieved by adopting a stance of unconditional positive regard, a concept rooted in humanistic psychology. Unconditional positive regard involves accepting the client fully and without judgment, regardless of the content of their disclosures. By embodying this principle, counselors affirm the client's right to their own experiences and perspectives, fostering a sense of trust and safety.

Transparency about the counselor's role and the therapeutic process further reinforces trust. Great care must be taken by the professional at this point to ensure that clients are not promised the answers to all their questions or that certain outcomes are guaranteed. Clients benefit from understanding what to expect from therapy, including the counselor's approach, goals, and limitations. Hence the importance of Informed Consent which clearly delineates the therapeutic process. For example, counselors can explain that their role is not to validate or invalidate the objective reality of the client's paranormal experiences but to explore their subjective significance and emotional impact. This clarity helps manage the client's expectations and reduces the potential for misunderstandings, thereby strengthening the therapeutic alliance.

Trust becomes especially critical when working with clients who feel marginalized or misunderstood because of their paranormal experiences. Such clients may approach therapy with a heightened sense of vulnerability or skepticism, fearing that their narratives will be dismissed or pathologized. By fostering a trusting relationship, counselors can help these clients feel seen, heard, and respected, enabling them to share their most vulnerable thoughts and emotions. This openness paves the way for deeper therapeutic work, as clients who trust their counselor are more likely to engage fully in the process and explore the underlying emotions, beliefs, and meanings associated with their experiences. Moreover, trust allows clients to take risks within the therapeutic setting. For instance, a client who trusts their counselor may feel more comfortable delving into painful memories, confronting unresolved conflicts, or exploring existential questions raised by their paranormal encounters. In this sense, trust acts as a catalyst for therapeutic growth, empowering clients to move beyond fear and self-doubt toward greater self-awareness and healing.

The principle of therapeutic trust is indispensable in counseling, serving as the foundation upon which all other aspects of the therapeutic relationship are built. By maintaining confidentiality, demonstrating reliability, and showing empathy and respect, counselors create a space where clients feel safe to share their most sensitive experiences. Verbal and non-verbal communication, the creation of a non-judgmental environment, and transparency about the therapeutic process further enhance this trust, particularly for clients who feel marginalized or misunderstood. Ultimately, by fostering trust, counselors empower clients to engage deeply in the therapeutic journey, facilitating meaningful growth and transformation.

CONCLUSION

In summary, this chapter sought to provide a comprehensive guide to helping professionals such as yourself effectively work with clients presenting anomalous or paranormal experiences. Through the GHOST framework—Genuine Graciousness, Holistic Hearing, Objective Observation, Sympathetic Searching, and Therapeutic Trust—you've been provided with a structured yet flexible approach to creating a safe, validating, and collaborative therapeutic relationship. Hopefully you have understood that while these skills are foundational to counseling in general, they take on unique significance when applied to clients dealing with experiences that challenge the boundaries of conventional understanding...as the paranormal so powerfully does!

Personal Reflection Questions for Chapter 4

When you think about creating a safe and trusting therapeutic environment, what challenges might arise when working with clients who share paranormal or anomalous experiences, and how would you approach those challenges?

Carl Rogers' person-centered therapy emphasizes empathy, acceptance, and non-judgment. How do these principles resonate with your own counseling style, and how might you apply them when using the GHOST Method with clients who feel misunderstood or dismissed?

Reflect on your own beliefs about paranormal or unexplained phenomena. In what ways could your personal perspectives either help or hinder your ability to provide genuine, nonjudgmental support to clients presenting these types of experiences?

REFERENCES

Roxburgh, E. C., & Evenden, R. (2016). 'They daren't tell people': Therapists' experiences of working with clients who report anomalous experiences. *European Journal of Psychotherapy and Counselling, 18*(2). https://doi.org/10.1080/13642537.2016.1170059

Russo-Netzer, P., & Icekson, T. (2023). An underexplored pathway to life satisfaction: The development and validation of the synchronicity awareness and meaning-detecting scale. *Frontiers in Psychology*, pp. 01–17. https://doi.org/10.3389/fpsyg.2022.1053296

Sacco, R. G. (2020). Synchronicity research: A review, taxonomy, and agenda. *International Journal of Jungian Studies, 13*(1), pp. 41–68. https://doi.org/10.1163/19409060-20201002

Chapter 5

Voices of the Ancestors

Investigating the Cultural Backdrop

INTRODUCTION

Paranormal and anomalous experiences—events or phenomena that seem to defy conventional explanation—have intrigued humanity for centuries. From ghostly apparitions and near-death experiences to telepathy and unidentified aerial phenomena, these occurrences often carry profound personal and cultural significance. While some individuals view such experiences as spiritual awakenings or messages from ancestors, others might perceive them as mere coincidences, hallucinations, or even signs of mental illness. These differing interpretations underscore the critical role culture plays in shaping how individuals and communities understand and respond to the paranormal. The purpose of this chapter is to take a deeper look into the multicultural perspectives on paranormal and anomalous experiences, emphasizing their significance within diverse cultural contexts. For mental health professionals, understanding these perspectives is not merely academic; it is a practical necessity. Counselors and therapists are increasingly encountering clients who describe unexplained phenomena, and their ability to navigate these conversations with cultural sensitivity can profoundly impact therapeutic outcomes. We, as authors, hope to provide some practical tools and strategies for counselors and people professionals to navigate discussions about paranormal experiences with cultural sensitivity. These include methods for exploring clients' cultural frameworks, fostering nonjudgmental dialogue, and integrating culturally informed approaches into treatment planning.

By equipping therapists with these skills, our goal is to bridge the gap between cultural understanding and clinical practice. Ultimately, we want to underscore the critical importance of multicultural competence in

DOI: 10.4324/9781003529477-5

addressing paranormal and anomalous experiences within counseling and mental health settings.

CULTURAL PERCEPTIONS OF PARANORMAL EXPERIENCES

Cultural context serves as the lens through which people make sense of their world, including their encounters with the extraordinary. Different cultures define and interpret paranormal phenomena vastly based on their specific beliefs, folklore, and historical context, with variations in the types of spirits, their motivations, and how they manifest, even though the core concept of "a presence beyond the normal" might be shared across cultures. According to research, a significant majority of cultures across the globe, often estimated around 90% or more, hold some form of supernatural belief, with most cultures utilizing supernatural explanations for natural phenomena like disease, food scarcity, and natural disasters, indicating a widespread acceptance of supernatural explanations for life events; however, the exact percentage can vary depending on the specific belief system and cultural context being studied (Young, 2023). Humans worldwide use supernatural beliefs to explain events, with a tendency to attribute natural phenomena like storms or disease to supernatural causes more than social phenomena such as murder or warfare. In their study analyzing 114 diverse societies, Jackson et al. (2023) found that this aligns with theories suggesting religious belief arises from a human tendency to perceive intent in the natural world. Interestingly, urbanized and socially complex societies were more likely to use supernatural explanations for social phenomena, highlighting how the use of such beliefs varies between small-scale communities and larger, more anonymous groups.

EXPLORATION OF HOW DIFFERENT CULTURES DEFINE AND INTERPRET PARANORMAL PHENOMENA

In many Indigenous cultures, paranormal experiences are often interwoven with spiritual beliefs and community traditions. These phenomena might be seen as signs of ancestral communication, natural imbalances, or spiritual lessons. In contrast, Western frameworks, influenced heavily by scientific materialism, often lean toward pathologizing or dismissing such experiences unless they can be empirically validated. Both perspectives are valid within their cultural domains, but the tension between them can create challenges for clients and counselors alike. For mental health professionals, being attuned to cultural characteristics that influence clients' perceptions of the paranormal is essential. Cultural competence enables therapists to recognize that an individual's interpretation of an anomalous experience is often deeply tied to their cultural background. For instance, a client from a collectivist society may perceive a paranormal event as a shared familial or community experience, while someone from an individualist culture might internalize it as a personal and isolated phenomenon. Without this understanding, counselors risk misinterpreting or invalidating their clients' experiences, which can lead to mistrust, disengagement, and ineffective treatment. Here are five major world cultures and examples of their cultural narratives regarding the paranormal. Let's highlight how these narratives can and do shape individual beliefs around the paranormal mindset:

1. ***Western Culture (European and American Traditions)***
   - *Cultural Narrative*: Ghost stories, such as those rooted in Gothic literature, and beliefs in haunted places (e.g., Salem witch trials or Halloween traditions). Western culture, particularly in Europe and America, has a rich tradition of ghost stories and supernatural narratives deeply embedded in its history and literature. These stories often serve as reflections of societal fears, moral lessons, or explorations of the unknown, contributing significantly to the cultural identity of the West. From Gothic literature to localized folklore, ghost stories have evolved to both entertain and provoke thought about life, death, and the afterlife.

     One of the most notable influences in this realm is Gothic literature, which emerged in 18th-century Europe and quickly gained popularity. Works like Mary Shelley's Frankenstein or Edgar Allan Poe's chilling tales of madness and death captivated readers with their haunting atmospheres and supernatural elements. These stories often explored themes of human fragility, the consequences of hubris, and the eerie liminality between life and death. Ghosts and other supernatural entities were not just plot devices but also symbolic representations of unresolved emotions, guilt, or societal issues.

     In America, ghost stories have been intertwined with historical events, such as the Salem witch trials. These trials, driven by mass hysteria and fear of the occult, left a profound mark on American cultural consciousness. Today, Salem is renowned for its haunted places and ghost tours, attracting visitors fascinated by its dark history. Similarly, Halloween traditions—rooted in the Celtic festival of Samhain—have evolved in the West into a celebration that blends playful engagement with the supernatural, such as dressing up as ghosts or holding séances, with lighthearted fun like trick-or-treating.

The cultural narrative of ghosts also reflects a duality in Western thought: a blend of skepticism and fascination. While the Age of Enlightenment emphasized reason and rationality, the enduring popularity of ghost stories suggests a persistent human curiosity about the mysteries of the afterlife and the unknown. This duality is evident in practices like séances, which became popular in the 19th century as people sought to communicate with spirits, blending scientific curiosity with spiritual belief. Ghost tours, often centered around historically significant or reputedly haunted locations, continue to draw people seeking both thrills and a deeper connection to history.

- *Role*: These narratives shape beliefs in spirits, supernatural encounters, and the afterlife, often blending skepticism with fascination and contributing to traditions like séances or ghost tours. These supernatural narratives have played an important role in shaping Western perceptions of life and death. By exploring the boundaries of the known and unknown, they foster a sense of wonder and curiosity while allowing individuals to confront fears and uncertainties. Ultimately, ghost stories in Western culture are not merely tales of fright but reflections of collective imagination, offering insights into human nature and this society's evolving relationship with the supernatural.

2. ***East Asian Culture (China, Japan, Korea)***
   - *Cultural Narrative*: East Asian culture, encompassing the traditions of China, Japan, and Korea, is deeply rooted in a shared respect for the spiritual world and its interplay with daily life. Central to these cultures are their rich narratives about ancestral spirits, ghosts, and supernatural entities, which have been passed down for generations through folklore, literature, and oral traditions. These beliefs are not merely stories but serve as frameworks for understanding the world, guiding behavior, and maintaining social harmony.

   In China, the concept of souls is often described through the duality of *hun* and *po*. The *hun* represents the ethereal, yang-associated soul, while the *po* is the corporeal, yin-associated counterpart. This duality underscores the balance between the spiritual and physical realms, a concept central to Chinese cosmology. Ancestral spirits are believed to remain connected to the living, and their well-being is maintained through rituals such as offerings and ceremonies. The Hungry Ghost Festival, celebrated during the seventh lunar month, exemplifies this connection. During this time, the living offer food, incense, and other gifts to appease wandering spirits, ensuring familial harmony and warding off misfortune.

In Japan, beliefs in ghosts (*yūrei*) and supernatural beings like *yōkai* are integral to cultural narratives. *Yūrei* are often depicted as restless spirits bound to the world by unresolved emotions, such as vengeance or sorrow, while *yōkai* encompass a diverse range of entities, from mischievous tricksters to malevolent forces. Stories of *yūrei* are cautionary tales, warning against neglecting moral obligations or mistreating others, as such actions could lead to hauntings. Similarly, *yōkai* legends often serve as allegories for natural phenomena or societal fears, blending superstition with practical wisdom. Festivals like Obon, where families honor the spirits of their ancestors through dance, lantern lighting, and offerings, reflect the enduring importance of these beliefs.

In Korea, ancestral veneration is deeply ingrained in practices such as *jesa* (ancestral rites), where families honor their forebears by preparing offerings and performing rituals. Ghosts, known as *gwishin*, are believed to linger due to unfinished business or emotional ties, and their stories often highlight the consequences of moral failings or unfulfilled duties. Folktales involving *dokkaebi* (goblin-like spirits) and other supernatural entities are similarly instructive, blending humor and cautionary lessons.

- *Role*: Across these cultures, the role of such narratives extends beyond entertainment. They reinforce a sense of respect and duty toward ancestors, promote ethical behavior, and offer frameworks for coping with the unknown. Rituals and festivals associated with these beliefs foster community cohesion and serve as reminders of the interconnectedness of the living and the dead. In modern times, these traditions continue to shape cultural identity, providing a bridge between the past and present while preserving the rich heritage of East Asian spirituality.

3. ***African Cultures***
   - *Cultural Narrative:* African cultures are deeply rooted in spiritual traditions and beliefs that emphasize the interconnectedness of the physical and supernatural realms. Across the continent, traditional narratives highlight the enduring influence of spirits, witchcraft, and ancestors on daily life. These elements are integral to African cosmology, shaping social norms, practices, and values while providing frameworks for understanding and addressing life's challenges. Central to many African cultural

narratives is the belief in the continuing presence and influence of ancestors. Ancestors are regarded as spiritual guardians who watch over their descendants, offering guidance, protection, and blessings. Maintaining a harmonious relationship with these forebears is crucial, as it ensures the well-being of both individuals and the broader community. Rituals such as libations, offerings, and ceremonies are performed to honor and appease the ancestors, reinforcing the importance of kinship and intergenerational respect.

The concept of witchcraft also plays a significant role in many African cultures. Witchcraft is often seen as a source of both fear and explanation for misfortune, illness, or conflict. It is believed that individuals can harness supernatural powers, either benevolently or malevolently, to influence events or harm others. This belief fosters a strong sense of accountability and moral vigilance within communities, as actions and intentions are scrutinized for their potential spiritual consequences. At the same time, accusations of witchcraft can be contentious and carry significant social implications.

Spiritual healers, such as *sangomas* in Southern Africa, embody the connection between the physical and unseen worlds. These healers serve as mediators, using their knowledge of rituals, herbs, and divination to diagnose and address spiritual ailments. Their role extends beyond physical healing to include resolving disputes, seeking justice, and offering protection from malevolent forces. *Sangomas* and similar figures are deeply respected for their wisdom and their ability to interpret the will of ancestors and spirits.

- *Role*: These beliefs and practices collectively guide key aspects of daily life, and play key roles in health, relationships, and governance. For instance, divination rituals may be conducted to uncover the root causes of illness or misfortune, emphasizing the spiritual dimension of challenges. Similarly, community justice systems often incorporate traditional beliefs, ensuring that disputes are resolved in ways that align with spiritual and cultural principles. In modern times, these traditions continue to coexist with contemporary religious practices and influences. Many Africans integrate their traditional beliefs with Christianity, Islam, or other faiths, creating a dynamic cultural tapestry. Despite changes brought by globalization and modernization, the core values of spiritual connection, respect for ancestors, and the balance between the seen and unseen remain central to African identities. These enduring narratives underscore the resilience and adaptability of African cultures, ensuring their relevance and vitality across generations.

4. ***Indigenous Cultures (Native American, Aboriginal Australian, etc.)***
   - *Cultural Narrative*: Indigenous cultures, such as those of Native Americans, Aboriginal Australians, and Hawaiian/Polynesian cultures, are deeply rooted in animistic worldviews, where the natural world is seen as alive and imbued with spiritual significance. These cultures share profound narratives of spirits associated with natural elements, sacred places, and mythical beings, which shape their understanding of the universe and humanity's role within it. These stories are not merely myths but serve as foundational frameworks that guide spiritual practices, ethical behaviors, and ecological stewardship.

     In Native American traditions, *animism* is evident in the belief that everything in the natural world—animals, plants, rocks, rivers, and even the wind—possesses a spirit or essence. Trickster spirits, such as Coyote in many Plains and Southwestern tribes, play significant roles in these narratives. Often depicted as cunning, mischievous, or paradoxically wise, tricksters are central to stories that teach moral lessons, explain natural phenomena, or highlight human flaws. These tales serve as both entertainment and ethical instruction, emphasizing respect for the natural order and caution against arrogance or greed.

     Similarly, Aboriginal Australian culture revolves around the concept of the *Dreamtime*, a spiritual framework that explains the origins of the world and its sacred connection to the people. The *Dreamtime* recounts the creation of the land, animals, and human beings by ancestral spirits, who shaped the landscape and left their essence in sacred sites. These spirits, often represented by beings such as the Rainbow Serpent, embody the interconnectedness of all life. Aboriginal lore emphasizes the importance of caring for the land, not only as a physical resource but as a spiritual inheritance that sustains cultural identity and continuity.

     In Hawaiian culture, spirits, or *'aumākua*, are considered ancestral guardians that watch over individuals and families. These entities often take the form of animals, such as sharks, owls, or turtles, and serve as protectors and guides. Belief in 'aumākua reinforces the importance of respecting nature and familial bonds. Hawaiian legends also include entities such as *night marchers* (*huaka'i pō*), ghostly processions of ancient warriors that traverse sacred paths. These spirits are said to punish those who disrupt their journey or fail to show proper reverence, underscoring the need to honor traditional practices and sacred spaces. Similarly, Polynesian cultures, including those in Tahiti, Samoa, and Tonga, feature rich spiritual narratives involving deities, spirits, and mythical beings. Across the islands, *mana*—a supernatural force or spiritual energy—is a central concept. *Mana* is believed to reside in people, places, and objects, influencing their power and significance. Polynesian legends also tell of mischievous or malevolent spirits, such as *aitu* in Samoa, who can bring harm or misfortune if offended. These stories often serve as cautionary tales, instilling respect for customs, elders, and sacred traditions.

- *Role*: The role of these narratives extends far beyond storytelling. They shape cultural practices and beliefs about the interconnectedness of humans and nature. Rituals to honor spirits are central to both Native American, Aboriginal, and Hawaiian/Polynesian traditions. These ceremonies, which may include dances, songs, offerings, or art, are performed to maintain harmony with the spiritual realm, ensure the well-being of the community, and express gratitude for nature's gifts. Failing to honor these spirits or offending them through disrespect or environmental destruction is believed to bring misfortune, illness, or imbalance. These sacred activities provide explanations for natural phenomena, guide ethical behavior, and maintain social harmony. Rituals and ceremonies are central to honoring spirits and deities, ensuring balance and protection. For instance, offerings of food or chants may be made to appease spirits or invoke their guidance.

These traditions also serve as ecological guidelines, fostering sustainable practices and deep respect for the environment. For example, hunting and gathering are often accompanied by rituals to thank the spirit of the animal or plant, reflecting an acknowledgment of mutual dependence. In contemporary times, Indigenous cultures face challenges due to colonization, globalization, and environmental degradation. However, the resilience of these animistic narratives continues to inspire efforts to preserve their cultural heritage and advocate for environmental justice. By emphasizing the interconnectedness of all life, Indigenous worldviews offer timeless lessons on coexistence, respect, and sustainability, reminding humanity of its shared responsibility toward the Earth.

5. ***South Asian Culture (India and Surrounding Regions)***
   - *Cultural Narrative*: South Asian culture, encompassing India and its surrounding regions, is deeply intertwined with spiritual beliefs that reflect its rich religious and cultural diversity. Central to these traditions are narratives about ghosts, spirits, and reincarnation, which are rooted in Hindu, Buddhist, and other regional cosmologies. These beliefs not only explain the mysteries of life, death, and the afterlife but also shape daily practices, rituals, and moral values.

     In Hindu cosmology, the concept of the *atman* (soul) and its journey through cycles of birth, death, and rebirth (samsara) is central. Spirits of the deceased, such as *bhut* or *preta*, are believed to linger in the earthly realm if proper funeral rites are not performed or if they meet untimely or violent deaths. These spirits may become restless or vengeful, influencing the living in various ways. Similarly, Buddhist teachings emphasize the impermanence of life and the potential for spiritual liberation (*nirvana*), with beliefs in *hungry ghosts* (*preta*) who suffer due to unresolved desires or karmic debts. These narratives explain the existence of supernatural entities and encourage practices that promote spiritual balance and harmony.

     Folklore across South Asia is rich with stories of vengeful spirits, such as *chudail* (a ghostly female figure in North Indian lore) or *yakshi* (a similar figure in South Indian and Sri Lankan traditions). These spirits are often depicted as women who died unjustly or tragically, seeking retribution against wrongdoers. On the other hand, protective deities and benevolent spirits are also prominent, offering guidance and safeguarding communities from harm. Shrines and temples dedicated to such entities are common, serving as focal points for worship and communal bonding.
   - *Role*: The role of these beliefs extends into daily life and spiritual practices. Funeral rites are of paramount importance in South Asian culture, as they ensure the peaceful transition of the soul to the afterlife. Rituals like cremation, offerings of food, and prayers are performed to help the departed attain liberation or a favorable rebirth. Failure to conduct these rites properly is believed to result in restless or malevolent spirits. Additionally, rituals such as exorcisms, performed by priests or spiritual healers, address the influence of malevolent entities. These practices are guided by ancient texts, traditions, and local customs, blending spiritual wisdom with cultural heritage. The influence of these beliefs also extends to ethical behavior, promoting adherence to

moral values such as compassion, honesty, and respect for others. Acts of kindness and generosity are seen as ways to accumulate good karma, ensuring a favorable spiritual journey.

In modern times, South Asian narratives of spirits and reincarnation remain relevant, blending with contemporary practices and global influences. Festivals, rituals, and storytelling continue to preserve these traditions, connecting communities to their ancestral roots and offering a framework for understanding life's deeper mysteries. These beliefs not only shape individual spirituality but also foster social cohesion and cultural continuity in a rapidly changing world. These cultural narratives not only help explain the paranormal but also guide rituals, moral behaviors, and a sense of continuity between the physical and spiritual realms.

MEANING-MAKING, RESILIENCE, AND COPING

Cultural narratives about the paranormal often provide individuals with tools for meaning-making, resilience, and coping. Consider the role of spirits and ancestors in African and Afro-Caribbean traditions, where contact with the supernatural is often seen as a source of guidance or protection. Similarly, in many Asian cultures, experiences such as seeing ghosts or communicating with the deceased are sometimes interpreted as opportunities to restore harmony or address unfinished business. These cultural frameworks can offer clients a sense of purpose or clarity that might otherwise be overlooked in therapeutic settings that default to a Western perspective. Acknowledging and validating these cultural dimensions is not only respectful but also therapeutically beneficial. When counselors approach their clients' paranormal experiences with curiosity and cultural humility, they create a safe space for exploration. This approach allows clients to reflect on their beliefs, values, and attitudes, ultimately fostering deeper self-awareness and healing. Conversely, dismissing or pathologizing these experiences without consideration of cultural context can exacerbate feelings of isolation or confusion, particularly for clients who already feel marginalized or misunderstood.

IMPLICATIONS AND METHODS FOR MENTAL HEALTH PROFESSIONALS

The importance of cultural competence extends beyond understanding clients' interpretations of paranormal events. It also involves recognizing the broader societal and historical factors that shape these perspectives.

For example, colonialism and globalization have often disrupted Indigenous belief systems, leading to hybrid or syncretic interpretations of the supernatural. Mental health professionals must be aware of these dynamics to appreciate the nuanced ways in which cultural heritage and contemporary influences intersect in clients' worldviews. As cultures differ significantly in their approaches to these phenomena, therapists must develop a deep appreciation for the diversity of human experience. This understanding not only enriches the therapeutic process but also affirms clients' humanity and dignity. By embracing the complexity of cultural perspectives, mental health professionals can better support their clients in finding meaning and healing in even the most extraordinary of experiences. Take the time to truly listen to the rich tapestry of cultural voices around you and those whom you work with. Immerse yourself in their stories, traditions, and experiences, and let their perspectives guide your understanding. By doing so, you honor their deep connections to the past, celebrate their influence on the present, and embrace their vision for the future. This journey of listening and learning enriches not only your understanding but also your ability to connect authentically with others. Let's discuss three important topics when addressing clients who report paranormal experiences. As always, it is vital to approach the topic with sensitivity and a culturally informed perspective. The following methods outline strategies to engage effectively and therapeutically.

Exploring Clients' Cultural Frameworks

Understanding a client's cultural background is essential when working with individuals who report paranormal experiences. Different cultures have varying beliefs, traditions, and explanations for phenomena that may be considered supernatural. Counselors can:

- Ask about cultural beliefs: Invite clients to share their understanding of the experience within the context of their cultural or spiritual framework. This can include beliefs in ancestors, spirits, energy, or otherworldly entities.
- Learn about cultural narratives: Gain knowledge about folklore, traditions, and spiritual practices associated with the client's background. This can provide a framework to interpret their experiences respectfully and accurately.
- Acknowledge the role of culture in meaning-making: Understand how cultural values shape the client's interpretation of events and how this meaning influences their emotions, behaviors, and coping strategies.

Fostering Nonjudgmental Dialogue

Creating a safe, open, and accepting environment is fundamental when clients share potentially stigmatized or misunderstood experiences. Counselors can help and support their clients by implementing the following strategies:

- Adopt an open-minded stance: Avoid dismissing or pathologizing the client's accounts, even if they challenge conventional understanding. Instead, express curiosity and empathy.
- Validate their emotions: Focus on the emotions and impacts associated with the experience, such as fear, confusion, or a sense of wonder, rather than debating the reality of the phenomena.
- Use reflective listening: Paraphrase the client's words to demonstrate understanding and ensure the client feels heard without judgment or skepticism.

Integrating Culturally Informed Approaches into Treatment Planning

Tailoring interventions to align with a client's cultural and spiritual worldview enhances the therapeutic process. Steps include:

- Incorporating culturally relevant practices: When appropriate, explore traditional healing practices or rituals the client finds meaningful, such as ceremonies, blessings, or consulting a spiritual leader.
- Collaborate on treatment goals: Work with the client to integrate their beliefs into treatment objectives. For example, a goal may involve finding ways to coexist peacefully with perceived paranormal phenomena or reducing anxiety about such experiences.
- Bridge cultural and psychological approaches: Combine culturally specific interventions with evidence-based psychological treatments. For instance, mindfulness or grounding exercises might be adapted to align with spiritual practices relevant to the client's culture.

By exploring clients' cultural contexts, maintaining a nonjudgmental attitude, and weaving cultural sensitivity into treatment planning, counselors can create a supportive environment that validates clients' experiences while addressing their emotional and psychological needs. By doing so, counselors are more likely to foster trust, empower clients, and demonstrate respect for the diversity of human experience.

KEY TOOLS FOR COUNSELORS AND PEOPLE PROFESSIONALS

Culturally sensitive assessment techniques for counselors include: asking open-ended questions about cultural practices and beliefs, using culturally relevant language, allowing clients to explain their experiences in their own words, considering the impact of cultural stigma, actively listening for cultural nuances, and adapting assessment tools to fit the client's cultural context; essentially, prioritizing understanding a client's cultural background and incorporating it into the assessment process without making assumptions.

Inquiring About Cultural Identity

"Can you tell me a bit about your cultural background and how it shapes your life?"

This question invites the individual to share their unique cultural experiences and how these shape their worldview. It opens a dialogue about traditions, beliefs, and values that might influence their daily life, relationships, and personal identity. By asking this question, a practitioner demonstrates an interest in understanding the cultural nuances that contribute to the person's sense of self, fostering trust and creating space for the client to feel seen and respected.

Exploring Cultural Values

"How important is family to you and how does that influence your decision-making?"

Family plays a central role in many cultures, influencing priorities, career choices, and interpersonal dynamics. By asking this, you explore how family values guide the person's decisions, responsibilities, and conflicts. This insight helps to understand how family expectations and relationships may affect the client's goals and challenges, such as balancing personal desires with collective obligations, and informs culturally attuned support strategies.

Understanding Cultural Practices

"Are there any traditional practices or rituals that are significant to you?" This question allows the individual to share meaningful cultural or religious practices that may impact their routines, identity, or emotional well-being. Recognizing these traditions highlights their importance and allows practitioners to respect and integrate these elements into the care plan. Whether it's participating in specific ceremonies or following dietary restrictions, such practices can be central to a person's sense of balance and belonging.

Assessing Cultural Stigma

"Do you feel like there are any cultural beliefs that might make it difficult to seek help for your concerns?" This question provides a safe space to discuss cultural stigmas, such as those surrounding mental health or certain behaviors. It helps identify barriers the client might face in accessing or accepting support, such as fear of judgment, shame, or misunderstanding within their community. Understanding these challenges can guide the adaptation of interventions to reduce stigma and encourage the client's participation in services.

Language Considerations

"Do you prefer to speak in your native language or English?" Language is a vital aspect of effective communication and cultural expression. Asking this demonstrates respect for the client's preferences and comfort, ensuring they can express themselves authentically. For some, speaking in their native language may evoke a deeper emotional connection or clarity, while others might prefer the practicality of English in certain contexts. Addressing this choice ensures mutual understanding and fosters trust.

Adapting Assessment Tools

Modifying standard assessment questions to be culturally relevant involves tailoring the language and examples to resonate with the client's cultural context. For instance, instead of referencing Western holidays or traditions, use culturally specific events or practices familiar to the client. This personalization makes assessments more relatable and accurate, enhancing the relevance of the insights gathered and ensuring that interventions align with the client's lived experience. There are some key points to remember when using culturally sensitive assessment techniques.

Be mindful of your own biases: Regular self-reflection is essential to identify and address unconscious biases that may affect your interactions. By being aware of your own cultural lens, you can engage with clients more openly and avoid making assumptions that might alienate or misinterpret their experiences.

Show genuine curiosity: Approach every client interaction with a sincere desire to learn about their cultural background and how it shapes their life. This demonstrates respect and fosters a collaborative relationship where the client feels valued and understood.

Validate client experiences: Recognize the significant role culture plays in shaping a client's identity, struggles, and coping mechanisms. Acknowledging these influences validates their lived experience and strengthens their sense of dignity and self-worth.

Seek additional knowledge: If faced with cultural contexts you are unfamiliar with, consult resources, cultural experts, or community organizations. This ensures you provide informed and respectful care while demonstrating a commitment to understanding the client's unique background.

CONCLUSION

Understanding multicultural perspectives on paranormal experiences is essential for counselors and mental health professionals, as such experiences are often deeply intertwined with cultural values, worldviews, and traditions that shape how clients interpret the unexplained. Across cultures, paranormal or anomalous phenomena are not only defined differently but also carry varied implications for personal identity, meaning-making, and community belonging. For example, one culture may view a spiritual visitation as a sacred ancestral connection, while another may interpret it as a psychological or pathological event. Without a grasp of these cultural lenses, counselors risk imposing their own assumptions and potentially invalidating clients' lived experiences. Cultural sensitivity, therefore, becomes more than a professional courtesy is a critical skill for building trust and offering effective care. By approaching clients with openness, humility, and curiosity, counselors can better explore the underlying beliefs, values, and behaviors that inform how individuals conceptualize paranormal encounters. This sensitivity allows professionals to appreciate the broader human dynamics at play and design treatment approaches that honor both the client's cultural framework and their unique psychological needs. Emphasizing multicultural competence also helps practitioners avoid reductionist explanations that may alienate or marginalize clients, replacing them instead with insights and perspectives grounded in respect, empathy, and holistic understanding.

The counselor's role is not to determine whether the experience is "real" but to validate the meaning it holds within the client's cultural context and to support their process of integration. In this way, mental health professionals can serve as bridges, helping clients navigate between traditional cultural interpretations and modern clinical perspectives without erasing either. The call to action for the profession is clear: prioritize cultural awareness as a foundational element of practice. Just as counselors are trained to recognize developmental, systemic, and social influences, so they, too, must-actively develop competencies in multicultural perspectives on the paranormal. This requires ongoing education, engagement with diverse cultural narratives, and reflection on personal biases that may shape clinical judgment. Ultimately, embracing cultural sensitivity is not only a matter of ethical responsibility but also a path toward more inclusive, compassionate, and effective counseling. By recognizing that paranormal experiences often lie at the intersection of culture, spirituality, and psychology, mental health professionals can help clients find meaning, resilience, and healing in ways that affirm their identities and honor their traditions.

Personal Reflection Questions for Chapter 5

How have your own cultural background, beliefs, or values shaped the way you interpret or respond to paranormal or unexplained experiences, either your own or those shared by others?

When working with clients from cultural traditions different from your own, what steps can you take to ensure that you approach their paranormal or anomalous experiences with genuine curiosity, respect, and cultural humility?

Reflect on a time when you encountered a belief or experience that challenged your worldview. How did you respond, and what does that reveal about your level of multicultural competence as a counselor or helping professional?

REFERENCES

Jackson, J. C., Dillion, D., & Bastian, B. *et al* (2023). Supernatural explanations across 114 societies are more common for natural than social phenomena. *Nature Human Behaviour*, 7, 707–717. https://doi.org/10.1038/s41562-023-01558-0.

Young, E. (May 09, 2023). Ghosts and gaps: Supernatural beliefs fill similar unknowns across cultures. *BPS Research Digest*, pp. 1–5. https://www.bps.org.uk/research-digest/ghosts-and-gaps-supernatural-beliefs-fill-similar-unknowns-across-cultures

Chapter 6

God and Ghosts

Integrating Spirituality, Faith, and the Paranormal

INTRODUCTION

The design of this chapter focuses on the profound spiritual implications of dealing with paranormal experiences and their impact on mental health. The chapter will highlight the importance of understanding spirituality and beliefs within a client's cultural and familial context. Our hope is that you as a mental health and/or helping professional will be guided through the significance of these spiritual dimensions, which often play a key role in shaping the client's worldview and how they interpret paranormal encounters. Special attention will be given to developing therapeutic strategies that encourage clients to integrate their paranormal experiences with their personal spiritual beliefs. Counselors will be provided with tools for facilitating this process, such as promoting spiritual introspection, helping clients identify their foundational faith beliefs, and fostering flexibility within these beliefs. Supporting clients with strong, conservative faith backgrounds can be a challenging endeavor. Many may struggle to reconcile their paranormal experiences within the rigid frameworks of their established faith. For these clients, the tension between their spiritual beliefs and the paranormal can create inner conflict and distress, as they may perceive these experiences as contradictory to their religious teachings. It is important for professionals to learn about those practical strategies which may help clients navigate this conflict, encouraging them to find space within their belief systems to accommodate these experiences without feeling they are betraying their faith. Spiritual flexibility must always be a central

DOI: 10.4324/9781003529477-6

theme, as it enables clients to adjust and evolve their beliefs in ways that are personally meaningful.

Exploring the deep connection between spiritual beliefs and the paranormal can help individuals interpret and respond to paranormal phenomena that are often intertwined with their spiritual outlook. For many, paranormal experiences may serve as catalysts for deeper spiritual inquiry or transformation, pushing them to question or expand their spiritual frameworks. There is strong evidence to suggest that the greater one's religious beliefs are, the more open he or she may be to the acceptance of the paranormal (Orenstein, 2002). Mental health professionals would do well to learn how to assess and work with their clients' spiritually based perspectives, particularly in cases where these perspectives significantly influence their mental and emotional well-being.

Professionals can also help their clients examine the search for meaning in life and how it relates to religiosity, spirituality, and belief in the paranormal. Understanding this connection is crucial for therapists, as many clients turn to spirituality and paranormal experiences in their quest for significance, purpose, and belonging. The human psyche varies from person to person, and personality traits often are intricately associated with how one processes the paranormal, fueling the need to address existential concerns and the human drive to find meaning. Ultimately, our goal in this chapter is to equip therapists with the knowledge and some strategies to effectively integrate spirituality into their therapeutic work, especially when addressing clients' paranormal and anomalous experiences.

As the understanding of mental health expands, the importance of integrating spirituality into therapeutic approaches, particularly for clients who report paranormal experiences, becomes increasingly evident. Often professionals overlook the intricate relationship between spirituality and the paranormal and how these elements intersect with mental health practices. There is a tendency for many mental health providers to shy away from the topic of spirituality. But there is a way to incorporate spirituality into your practice in a culturally sensitive and effective manner. The wise counselor will recognize the diverse interpretations of spirituality that exist across cultures and how these interpretations shape individuals' perceptions of their experiences, including paranormal ones. Ultimately, we hope this chapter will provide a comprehensive overview of the importance of incorporating spirituality into mental health care, particularly for clients who have encountered paranormal phenomena. By embracing a culturally sensitive approach and recognizing the value of spirituality, therapists can offer more holistic and effective support to their clients. Let's begin!

THE ROLE OF SPIRITUALITY IN MENTAL HEALTH

Let me (Dr. Bain) begin this section by discussing the power of faith and belief. Travelling to the pilgrimage town of Fatima, Portugal, in 2024, I really had no idea what to expect apart from what I knew from its veneration and respect by Catholic people across the globe. Over 100 years ago, three children claimed to have had an extraordinarily anomalous experience involving none other than Mary, the mother of Jesus. Hailed as our Lady of Fatima, the children, ages 8–13, received both general and specific messages from the Holy Lady. The main focus of this story is not to accentuate the purported messages the children articulated, but to delve into the depth of their belief in the miracle of revelation they received.

The story of the three children of Fatima—Lucia dos Santos and her cousins Francisco and Jacinta Marto—centers around the apparitions of the Virgin Mary that they witnessed in 1917 in Fatima, Portugal. The children reported seeing a lady, whom they later identified as the Virgin Mary, on six occasions between May and October of that year. The apparitions conveyed messages of prayer, repentance, and devotion to the Immaculate Heart of Mary. Initially, the children faced skepticism from local authorities, clergy, and even their families, who did not believe their claims. The children were eventually summoned to meet with the local police, who pressured them to recant their story. In August 1917, the three were imprisoned by the civil authorities, who attempted to force them to admit that they had fabricated the apparitions. They were threatened with execution, but despite intense pressure and fear, the children refused to back down from their belief in what they had seen.

After being jailed for several days, the children were released, and their faith in the apparitions remained unwavering. Eventually, many people came to believe in the children's testimony, and the events at Fatima became one of the most significant Marian apparitions in Catholic history. Lucia, Francisco, and Jacinta later led very different lives, but the legacy of their experiences endured, with the Catholic Church officially recognizing the apparitions and the children's visions. Francisco and Jacinta died young, but Lucia went on to become a Carmelite nun and lived to see their beatifications.

Their story accentuates how spirituality, a concept that transcends religious boundaries, plays a significant role in the personal growth and mental well-being of many individuals. Spirituality encompasses a wide range of beliefs and practices that give meaning to life, often influencing how clients perceive their experiences, including those of a paranormal nature. As you move through this chapter, we want to help define spirituality and highlight its diverse interpretations across different cultures. We need to explore how spiritual beliefs can profoundly affect mental health, drawing on research findings that demonstrate the positive impact of spirituality on psychological well-being. You will also have an opportunity to consider actual stories of people's encounters with the paranormal. These will be presented to illustrate the effective integration of spirituality into therapeutic practices, showing how a spiritual perspective can enhance mental health outcomes.

The relationship between spirituality and the paranormal has been a subject of interest throughout history. Different cultures interpret spirituality in a myriad of ways, and these interpretations affect how clients understand their spiritual and paranormal experiences. For example, what might be considered a paranormal experience in one culture could be seen as a spiritual awakening in another. By recognizing the connection between spirituality and the paranormal, the effective professional can more effectively address the needs of clients who hold these beliefs. Understanding the cultural context of a client's spiritual beliefs is essential for mental health practitioners. A therapist who is culturally competent can offer more meaningful support to clients, helping them navigate their spiritual experiences in a way that aligns with their cultural and personal belief systems.

I was licensed and ordained as a minister (Dr. Bain) in 1979 and early on in my ministerial career, I discovered there were many issues people were facing that could not easily be addressed with a simple prayer and select readings from the Holy Bible. By the time I finished my undergraduate work, I realized the seminary education I was getting did not fully equip me in the area of mental health counseling. In 1987, I enrolled at Memphis State University (now the University of Memphis) and received my Master of Counseling degree in 1988. I remember my old professor, Dr. Burl Gilliland used to say, "As a professional counselor, you are going to see and experience things that are not covered in the DSM III." He had no idea how prophetic his words were to me. I soon began to deal with things that could not be readily dismissed with the most contemporary psychological or theological ideologies of the time. Of all the anomalous experiences I had in my 34-year career as a pastor, I remember one very distinctly.

When I was a young pastor, a married woman in her early 30s was brought to me for counseling. She had made extraordinary claims of having daily conversations with Jesus, which, according to her, included a range of intimate experiences. One of her most unusual assertions was that she and Jesus had engaged in sexual intercourse while she rested in a hammock in the backyard of her country home. When we met, she spoke in a gentle and pleasant voice. Early in our session, she asked, "Do you mind if I pray for us?" I agreed, and she began with what appeared to be a simple, sincere prayer. Without warning, however, her voice dropped several octaves, and in a startlingly deep tone she began speaking in the third person: "Listen to what my servant, Butterfly, has to say. She is my voice." Immediately, I felt a profound sense of unease. I responded, "Whoever you are, the Lord does not need you to communicate through her. The true God speaks directly to whomever He chooses." At that moment, it was as if something released her. She collapsed onto the floor of my living room, appearing to lose consciousness. Two others who were present witnessed the entire event. Later, she firmly stated that she had no memory of what had occurred.

Some might describe this as demonic possession; others might interpret it differently. Whatever it was, I quickly realized I had no training or tools to address such an encounter. Both theology and psychology, as I understood them at the time, failed to provide me with an explanation, and I was left deeply unsettled. In the sessions that followed, she sincerely sought to understand her experiences. Yet I knew I was not equipped to guide her on such a complex journey. Ultimately, I referred her to professional services, recognizing that she needed a level of care beyond what I could provide.

BRIDGING THE DIVERGENT WORLDS OF SPIRITUALITY AND THE PARANORMAL

The spiritual implications of dealing with the paranormal can be profound, often shaking the very foundation of a person's belief system. Whether an individual encounters ghosts, spirits, UFOs, or other unexplained phenomena, such experiences frequently challenge one's concepts and understanding of reality and provoke deep questions about life, death, and the existence of a higher power. These encounters can lead to confusion, fear, and anxiety, particularly for those who come from cultural or religious backgrounds that interpret the paranormal in specific ways.

Therefore, addressing these spiritual dimensions is vital in the therapeutic process, especially when mental health professionals are working with clients from diverse cultural, religious, or spiritual backgrounds. Spirituality, as a common and core component of one's personal identity, must not be understated. In recent years, mental health professionals have increasingly recognized the importance of incorporating clients' spirituality and religious beliefs into counseling. As a young counselor in training (Dr. Bain), I remember how traditional Western psychology dismissed or pathologized paranormal experiences. It was considered ludicrous to consider spiritual components within the counseling process. Fortunately, modern approaches are more integrative, acknowledging that for many individuals, these experiences carry significant spiritual meaning. Consequently, counselors and therapists must be equipped to navigate the intersection between mental health, spirituality, and paranormal experiences in a sensitive and supportive manner. This involves understanding the cultural and familial context of the client, as well as offering strategies that help them integrate their experiences into their spiritual worldview.

UNDERSTANDING THE CULTURAL AND FAMILIAL CONTEXT

One of the first steps mental health professionals must take when working with clients who report paranormal experiences is to understand the cultural and familial context that informs their spirituality. Beliefs about the paranormal vary widely between cultures and religious traditions. A significant aspect of spirituality that must be addressed in therapy is how it is transmitted through families. Familial transmission of spiritual values plays a key role in shaping an individual's beliefs and practices. These values are often passed down from generation to generation and can deeply influence how a person perceives and copes with their mental health and spiritual experiences. Therapists must equip themselves with techniques to assess and understand a client's spiritual background, which includes exploring the influence of their family dynamics and cultural heritage on their spiritual outlook. Moreover, as mental health professionals increasingly encounter clients from diverse cultural and spiritual backgrounds, understanding the spiritual significance of their experiences is crucial. Spiritual beliefs often provide a framework for understanding life events, including paranormal phenomena, and can offer a sense of meaning, comfort, and guidance. In working with your clients and patients, you must approach these experiences with an open mind and a willingness to explore how they fit into that individual's overall mental health and well-being.

To effectively support clients, mental health professionals need to conduct culturally sensitive assessments that honor the diversity of spiritual beliefs. These assessments are critical not only for understanding a client's spiritual background but also for helping them integrate their spiritual beliefs into their mental health care. This is especially important for clients who report paranormal experiences, as these experiences can sometimes be misunderstood or dismissed in traditional therapeutic contexts. By acknowledging the spiritual implications of such experiences, therapists, counselors, and support professionals can create a safe and supportive environment for clients to explore and integrate these aspects of their lives into their mental health journey. In addition, it will highlight the importance of building trust and fostering a non-judgmental therapeutic environment where clients feel comfortable discussing their spiritual and paranormal experiences. Through this integrative approach, therapists can better support their clients' overall mental, emotional, and spiritual health.

For instance, in some Indigenous cultures, spirits and ancestors are seen as an integral part of the living world, and encounters with them are viewed as normal and even desirable. On the other hand, in some branches of Christianity, paranormal experiences might be interpreted as demonic or as temptations that should be resisted. Similarly, Eastern spiritual traditions such as Buddhism or Hinduism might interpret paranormal phenomena in terms of karma, reincarnation, or the illusory nature of the material world. Understanding these nuances is crucial because clients often process their paranormal experiences through the lens of their upbringing and belief systems. Family beliefs and expectations can also influence how an individual interprets and reacts to such encounters. A client raised in a strict religious household may feel shame or fear about experiencing something paranormal, while someone from a more spiritually open environment might embrace the encounter. Therefore, mental health professionals should engage in a careful assessment of the client's spiritual background, exploring not only their individual beliefs but also the broader cultural and familial narratives that shape their worldview.

THE CONSTANT SEARCH FOR COMPATIBILITY BETWEEN SPIRITUALITY AND THE PARANORMAL

Over the last century, a notable divergence has emerged between religious beliefs and the concept of the paranormal, driven in large part by developments in modern psychology and scientific thought. Traditionally, religion and the paranormal often occupied overlapping spaces in human understanding, with both systems addressing the unknown, the supernatural, and the spiritual. In many cultures, religious explanations for phenomena like spirits, miracles, and divine interventions provided a framework for understanding mysterious or unexplainable events. However, the 20th and 21st centuries have seen a shift, largely due to the rise of scientific inquiry and psychological analysis. Only in the past few decades has there been a significant return to the possibility of incorporating the paranormal into one's framework of existence and being. Recently, the UFO/UAP phenomenon has come to the forefront with testimonies by extremely credible and respected sources so much so that the United States Congress opened special hearings and investigations to these unexplained aerial phenomena. Like UFO/UAP, very credible and respected people are feeling at liberty to openly discuss their own paranormal or anomalous experiences. The times seem to be changing for a more open, sincere, and robust discussion about the subject.

In the recent past, modern psychology, particularly through the work of figures like Sigmund Freud, Carl Jung, and William James, began to explore human experiences of the paranormal—such as visions, ghost sightings, and mystical encounters—not as external supernatural events, but as projections of the mind or reflections of unconscious psychological processes. For instance, Freud's psychoanalytic theory often interpreted religious and paranormal experiences as expressions of repressed desires or unresolved emotional conflicts. Jung, while more sympathetic to the mystical side of human experience, also framed paranormal phenomena within the context of the collective unconscious and archetypal imagery rather than attributing them to external supernatural forces.

Simultaneously, advancements in scientific thought have increasingly sought to explain phenomena that were once considered supernatural through naturalistic frameworks. For example, developments in neurology and cognitive science have shown how hallucinations, sleep paralysis, and mental illnesses like schizophrenia can account for many paranormal experiences. Furthermore, the scientific method has emphasized empirical evidence and skepticism of claims that cannot be measured or tested, creating a growing gap between science-based perspectives and traditional religious or paranormal beliefs. This divergence highlights the tension between faith-based worldviews and the empirical demands of science, with the paranormal often falling into a liminal space, neither fully embraced by religious institutions nor accepted by mainstream science.

A study conducted in New Zealand by Wilson et al. (2014) delved into the differences and similarities between religious and paranormal beliefs, revealing intriguing insights into how these beliefs impact individuals' lives. Their findings highlighted that supernatural thinking plays a significant role in shaping overall life satisfaction, happiness, and feelings of social belonging. This suggests that regardless of whether a person's beliefs are rooted in religion or the paranormal, such beliefs have a profound effect on their emotional and social well-being. Expanding on these ideas, Sparks (2001) offered a nuanced perspective on the relationship between paranormal beliefs and religious beliefs. He noted that the connection between these two types of beliefs is far more complex than it might initially seem.

On the surface, one might assume that both religious and paranormal beliefs involve a similar acceptance of supernatural phenomena. However, the reality is more intricately complicated. For example, individuals who are traditional spiritualists or religionists, such as Christians who believe in the miracles described in the Bible, may readily accept supernatural occurrences within the context of their religious framework. These believers may view miracles, divine interventions, and other religiously framed supernatural events as integral components of their faith. However, when it comes to paranormal phenomena outside their religious context—such as ghosts, psychic abilities, or UFOs—they may be skeptical or even dismissive. Sparks (2001) concluded: "The tendency to report a paranormal experience is not the same as expressing belief in the paranormal, but those who report experiences would almost certainly report strong belief in the existence of that which they had supposedly encountered directly" (pp. 55–56). From a historical perspective, it may be accurate to assume that the acceptance or rejection of the paranormal is different in this modern era as opposed to those who lived only a couple of centuries ago.

In discussing the curious relationship between religious beliefs and paranormal beliefs, Baker et al. (2016) deduced from their research: "Once the generalized negative effects of organizational and exclusive religious participation on paranormalism are accounted for, it is indeed only a small-step from being touched by an angel to believing in ghosts, UFOs, and trying to contact the dead" (p. 24). But current skepticism from established religion can stem from a perceived threat to an organization's religious beliefs or from teachings that discourage belief in non-religious supernatural events. The disparity in how religious individuals view different forms of supernatural phenomena can often be traced back to their upbringing and the religious teachings they were exposed to during their formative years. Those raised in devout religious households may have been taught to believe in the supernatural events described in their religious texts, while simultaneously being warned against believing in non-religious supernatural phenomena, which might be seen as contrary to their faith.

Conversely, individuals who are skeptical of the paranormal often approach such beliefs from a scientific or rational perspective. Their disbelief may stem from a worldview that prioritizes empirical evidence and logical reasoning. For these skeptics, belief in the paranormal is often viewed as a violation of the principles of the scientific method, which relies on observation, experimentation, and reproducibility. Paranormal phenomena, which often lack scientific validation, are therefore dismissed as implausible or unworthy of serious consideration.

Interestingly, for religious individuals, belief in paranormal phenomena may also be seen as a violation of traditional religious teachings. This is particularly true for those whose religious beliefs have been reinforced through personal experiences or deep spiritual journeys. For these believers, accepting paranormal phenomena outside the context of their religion might be perceived as undermining the authority of their religious teachings or as inconsistent with their faith.

The relationship between religious and paranormal beliefs can also be influenced by cultural and societal factors, as previously discussed in Chapter 5. In some cultures, religious and paranormal beliefs may coexist harmoniously, with individuals viewing both as part of a broader supernatural framework. In other societies, however, there may be a stronger distinction between religious and paranormal beliefs, with the latter being regarded as fringe or unconventional. This complexity is further compounded by the fact that people's beliefs can evolve over time. An individual who starts out with a strong belief in traditional religion might, over time, develop an interest in paranormal phenomena, or vice versa. This shift can be influenced by personal experiences, exposure to new ideas, or changes in social or cultural environments. For example, a religious person who has a paranormal experience might begin to explore paranormal beliefs, leading to a broader acceptance of supernatural phenomena. Alternatively, a person who begins to question their religious beliefs might turn to paranormal explanations as a way to make sense of their experiences or the world around them.

THE ETHICAL JOURNEY OF INTEGRATION OF SPIRITUAL BELIEFS WITH PARANORMAL REALITY

The relationship between religious and paranormal beliefs is far from straightforward. It is here the mental health professional must tread carefully. As outlined in Chapter 4, professionals are guided by fundamental, ethically grounded principles that help us model genuine graciousness, practice holistic listening, engage in objective observation, and pursue compassionate exploration–all while building therapeutic trust. For many of the people you will work with, discussing the paranormal is most likely a departure of the safe waters of religious dogma wherein they discover there is more to their spiritual and physical world than what they were led to believe. Perhaps one of the best therapeutic approaches is to show how religious beliefs have room to embrace a richer, more diverse, and wildly exotic landscape than denominational doctrines often allow.

As was mentioned in Chapter 1, Kris and I debuted our conceptual theme of this book during a national conference in New Orleans (the perfect paranormal place, right?!) in February 2024. We were both delighted and shocked at the amazing reception of the professional counselors, counseling educators, mental health experts, and university professors connected to the mental health theme. We addressed six key issues related to our topic of "An Ethical Haunting" which sought to address the ethical considerations when working with people who have experienced paranormal or anomalous events. Here's what we encouraged the attendees to keep in mind when working with this special population:

1. Always remember that as a counselor, therapist, clergy, life coach, or support professional, we are NOT there to be ghost investigators! This emphasizes that our role is not to search for or confirm the existence of ghosts or supernatural entities. Instead, the focus is on providing professional, respectful, and non-judgmental support for

individuals who are experiencing distress or curiosity about unusual events in their lives. This distances the practice from sensationalism and reinforces that the goal is to help people, not to prove or disprove paranormal phenomena.

2. We must provide support to people who experience unexplained phenomena. Many people report experiences that they cannot easily explain, which can be unsettling and isolating. This point underscores the importance of offering empathetic and supportive responses to these individuals. Rather than focusing on finding definitive explanations, the objective is to be there for clients, validate their feelings, and help them navigate their experiences.
3. We should leave pre-conceived notions at the door and practice bracketing! "Bracketing" is a technique often used in phenomenological research and practice, where practitioners set aside their personal beliefs and biases to fully understand the client's perspective. This point calls for practitioners to approach each case with an open mind, avoiding assumptions about what is "real" or "impossible" and instead focusing on understanding the client's experiences as they perceive them.
4. It is essential to approach each case without immediately attributing the client's experiences to mental health conditions like schizophrenia or psychosis. This reminder suggests that unusual experiences are not inherently signs of mental illness and that practitioners should assess each case on its own merits, avoiding stigmatizing or pathologizing clients based on the unusual nature of their experiences.
5. We have ethical obligations to practice and model non-maleficence, beneficence, and veracity. This point refers to the ethical principles of:
   - Non-maleficence: Avoid causing harm.
   - Beneficence: Act in the best interest of the client.
   - Veracity: Be truthful and transparent. These principles ensure that practitioners prioritize the well-being of clients, offer genuine support, and avoid causing harm through judgment or exploitation. Practicing these values builds trust and integrity within the profession and provides clients with a safe environment to share their experiences.
6. We should remember that paranormal beliefs and anomalous experiences are usually culturally normal and nonharmful. Many cultures around the world hold beliefs in spirits, the supernatural, and other paranormal concepts. This point encourages practitioners to recognize

and respect the cultural context of a client's beliefs and experiences. Acknowledging that such beliefs are often typical and not inherently harmful helps prevent unnecessary pathologization and allows for a more compassionate and culturally sensitive approach. Each of these principles helps foster a supportive, non-judgmental environment that respects the individual's experiences, beliefs, and well-being.

WHAT DO SACRED TEXTS HAVE TO SAY ABOUT THE PARANORMAL?

Sacred texts from Christianity, Islam, Hinduism, and Judaism offer varying perspectives on ghosts and the paranormal:

Christianity

The Bible doesn't explicitly mention ghosts, but it does include passages that touch on the supernatural and spirits. Some interpret these passages as referring to an intermediate state where the spirits of the dead await resurrection. The Bible also warns against trying to contact the dead for divination. But there are some very interesting passages in the Bible that make for further investigation. In Matthew 14: 24-31, Jesus walks on the water (how's that for paranormal?!) and when the disciples see him coming to them in the boat, they cry out in fear "It's a ghost!" The Greek word here is "phantasma" from a root word "phantazein" that means to make visible. So phantasma means "image" or "phantom". After His resurrection (another amazing paranormal event), Jesus appears to the disciples in Luke 24:36-43 and quietens them by reassuring them "I m not a ghost!" As having a seminary degree and an avid student of the Bible, I find it very interesting that Jesus doesn't say "Guys, there are no such things as ghosts!" He simply says, "I'm not one! I am real!" I also find a passage in Genesis 4:10 quite interesting as God interrogates Cain after he murdered his own brother. Cain at first denies knowing what God is talking about, but the Lord says: "What have you done? Listen! Your brother's blood cries out to me from the ground!" Is this a potential reference to residual paranormal energy?

Islam

The Quran and Hadith, central texts in Islam, reference supernatural beings known as jinn, who, like humans, possess free will and can choose to do good or evil. They are created from "smokeless fire" and exist in an unseen realm, occasionally interacting with humans. Islamic teachings also acknowledge the existence of witchcraft, often associated with harmful practices that manipulate jinn or other forces to influence people's lives negatively. Additionally, the concept of the "evil eye" refers to a harmful glance believed to cause misfortune or illness, which is combated in Islam through specific prayers and protective practices. These elements underscore a belief in unseen forces that can impact the material world, emphasizing the importance of spiritual protection.

Hinduism

In the Bhagavad Gita, ghosts, referred to as bhuta-ganan, are described as the spirits of individuals who, after death, remain trapped in a liminal state due to their inability to achieve atman (true self) or Brahman (ultimate reality) realization. These souls are unable to transcend to higher spiritual planes or rebirth because they are weighed down by unresolved desires, attachments, or ignorance from their earthly lives. In Hinduism, the soul (atman) is eternal and indestructible; it transcends the physical body and undergoes a continuous cycle of rebirth (samsara) until it attains liberation (moksha), ultimately merging with Brahman.

Judaism

The Torah's most well-known ghost story involves King Saul, who, facing a looming battle with the Philistines and desperate for guidance, sought out a medium in the town of Endor. Despite having banned witchcraft in Israel, Saul disguised himself and visited the Witch of Endor, requesting that she summon the spirit of the deceased Prophet Samuel. When Samuel's spirit appeared, he foretold Saul's defeat and eventual death, delivering a grim prophecy that left Saul terrified. This story highlights the themes of divine authority, forbidden practices, and the limits of human power in seeking supernatural insight.

While both religion and paranormal beliefs involve divergent credence of the supernatural, the specific nature of these beliefs, how they are integrated into a person's worldview, and how they affect their life satisfaction and social belonging can vary widely. Religious individuals may accept supernatural phenomena within the context of their faith but reject the paranormal phenomena that fall outside of it. On the other hand, skeptics may reject both religious and paranormal beliefs based on a commitment to scientific principles. Ultimately, the intersection of religious and paranormal beliefs is shaped by a complex interplay of cultural, societal, psychological, and personal factors, making it a rich area for further exploration and understanding.

THREE COUNSELING STRATEGIES FOR INTEGRATION OF THE PARANORMAL WITH SPIRITUAL BELIEFS

It is imperative for the mental health or helping professional to remain flexible, open-minded, and responsive to the unique needs and perspectives of each individual when working with issues that touch on the supernatural. Understanding paranormal and anomalous experiences is a work in progress. There is so much we do not and cannot understand at this point. But that does not mean we shouldn't keep trying. Imagine the amazing progress made in the past 100 years regarding technology, biology, medicine, and physical science. We simply didn't have the tools and conceptualization to understand penicillin, vaccines, the makeup of DNA, the internet, the personal computer, television, and a host of other important discoveries that we now take for granted. As time moves on, perhaps tools to detect, measure, and understand the paranormal will be developed and then we can integrate this mysterious subject into our everyday existence. Before we delve into outlining some key strategies, we want to offer an important disclaimer.

The approaches we will discuss are just *some* potential strategies that could help a client or patient integrate their experiences into their faith system. However, it's crucial to recognize that these are not definitive or exhaustive solutions. The nature of supernatural experiences—whether spiritual, psychological, or both—varies significantly from person to person, and the ways in which individuals process and interpret these experiences can be deeply personal and unique. It would be unwise to assume there is a finite set of tactics or methods that apply universally to all individuals facing supernatural challenges or spiritual crises. Each person's background, belief system, and level of spiritual engagement will influence how they understand, respond to, and ultimately integrate such experiences into their worldview. And this is also true for the helping professional. Each of us brings our own unique personality, approaches, and perspectives to the table when helping our clients/patients. With that said, let's begin.

Encourage Spiritual Introspection and Reflection

One of the most effective counseling strategies for helping clients integrate their paranormal experiences with their spiritual beliefs is encouraging spiritual introspection. This involves creating a safe space for clients to explore the personal significance of their experiences without judgment. The goal is not to validate or invalidate the paranormal occurrence itself but to focus on the meaning the client derives from the experience. Spiritual introspection can help clients ask deep, meaningful questions: *What might this experience mean for my spiritual journey? How does it challenge or reinforce my faith? What emotions arise when I think about this experience, and what do they tell me about my beliefs?*

Therapists can guide clients in reflecting on how these paranormal experiences might fit into their broader spiritual narrative. For example, a person who believes in life after death might interpret an encounter with a deceased loved one as a comforting confirmation of their faith, while another client might need to reconcile feelings of fear or doubt after an unsettling experience. In these cases, spiritual introspection allows the client to explore how their faith can provide a framework for understanding and integrating the paranormal in ways that feel authentic to them. Tools such as journaling, meditation, or guided visualization exercises can help facilitate this process. By encouraging clients to engage in deep reflection on their experience, mental health professionals can help them move from a place of confusion or fear to one of spiritual clarity and acceptance.

Identify and Strengthen Foundational Faith Beliefs

Another important strategy is helping clients identify and strengthen their foundational faith beliefs. When someone experiences the paranormal, it can sometimes cause them to question their faith or spiritual beliefs, especially if the experience contradicts what they've been taught. For example, a devout Christian may struggle to reconcile a ghostly encounter with their understanding of heaven and hell. A person from a secular background may be confused or frightened by an experience they cannot explain through rational thought. In these cases, mental health professionals can help clients identify the core beliefs that give them strength and peace. This involves helping clients distinguish between the elements of their faith that are essential to their sense of well-being and those that may be more flexible or open to interpretation. For example, a client may come to realize that their belief in a loving higher power is more important to them than adhering to strict religious doctrines about the afterlife. By focusing on these core beliefs, therapists can help clients regain a sense of spiritual stability even as they grapple with the mysteries of the paranormal.

Additionally, exploring foundational beliefs can empower clients to create a more nuanced understanding of their spirituality. Clients often interpret paranormal experiences through the lens of their existing spiritual or religious beliefs. You as a counselor, life-coach, minister, or similar professional have the opportunity to guide clients in exploring how the experience aligns or conflicts with their faith. This process may involve discussing sacred texts, consulting spiritual leaders, or reflecting on personal interpretations of spirituality. This approach helps clients to find meaning in the experience without dismissing or devaluing their spiritual worldview. With this approach, your clients may decide that their faith can accommodate both the teachings of their religion and the reality of paranormal experiences. By validating their core beliefs while remaining open to the new, the client can integrate their experiences in a way that strengthens their spiritual identity.

Foster Flexibility Within Beliefs

Fostering and encouraging flexibility within a client's belief system is another key counseling strategy. Paranormal experiences often defy logical explanation, and trying to fit them neatly into an existing belief system can be challenging. Mental health professionals can help clients by encouraging them to approach their beliefs with a sense of openness and adaptability. In this approach, the counselor works with the client to develop a more fluid and dynamic spiritual worldview that can accommodate even the mysterious. This doesn't necessarily mean that clients must change their fundamental beliefs; rather, they can learn to embrace uncertainty and hold space for experiences that they may not fully understand. For instance, a person may continue to believe in a benevolent God while also acknowledging that some spiritual phenomena might exist outside the framework of their religious teachings. By fostering this flexibility, therapists can help clients reduce the cognitive dissonance that often arises from paranormal encounters. Clients can come to see their spiritual beliefs as evolving rather than static, and this can help them find peace with their experiences, even if they don't have all the answers. Encouraging flexibility allows clients to explore different perspectives without feeling that they are betraying their faith or spiritual identity.

As the authors have both come from conservative religious backgrounds, we believe it's important to address working with clients with strong, conservative faith backgrounds. There are some definite internal struggles these individuals face when confronted with paranormal experiences that conflict with their religious beliefs. This becomes a fertile opportunity for counselors and mental health professionals to bridge the gap between faith and paranormal experiences, offering therapeutic approaches that support clients in reconciling these often-conflicting aspects of their lives. You as a professional will find listening, gently interrogating their reality, and offering opportunities to accept and assimilate these experiences into their lives to be powerful tools for personal progress. By understanding the challenges faced by clients with rigid faith structures, therapists can better assist them in finding a path to spiritual and psychological harmony.

FINDING MEANING IN LIFE THROUGH SPIRITUALITY AND PARANORMAL BELIEFS

Recently, I was waiting to tee off at a local golf course with a new teammate, Michael. I was pleasantly surprised and intrigued at the most interesting conversation with this former golf coach and retiree. I mentioned the book my colleague and I were writing and this topic of finding the meaning of life through paranormal experiences came up. He said, "I can tell you something about that." And he launched into an experience he had after losing his mother to death only three years earlier. Upon a particular morning, he was shocked to hear his mother's voice (which he immediately recognized) whispering to him the words "I'm all right. You will be also, Sweetie!" He told me very confidently that experience helped him process and reconcile her death. Although he had never experienced or thought about the paranormal, he was profoundly impacted by this as he found great peace and joy in hearing her voice. Subsequently, he was able to intertwine this experience into his personal life through counseling and personal introspection. Why did I find this unexpected conversation so refreshing? Because he was adamant that he needed to make sense of her death and find meaning in his grief and loss. I followed this up with two main questions for my newfound friend:

1. Up until the time you had this experience, what were you looking for as you sought to process your mom's death?
2. Why do you suppose you were able to embrace that experience without hesitancy as genuine and valid?

Mike emphasized that he was looking to find meaning to help him make his own life better. He told me how he didn't have a clue how to begin the search for meaning or how to navigate the pathway of grief. When he experienced this paranormal event, he said he knew it wasn't anything driven by a hallucination or too much alcohol the night before. He took the event as a sign from her that she would always be with him and for him never to worry about her well-being. It was a welcome relief to this man who was the baby of the family and so very close to his mom. His intriguing story left me with more questions than answers. I found myself asking: *Why do people search for the meaning of and the meaning in death as well as the meaning of life? What religious, cultural, or personal factors preclude us from finding this meaning or even starting the journey to find answers? And why are people so hesitant to discuss something so personal as a paranormal experience?*

Professionals such as clergy, counselors, therapists, life coaches, personal trainers, psychologists, psychiatrists, and social workers can encourage and motivate people to be more open to finding meaning in their paranormal experiences. Spirituality and paranormal beliefs often play a significant role in many people's quests for meaning and purpose in life. These concepts go beyond the material world, offering individuals a way to connect with something greater than themselves. Spirituality typically involves a sense of connection to a higher power, the universe, or deeper aspects of existence. It provides comfort, guidance, and a sense of belonging, which can help people navigate the complexities and challenges of life. For some, spiritual practices such as meditation, prayer, or mindfulness foster a sense of inner peace and clarity, allowing them to reflect on their purpose and values. This connection to something greater often instills hope, resilience, and a sense of direction, especially in times of difficulty or uncertainty. Spirituality, in this way, becomes a source of meaning, offering people a framework through which they interpret their experiences and understand their place in the world. Similarly, paranormal beliefs, which include concepts such as life after death, ghosts, or supernatural forces, offer alternative or supportive ways of understanding reality. While these beliefs may not be grounded in scientific evidence, they often provide comfort and meaning to those who hold them. The idea that there is more to life than what we can see or explain opens the door to the possibility of an existence beyond death, an unseen force guiding events, or even a deeper connection between people and the universe.

CONCLUSION

For many individuals, spirituality and paranormal beliefs are integral to their search for meaning and purpose in life. The spiritual implications of dealing with paranormal experiences are deeply personal and complex. For them, these encounters can provoke profound questions about their faith, spirituality, and the nature of reality. Mental health professionals play a crucial role in helping clients navigate these experiences by integrating spirituality into the therapeutic process through a culturally sensitive approach. By understanding the client's cultural and familial background, therapists can provide more meaningful support. Counseling strategies such as encouraging spiritual introspection, identifying foundational faith beliefs, and fostering flexibility within belief systems offer powerful tools for helping clients reconcile their paranormal experiences with their spiritual worldview. In the end, helping clients view their paranormal experiences as opportunities for growth can be beneficial. Counselors can frame these events as catalysts for deepening their spiritual understanding or enhancing personal resilience. By encouraging clients to reflect on how the experience contributes to their overall spiritual journey, the counselor fosters a sense of empowerment and integration. Through this integrative approach, mental health professionals can guide clients toward a place of spiritual acceptance, growth, and peace. As a professional, how will you guide, support, encourage, and educate your clients in relation to their paranormal experience? And how might this approach awaken the depth and reality of your own spiritual journey?

Personal Reflection Questions for Chapter 6

How might your own spiritual or religious background influence the way you interpret and respond to a client's paranormal experience?

In working with clients whose belief systems differ significantly from your own, what strategies can you use to balance respect for their worldview with the need to promote psychological flexibility and growth?

How can counselors integrate clients' spiritual and cultural frameworks into therapeutic goals in a way that supports both healing and the search for significance, purpose, and belonging?

REFERENCES

Baker, J. O., Bader, C. D., & Mencken, F. C. (2016). A bounded affinity theory of religion and the paranormal. *Sociology of Religion*, *77*(4): 334–358. http://dx.doi.org/10.1093/socrel/srw040

Orenstein, A. (2002). Religion and paranormal belief. *Journal for the Scientific Study of Religion*, *41*, 301–311. https://doi.org/10.1111/1468-5906.00118

Sparks, G. G. (2001). The relationship between paranormal beliefs and religious beliefs. *Skeptical Inquirer*, *25*(5), 50–6.

Wilson, M. S., Bulbulia, J. A., & Sibley, C. G. (2014). Differences and similarities in religious and paranormal beliefs: A typology of distinct faith signatures. *Religion, Brain & Behavior*, *4*, 104–126.

Chapter 7

Accepting Without Accepting… Techniques and Bracketing

INTRODUCTION

Mental health professionals frequently encounter clients whose experiences challenge conventional understandings of reality, particularly those involving paranormal phenomena. This chapter aims to equip counselors with essential strategies for accepting a client's perspective on their paranormal experiences without necessarily integrating these beliefs into their own worldview. By exploring techniques for offering unconditional positive regard (UPR) and learning how to bracket personal beliefs, morals, and values, counselors can foster a therapeutic environment built on trust and respect. A critical component of this discussion involves distinguishing between chronic delusional thinking, potentially linked to mental illness, and paranormal beliefs, which may stem from unusual or anomalous experiences. Recognizing this distinction is vital in providing ethical and effective care. Additionally, this chapter advocates for a shift in perspective, encouraging mental health professionals to approach paranormal experiences as part of a broader spectrum of human experience rather than dismissing them outright. To support practitioners in this complex area, the chapter will also introduce essential self-care strategies for those working with clients who report paranormal encounters. Furthermore, it will explore the integration of emerging technologies, such as virtual reality (VR) therapy, into paranormal counseling practices, offering innovative ways to engage and support clients. Through these discussions, this chapter provides a framework for counselors to navigate the intersection of mental health and the paranormal with professionalism, empathy, and an open mind.

DOI: 10.4324/9781003529477-7

ACCEPTING THE CLIENT's PERSPECTIVE

Accepting the client's perspective on his or her paranormal experience without necessarily accepting it as a part of the counselor's own belief system can be challenging. This approach aligns with the principles of counselor neutrality and UPR, which are especially important when addressing topics like paranormal experiences that may not fit within the counselor's personal belief system. A key aspect of this approach is validating the client's experience, acknowledging it as real and meaningful to them, even if it differs from the counselor's own perspective. This validation fosters trust and rapport, creating a safe space for open dialogue. Rather than debating the factual nature of paranormal experience, the focus remains on its emotional and psychological impact. Exploring how the experience has shaped the client's thoughts, feelings, and behaviors allows for meaningful therapeutic engagement. Additionally, respecting the client's worldview, including their beliefs in the paranormal, is essential for honoring cultural, spiritual, and personal diversity. By embracing this respect, counselors help clients feel accepted and understood.

At the same time, maintaining professional boundaries is crucial. Counselors are not required to adopt or affirm paranormal beliefs but should remain open, curious, and nonjudgmental. This allows them to guide clients in exploring their own experiences without the imposition of external belief systems. Ultimately, this approach fosters a therapeutic environment that prioritizes the client's mental health and well-being, ensuring that their experiences are met with understanding and support.

PRACTICAL TIPS FOR THE PARANORMAL COUNSELOR

Here are some practical steps and tips for applying this approach when working with clients who have had paranormal experiences:

Create a Safe, Nonjudgmental Space

Active Listening: When the client shares their paranormal experience, listen actively and empathetically. Use open-ended questions to encourage them to elaborate.

Non-Verbal Cues: Ensure your body language, facial expressions, and tone of voice communicate openness and acceptance. Avoid any signals that might suggest disbelief or skepticism.

Example:

Client: "I saw a ghost in my house last night, and it's really scaring me."
Counselor: "That sounds like a really intense experience. How did it feel for you in that moment?"

Explore the Meaning Behind the Experience

Focus on Emotions: Ask the client how the experience made them feel, rather than focusing on whether the experience was "real" or not. This helps shift the conversation to the emotional impact.

Understand the Role of Beliefs: Explore how the client's beliefs about the paranormal are influencing their current thoughts, feelings, or behaviors. It could be tied to anxiety, fear, or even positive spiritual meaning.

Example:

Counselor: "It sounds like this experience has a lot of meaning for you. What do you think this event means in your life?"

Address Psychological and Emotional Impact

When clients disclose paranormal experiences in counseling, it is critical to explore not only the narrative details but also the psychological and emotional responses associated with the experience. Regardless of the counselor's belief in the veracity of the event, the emotional reality of the client must be the primary focus. Many clients report feelings of fear, confusion, shame, anxiety, or even awe following a paranormal experience. These emotions can impact their daily functioning, relationships, and sense of self. Addressing these psychological and emotional responses with empathy and clinical sensitivity helps foster a sense of safety and personal validation.

Validate the Experience

Validation is a central component of trauma-informed and person-centered care. It involves affirming the client's emotions and acknowledging that their experience, regardless of how unusual it may seem, feels real and significant to them. This validation can be a powerful therapeutic tool, especially for clients who have been dismissed or pathologized in the past. A counselor might say, "It sounds like this experience was overwhelming and left you feeling unsettled. That's completely understandable." Such affirming responses signal that the client is not alone or abnormal for having intense feelings about their encounter. Research consistently shows that when clients feel emotionally validated, they are more likely to engage in therapy, develop insight, and build resilience (Cain, 2010; Rogers, 1957).

If the paranormal experience is linked to ongoing distress, such as intrusive thoughts, hypervigilance, or difficulty sleeping, counselors should collaboratively develop coping strategies tailored to the client's needs. Techniques like grounding exercises, mindfulness meditation, progressive muscle relaxation, or breathing techniques can be particularly effective in reducing anxiety and restoring a sense of control. Psychoeducation may also be useful, helping clients understand how the body responds to stress or fear, and normalizing their emotional reactions. Counselors may also integrate cognitive-behavioral techniques to help clients reframe catastrophic thoughts or develop empowering narratives around their experience. The goal is not to explain away the paranormal event but to reduce its negative emotional hold on the client. Ultimately, helping clients manage their emotional responses allows them to regain stability and integrate the experience in a way that supports their mental health.

Example:

Counselor: "It seems like this experience has left you feeling anxious and unsafe in your own home. Would it be helpful if we worked on strategies to manage that anxiety?"

Apply Cultural and Spiritual Sensitivity

Respect Different Worldviews: Some clients may come from cultural or spiritual backgrounds where paranormal experiences are accepted or even celebrated. It's essential to approach the conversation with cultural humility.

Avoid Pathologizing: Be careful not to label the paranormal experience as delusional or indicative of a mental health issue unless there are clear signs of distress or dysfunction that require further evaluation.

Example:

Counselor: "In many cultures, experiences like yours are considered part of a spiritual connection. How does your culture or belief system interpret what you experienced?"

Balance Empathy with Professional Boundaries

Neutrality: While being empathetic, maintain a neutral stance about the truth of the paranormal event itself. The goal is not to confirm or deny the client's experience but to explore its impact on their well-being.

Redirect If Needed: If the conversation becomes overly focused on proving or debating the paranormal aspect, gently redirect the conversation back to the client's feelings and coping strategies.

Example:

Counselor: "Whether or not we can explain the experience, what's important is how it's affecting you. Let's talk about how we can support you moving forward."

Know When to Refer

While many clients who report paranormal experiences are psychologically healthy and simply seeking understanding or validation, counselors must remain vigilant for signs that such experiences may be masking or coinciding with underlying mental health conditions. Paranormal narratives—such as visions, voices, or spiritual encounters—can sometimes resemble symptoms found in disorders like schizophrenia spectrum disorders, post-traumatic stress disorder (PTSD), dissociative disorders, or severe anxiety. For this reason, it is essential that counselors approach each case with both empathy and clinical discernment.

All helping professionals, including licensed professional counselors, must be prepared to refer clients when the concerns presented go beyond the counselor's scope of practice or expertise. If a client's experiences are accompanied by disorganized thought, severe emotional dysregulation, hallucinations unrelated to cultural or spiritual beliefs, or significant impairment in functioning, it may indicate the need for a more comprehensive psychological or psychiatric evaluation.

Making a referral should not be viewed as dismissing the client's experience. Instead, it should be framed as an extension of care—ensuring the client receives the most appropriate and specialized support for their overall well-being. Collaborating with psychologists, psychiatrists, or trauma specialists can enhance treatment outcomes, especially when paranormal experiences intersect with unresolved trauma or serious mental health conditions. In rare cases, frequent or distressing paranormal experiences might be tied to underlying psychological issues (e.g., psychosis, trauma). If you suspect this, it is important to assess for other mental health conditions and consider appropriate referrals to specialists. Ultimately, ethical practice demands that counselors balance cultural sensitivity and open-mindedness with clinical responsibility. Knowing when to refer is not only a sign of professional competence but also a commitment to doing what is in the best interest of the client. By taking this balanced approach, counselors can help clients process their paranormal experiences without dismissing their worldview. It's a respectful and effective way to support the client's mental and emotional well-being

UNCONDITIONAL POSITIVE REGARD

Now we want to discuss some techniques to provide UPR along with how to bracket one's own belief system, morals, and values. Offering UPR while bracketing one's own beliefs, morals, and values—especially in situations involving paranormal experiences—requires thoughtful techniques. Below are some methods for doing this effectively, along with guidance on maintaining neutrality as a counselor.

Unconditional Positive Regard Techniques in Counseling Clients with Paranormal Issues

In client-centered therapy, UPR is one of the foundational conditions that facilitates personal growth, trust, and therapeutic progress. Originally developed by Carl Rogers (1957), UPR involves the consistent and unwavering acceptance and support of clients, regardless of what they share in the therapeutic space. This approach is especially important when working with clients who present with paranormal or anomalous experiences. Many of these individuals have previously encountered disbelief, ridicule, or pathologizing responses from others, which can result in feelings of shame or fear about sharing their experiences openly. Implementing UPR techniques—particularly those that emphasize nonjudgment, empathy, and emotional validation—can foster a healing and trusting therapeutic alliance.

Suspend Judgment

One of the first and most crucial techniques in demonstrating UPR is learning to suspend judgment. This means setting aside personal skepticism or cultural biases about the content of a client's paranormal experiences in order to prioritize the emotional and psychological needs of the client. Clients who disclose such experiences often worry about being dismissed or labeled as "crazy." When counselors meet them with active acceptance and affirmation, they help reduce the client's vulnerability and foster a sense of emotional safety.

Active Acceptance

Active acceptance involves embracing the client's story as real and valid from their perspective, even if it falls outside the counselor's own belief system or empirical understanding. This does not mean the counselor must confirm the existence of the paranormal; rather, it means acknowledging the emotional and cognitive impact the experience has had on the client.

Example:

Client: "I believe this ghost is trying to send me a message."
Counselor: "It sounds like this experience has deeply affected you. I can see that it's something really important to you."

This response validates the client's emotional truth while refraining from making a judgment about the objective reality of the event.

Affirmation

Using affirming language reinforces the client's worth and dignity, which is essential in maintaining a nonjudgmental stance. Even when a counselor is internally uncertain about the nature of the experience, affirmations like "That sounds really meaningful to you" or "You've clearly put a lot of thought into this" serve to honor the client's perspective. Research in person-centered therapy has consistently shown that such affirmation improves rapport and client engagement (Cain, 2010). Clients are more likely to explore vulnerable or complex experiences when they feel they are being seen and heard without evaluation.

REFLECTIVE LISTENING

Reflective listening is another key element of UPR, used to demonstrate empathy and deepen the therapeutic dialogue. Reflective listening helps counselors remain client-focused by reframing the client's words and feelings in a nonjudgmental way. This process not only clarifies the counselor's understanding but also affirms the client's internal world.

Paraphrase Without Judgment

When paraphrasing, the goal is not to reinterpret or reframe the experience based on psychological theory or the counselor's assumptions, but to simply echo back the client's emotions and concerns in a compassionate and neutral way. This supports the client's narrative without minimizing or overanalyzing the paranormal elements.

Example:

Client: "I woke up and felt a presence in the room. I think it was my grandfather who passed away."

Counselor: "You felt someone was there with you, and it brought up thoughts of your grandfather. That sounds like a powerful moment for you."

This response avoids debating the paranormal aspects and instead emphasizes the emotional resonance of the experience.

Ask Clarifying Questions

Open-ended questions serve as an invitation for the client to explore their thoughts and feelings more deeply. Clarifying questions can be especially useful when clients are processing complex, ambiguous, or frightening experiences. These questions must be framed with sensitivity and curiosity rather than skepticism.

Example:

Counselor: "How did you feel in the moment when you sensed that presence?"

Counselor: "What meaning do you think that experience holds for you?"

By asking such questions, the counselor demonstrates care and interest in the client's worldview. This also encourages emotional insight, which is more therapeutically productive than debating the literal existence of paranormal events.

Integrate UPR with Cultural and Emotional Awareness

It is important to note that UPR must be exercised alongside cultural competence and emotional awareness. In many communities around the world, paranormal beliefs are embedded in religious, ancestral, or cultural traditions (Cardeña et al., 2014). Counselors must therefore avoid the Western psychological impulse to pathologize or dismiss what may be deeply significant and normative within the client's cultural framework. UPR, in this context, becomes a tool of not only empathy but also of cultural humility. By using these techniques, suspending judgment, practicing active acceptance, employing affirming language, paraphrasing empathetically, and asking clarifying questions—counselors can create a healing space for clients who may have never had their experiences acknowledged with respect. This not only enhances the therapeutic relationship but also supports emotional integration and psychological resilience.

Normalize Emotional Responses

Empathy for the Feelings: Rather than addressing whether the paranormal experience is "real," validates the client's emotional reaction. Let them know it's normal to feel strong emotions when facing something mysterious or unknown.

Empathetic Statements: Use phrases like, "It's understandable that you feel…" to convey that their emotions, regardless of the source, are valid.

Example:

Counselor: "It makes sense that you would feel frightened after such an intense experience. Let's talk about how we can help you feel more in control."

BRACKETING ONE'S OWN BELIEF SYSTEM, MORALS, AND VALUES

In counseling clients who report paranormal or anomalous experiences, maintaining therapeutic neutrality is not just a preference, it is an ethical necessity. Counselors must often contend with personal beliefs that may not align with the worldview of their clients. This is particularly relevant in sessions involving spiritual or supernatural content, where judgments, skepticism, or subtle invalidations can harm the therapeutic alliance. To support the client authentically, the practitioner must consciously set aside—*or bracket*—their own assumptions, belief systems, and moral frameworks. The following practices can help clinicians maintain a neutral, nonjudgmental stance rooted in empathy, openness, and cultural humility.

What Is Bracketing in Counseling?

Bracketing, in the context of counseling, refers to the deliberate practice of setting aside one's own beliefs, assumptions, and interpretations to be fully present with the client's perspective. Originating from phenomenological philosophy and later adapted into qualitative research and psychotherapy, bracketing allows the counselor to suspend their internal dialogue and personal worldview so they can attune to the lived experience of the client without distortion. This is especially critical when working with clients who describe events that defy conventional logic, such as supernatural encounters, religious visions, or unexplained phenomena. In essence, bracketing does not require the counselor to adopt the client's beliefs—it requires that the counselor refrain from imposing their own. It is a form of respectful restraint that prioritizes the client's meaning-making over the clinician's need for explanation or coherence.

Bracketing, Self-Awareness, and Reflection

Acknowledge Your Biases: Before entering the session, counselors are encouraged to reflect on their own worldview, especially as it relates to the paranormal, spirituality, or other metaphysical concepts. This involves recognizing any emotional reactions, skepticism, fear, or even fascination that might unconsciously guide the therapeutic process. Awareness is the first step toward managing these internal responses.

Engage Mindful Detachment: Grounding techniques can help therapists detach from their own interpretive lens. A simple breathing exercise or self-directed affirmation such as "This session is about the client's experience, not my beliefs. I will focus on their emotional world," can reinforce a non-egocentric approach to counseling. This level of attunement supports deeper empathy and helps the client feel seen rather than scrutinized.

Use Neutral Language

Avoid Probing for Explanations: Clients who have had paranormal experiences often face social stigma or disbelief, leading them to approach therapy with hesitance or guardedness. Asking them to justify or explain their experiences can mirror societal invalidation. Instead, let the client guide the depth and direction of the conversation.

Stay Away from Disclaimers: Counselors should avoid phrases such as, "I don't believe in that, but..." or "That's unusual; however..." which insert the clinician's perspective into the dialogue. These qualifiers subtly shift the focus away from the client's lived experience and toward the counselor's worldview. Neutral responses maintain the session's therapeutic integrity.

Example:

Client: "Do you think I'm crazy for believing this?"
Counselor: "I'm here to listen to how this experience has impacted you and how we can work through any challenges it's brought up. Let's focus on what it means to you."

Maintain Focus on the Client's Perspective

Set Your Beliefs Aside: Therapists may hold strong opinions about spirituality, religious orthodoxy, or empirical science. However, these beliefs have no place in a session where the goal is to understand and validate the client's internal world. Remind yourself that the therapeutic space is for the client's narrative—not yours.

Reflect the Client's Words: When paraphrasing or summarizing, mirror the client's terminology. Replacing emotionally resonant words like "ghost," "angel," or "spirit" with more generic or skeptical language (e.g., "perception," "hallucination," or "phenomenon") can invalidate the client's experience. Using their language reinforces rapport and helps them feel heard.

Example:

Client: "I think this ghost is communicating with me."
Counselor: "You believe the ghost is sending you a message. How does that make you feel?"

Avoid Intellectualization

Don't Rationalize or Debunk: Even when clients describe experiences that appear to contradict scientific understanding, therapists should resist the urge to interpret or analyze them through psychological or biological frameworks—unless clinically warranted. Over-intellectualizing the client's account can shift the session into analysis instead of exploration. The goal is to help the client process their meaning, emotions, and coping strategies—not to seek empirical validation.

Example:

Client: "I keep seeing shadows and hearing whispers at night."
Counselor: "That sounds frightening. How have you been coping with those experiences?"

In summary, bracketing one's personal belief system is not a passive task—it requires ongoing self-reflection, linguistic mindfulness, and emotional restraint. Especially when working with clients who report paranormal or spiritual experiences, the counselor must remember that validation is not the same as agreement. It is possible—and ethically essential—to honor the client's reality without needing to adopt or refute it. By cultivating this skill, therapists can create a safe and supportive environment where clients feel respected, heard, and empowered to explore even the most unusual aspects of their lived experience.

Combining Unconditional Positive Regard with Bracketing

Prioritize Emotional Safety: It is vital to create an environment where the client feels their experience is being taken seriously, regardless of the counselor's own views. Ensuring that the client feels unconditionally accepted fosters emotional safety.

Example:

Client: "I feel like no one believes me, and it makes me anxious."
Counselor: "It sounds like you feel isolated because of how others have reacted. You don't have to worry about that here. I'm here to listen and support you."

Compassion Over Credibility

It is important to shift the conversation toward compassion and care, rather than validating or questioning the experience's credibility. Here the counselor can explore how the client has been affected, rather than debating the event's reality.

Example:

Client: "Do you think this is all in my head?"
Counselor: "What's important is how you've been feeling and how we can work together to help you feel better."

Boundaries Without Judgment: When clients ask for your personal opinion or seek validation that their paranormal experience is "real," it is important to respond with empathy while maintaining professional boundaries. Rather than affirming or denying the experience, acknowledge the client's feelings and the impact the event has had on their life. A gentle boundary might sound like, "What matters most here is how this experience has affected you and what meaning it holds for you." This approach keeps the focus on the client's emotional and psychological needs while avoiding judgment or personal bias.

Example:

Client: "Do you believe in ghosts too?"
Counselor: "My role is to support you through your experience, regardless of my personal beliefs. Let's focus on what this means for you."

INTEGRATING EMERGING TECHNOLOGIES INTO THE COUNSELING OF CLIENTS WITH PARANORMAL

As mental health professionals encounter clients whose distress is linked to reported paranormal experiences, such as encounters with spirits, anomalous presences, or unexplained events, there is increasing recognition of the need for innovative, sensitive, and multimodal therapeutic interventions. While traditional talk therapy remains foundational, it may not always provide sufficient relief or validation for individuals whose experiences defy conventional frameworks. With the rapid advancement of technology, particularly in the areas of VR therapy, biofeedback, and wearable health monitoring, counselors are now better equipped to offer tailored, trauma-informed interventions that are both experiential and integrative.

The Promise of Virtual Reality Therapy

VR therapy involves the use of immersive, computer-generated environments that simulate real or imagined scenarios for therapeutic purposes. In the treatment of trauma and anxiety-related disorders, VR has already shown promise by allowing clients to revisit distressing experiences in a safe, controlled setting, where they can process emotions, confront triggers, and rehearse coping strategies (Maples-Keller et al., 2017). This approach is particularly suited for clients who report anomalous or paranormal experiences that are deeply emotional, traumatic, or symbolic in nature. For example, a client who believes he or she experienced an encounter with a spirit in a childhood home may feel overwhelmed by traditional exposure therapy or verbal retelling. In a VR environment, this same client could be guided through a digitally constructed version of the setting, allowing them to revisit and explore the emotional dimensions of the event with the support of a trained therapist. The VR system might simulate spatial elements (e.g., dim lighting, ambient sounds) without replicating the perceived entity, thereby helping the client remain grounded while exploring symbolic associations.

Such use of symbolic representation can facilitate meaning-making without pathologizing the experience. This approach honors the phenomenology of the client's encounter while offering a therapeutic frame for integration and healing. In addition to reprocessing trauma, VR environments can be used for psychoeducation, coping skills rehearsal, breathwork, and mindfulness training, making the modality both flexible and client-centered (Freeman et al., 2017).

Applications for Anomalous Experiences

Clients who report paranormal phenomena often struggle to find culturally competent or non-dismissive care. Their accounts may be misinterpreted as delusional, especially if clinicians do not differentiate between culturally normative spiritual beliefs and signs of psychopathology. The use of VR in these cases can support therapists in validating and exploring a client's internal reality without asserting the "truth" or "falsehood" of the event. This approach is aligned with phenomenological counseling methods and supports bracketing the therapist's personal belief system (Spinelli, 2005).

Moreover, VR allows clients to externalize their inner experiences. In some cases, individuals might be encouraged to create representations of their paranormal encounters using VR drawing tools, spatial design, or avatar-based storytelling. By crafting a visual, immersive narrative, clients may gain psychological distance from traumatic content while simultaneously enhancing emotional expression and insight. Such techniques mirror narrative therapy and expressive arts interventions while taking advantage of the technological affordances of the digital medium (Rizzo & Koenig, 2017).

Biofeedback and Wearable Technologies

Another promising frontier in counseling individuals with anomalous experiences is the use of biofeedback and wearable health-monitoring devices. These tools allow clients and clinicians to monitor and respond to physiological signals such as heart rate, galvanic skin response, respiration rate, and muscle tension. This is particularly important in sessions where clients recount emotionally intense or frightening paranormal events. Biofeedback helps clients gain awareness of how their bodies react to specific triggers and teaches them to self-regulate physiological stress responses. For example, if a client experiences significant anxiety while discussing a sleep-paralysis episode involving shadow figures, real-time biofeedback could alert both the client and counselor to rising stress levels. The counselor can then guide the client through breathing exercises, progressive muscle relaxation, or grounding techniques to bring their nervous system back to equilibrium (Khazan, 2019). Some wearable technologies, such as the Empatica E4 wristband or the Muse headband, offer continuous monitoring of physiological data and can provide clients with visual feedback on how their mental states shift during therapeutic discussion. Over time, these tools support the development of interoceptive awareness—the ability to recognize and respond to internal bodily cues—a skill shown to be essential in trauma recovery and emotional regulation (Farb et al., 2015).

Supporting Clients Who Find Talk Therapy Limiting

Not all clients respond well to conventional talk therapy. For those whose experiences are ineffable, traumatic, or embedded in shame or fear of ridicule, expressive or somatic tools may offer more accessible entry points. Some individuals find it difficult to articulate what they felt or saw during an anomalous event, and instead respond more effectively to sensorimotor, visual, or experiential modalities. In these cases, technologies such as VR or biofeedback may supplement traditional therapy by offering new ways to explore internal states, reprocess difficult material, or rehearse safety and stabilization techniques. VR, for instance, can simulate relaxing environments—such as nature scenes, sacred spaces, or calming rituals—that promote safety and reduce hyperarousal. Biofeedback devices can reinforce these states by showing the client how their body responds in real time, thereby promoting empowerment and mastery over distressing symptoms. Moreover, these technologies can bridge cultural and spiritual gaps in the therapeutic process. For clients who identify as clairvoyant, spiritual mediums, or energy-sensitive, incorporating tools that monitor energetic or physiological responses can affirm their experiences in ways that feel less pathologizing or invalidating. When used respectfully, these tools can become part of a collaborative treatment plan that prioritizes the client's belief system without endorsing or rejecting its content.

Ethical and Clinical Considerations

While the integration of digital tools into psychotherapy offers exciting possibilities, it also raises important ethical considerations. Informed consent must be revisited to include the use of immersive and physiological technologies. Clients should understand the purpose, limitations, and potential side effects of any technology used in session. Confidentiality, data storage, and device reliability must also be addressed to ensure compliance with HIPAA and other relevant professional guidelines (American Psychological Association [APA], 2022).

Clinicians must also receive appropriate training in the use of these technologies to avoid misuse or overreliance. Technological interventions should never replace therapeutic rapport or diminish the role of human empathy. Rather, they should be viewed as adjunctive tools—complementary supports that enhance, not replace, the counselor's connection to the client.

As technology continues to evolve, mental health professionals are presented with innovative avenues for supporting clients who report paranormal or anomalous experiences. VR therapy, biofeedback, and wearable devices offer immersive, experiential, and embodied methods for exploring distress, building coping strategies, and validating subjective realities. When integrated ethically and with cultural sensitivity, these tools hold the potential to expand the therapeutic frame and improve outcomes for clients who may feel marginalized or misunderstood in traditional clinical settings. By leveraging these emerging technologies, clinicians can meet clients not only where they are—but also within the symbolic and emotional spaces that define their lived experiences.

CONCLUSION

By combining UPR with bracketing, counselors can support clients with paranormal experiences while maintaining neutrality and respect for differing worldviews. This approach is key to maintaining a client-centered, therapeutic environment where the client feels valued, understood, and accepted. Distinguishing between belief systems rooted in mental health conditions—such as chronic delusional thinking or significant distortions of reality—and those that arise from genuine, though often misunderstood, paranormal or anomalous experiences will be important for counselors and helping professionals to differentiate. This differentiation is vital in the context of counseling and psychological assessment, as it enables mental health professionals to approach clients with the appropriate level of clinical sensitivity and cultural humility. Chronic delusions are typically symptomatic of serious mental health disorders such as schizophrenia, schizoaffective disorder, or delusional disorder. These beliefs are usually fixed, resistant to evidence, and often disconnected from shared reality. In contrast, individuals who report paranormal experiences may do so within a coherent narrative that aligns with their cultural background, personal values, or spiritual worldview. Their experiences may involve perceiving or interacting with phenomena that fall outside conventional scientific explanations—such as sensing presences, seeing apparitions, or having premonitions—but these beliefs are not necessarily indicative of psychopathology.

Rather than viewing paranormal beliefs as inherently pathological, it is essential to assess the level of distress, functional impairment, and consistency with broader belief systems. For example, a person raised in a community where spirit communication is considered normal may describe encounters with deceased relatives as healing rather than delusional. On the other hand, if such beliefs are accompanied by disorganized thinking, paranoia, or severe disruptions in daily functioning, they may signal the need for clinical intervention. Therefore, clinicians must carefully evaluate the context, intensity, and impact of the reported experience. Misinterpreting culturally sanctioned or experientially grounded beliefs as psychotic symptoms can lead to misdiagnosis, unnecessary treatment, and a breakdown in the therapeutic alliance.

It is important for practitioners who may be unfamiliar with anomalous experiences or who may feel unequipped to explore them therapeutically to receive the proper training and consultation. Counselors and psychologists are increasingly encountering clients whose experiences do not fit neatly into diagnostic categories but who are nevertheless seeking meaning, support, and validation. Furthermore, there is a growing need for need for continued education on spiritual and transpersonal dimensions of human experience, particularly as they relate to mental health. This includes understanding the psychological impact of extraordinary experiences and recognizing when a client may benefit from referrals to culturally competent or spiritually informed practitioners. Ultimately, the goal is not to confirm or deny the veracity of a client's paranormal beliefs but to hold space for exploration while maintaining ethical and clinical boundaries. This balanced approach fosters trust, respect, and therapeutic efficacy, especially when working with individuals whose worldviews may fall outside the mainstream yet remain deeply meaningful to them.

As the field of mental health continues to evolve in response to growing cultural diversity and shifting societal norms, it is imperative that clinicians broaden their perspectives on what constitutes "normal" human experience. One such area demanding thoughtful consideration is the inclusion of paranormal or anomalous experiences within the therapeutic space.

Rather than viewing these experiences solely through a pathological lens, mental health professionals are encouraged to approach them as potentially meaningful and valid aspects of a client's worldview. The insistence on reducing all such phenomena to hallucinations, delusions, or cognitive distortions may not only alienate clients but also obscure valuable therapeutic insight. As professionals committed to holistic, client-centered care, we must actively challenge outdated clinical biases and begin to advocate for a broader model of psychological wellness—one that acknowledges the possibility that the paranormal may simply be part of the normal spectrum of human experience. This shift calls for more than passive acceptance; it requires active advocacy. Clinicians are urged to educate themselves about the various forms of anomalous experiences—from near-death and out-of-body experiences to spirit encounters and extrasensory perceptions—and to remain open-minded in how these are interpreted. By validating, rather than dismissing, these experiences, therapists can build trust and foster deeper therapeutic alliances. This approach does not require that the therapist share the client's beliefs, but rather that they respect them as significant and meaningful to the client's inner world. Validation alone can be transformative, particularly for clients who have long felt marginalized or discredited by mainstream mental health systems.

However, working with clients who report paranormal experiences can be emotionally and cognitively demanding. The stories may be intense, the emotional expressions raw, and the belief systems unfamiliar. Therefore, it is essential for mental health professionals to prioritize their own self-care. Practitioners should cultivate a regular self-reflective practice, such as journaling or clinical supervision, to process their reactions to clients' extraordinary narratives. Engaging in mindfulness, grounding exercises, and spiritual or existential exploration can help clinicians maintain emotional balance and preserve their sense of professional clarity. Additionally, creating peer consultation groups focused specifically on paranormal or spiritually transformative experiences can offer a supportive community of practice where clinicians can share challenges and strategies. Moreover, as technology continues to advance, there is growing potential to integrate digital tools into the counseling of individuals with paranormal experiences. VR therapy, for instance, offers immersive environments that can help clients reprocess traumatic anomalous encounters, explore symbolic representations of their experiences, or build coping strategies within a controlled digital setting. Biofeedback and wearable technology may also assist clients in regulating anxiety or physiological responses during discussion of paranormal events. These tools can be especially helpful for clients who find traditional talk therapy limiting or retraumatizing.

Personal Reflection Questions for Chapter 7

How might my own personal beliefs, morals, or values make it difficult to remain neutral when a client shares a paranormal experience, and what strategies can I use to bracket these reactions in session?

In what ways can offering UPR to clients who describe unconventional experiences strengthen the therapeutic alliance and promote trust?

How can I balance respecting a client's worldview while maintaining professional boundaries, particularly when their experiences challenge my own understanding of reality?

REFERENCES

American Psychological Association. (2022). *Ethical principles of psychologists and code of conduct.* https://www.apa.org/ethics/code/

Cain, D. J. (2010). *Person-centered psychotherapies.* American Psychological Association. https://doi.org/10.1037/12103-000

Cardeña, E., Lynn, S. J., & Krippner, S. (2014). *Varieties of anomalous experience: Examining the scientific evidence* (2nd ed.). American Psychological Association. https://doi.org/10.1037/14258-000

Farb, N. A. S., Segal, Z. V., & Anderson, A. K. (2015). Mindfulness meditation training alters cortical representations of interoceptive attention. *Social Cognitive and Affective Neuroscience, 8*(1), 15–26. https://doi.org/10.1093/scan/nsr007

Freeman, D., Reeve, S., Robinson, A., Ehlers, A., Clark, D., Spanlang, B., & Slater, M. (2017). Virtual reality in the assessment, understanding, and treatment of mental health disorders. *Psychological Medicine, 47*(14), 2393–2400. https://doi.org/10.1017/S003329171700040X

Khazan, I. Z. (2019). *The clinical handbook of biofeedback: A step-by-step guide for training and practice with mindfulness.* Wiley-Blackwell.

Maples-Keller, J. L., Yasinski, C., Manjin, N., & Rothbaum, B. O. (2017). Virtual reality-enhanced extinction of phobias and post-traumatic stress. *Neurotherapeutics, 14,* 554–563. https://doi.org/10.1007/s13311-017-0534-y

Rizzo, A. S., & Koenig, S. T. (2017). Is clinical virtual reality ready for primetime? *Neuropsychology, 31*(8), 877–899. https://doi.org/10.1037/neu0000405

Rogers, C. R. (1957). The necessary and sufficient conditions of therapeutic personality change. *Journal of Consulting Psychology, 21*(2), 95–103. https://doi.org/10.1037/h0045357

Spinelli, E. (2005). *The interpreted world: An introduction to phenomenological psychology* (2nd ed.). SAGE Publications.

Chapter 8

The W.H.O.L.E. Truth

Processing Trauma from Anomalous Experiences

INTRODUCTION

The relationship between trauma and paranormal phenomena is a complex and intriguing area of study that explores how profound psychological distress or life-altering experiences can influence individuals' perceptions of the paranormal. Trauma often impacts cognitive and emotional processing, potentially heightening a person's sensitivity to unusual or unexplained occurrences. Paranormal experiences—such as sensing a presence, seeing apparitions, or having precognitive dreams—are sometimes reported following traumatic events, leading researchers to consider the possibility of a link between the two. This chapter will explore the potential of trauma that may lead to anomalous experiences as well as anomalous experiences that may lead to trauma. It is possible both could occur simultaneously in their client's paranormal experiences.

One perspective suggests that trauma may lower the psychological barriers that typically filter sensory information, making individuals more attuned to subtle or unconventional stimuli. In this sense, paranormal experiences could be a byproduct of heightened awareness or altered states of consciousness triggered by trauma. Another view proposes that these experiences might serve as a coping mechanism, providing meaning, comfort, or a sense of control during times of emotional turmoil. For instance, perceiving the presence of a deceased loved one could offer solace in the face of grief. However, it is essential to differentiate between trauma-related phenomena, such as flashbacks or dissociation, and genuine paranormal encounters, as the two can sometimes overlap in subjective interpretation. While some experiences may stem from psychological or neurobiological responses to

DOI: 10.4324/9781003529477-8

trauma, others might align with cultural or spiritual frameworks that regard such phenomena as legitimate. Understanding this interplay requires a multidisciplinary approach, integrating insights from psychology, spirituality, and cultural studies, to appreciate how trauma and the paranormal intersect within human experience.

TRAUMATIC EVENTS AND THEIR IMPACT ON PARANORMAL EXPERIENCES

Certain traumatic events are frequently associated with reports of paranormal experiences, likely due to their profound impact on an individual's emotional, psychological, and even spiritual state. Below are some of the most common traumatic events that elicit paranormal phenomena:

> The loss of a loved one is one of the most emotionally intense experiences a person can face. Many individuals report sensing the presence of the deceased, seeing apparitions, or having vivid dreams where they communicate with the departed. These experiences are often interpreted as visitations or as part of the grieving process, providing comfort and closure to the bereaved. In some cases, these experiences may also involve auditory phenomena, such as hearing the deceased's voice or other symbolic signs that are perceived as messages.

One notable case involves the experience of Dr. Elisabeth Kübler-Ross, a renowned psychiatrist and pioneer in the study of death and dying, who documented a personal story in her writings. After the death of a close friend, Dr. Kübler-Ross reported what she interpreted as a visitation from the friend. Shortly after the friend's passing, Kübler-Ross was alone in her home when she distinctly heard the friend's voice calling her name. Startled, she turned and briefly saw her friend's figure standing in the doorway, smiling warmly. The figure then faded away.

Although Kübler-Ross initially dismissed the encounter as a grief-induced hallucination, she later reflected on the experience as being consistent with what many grieving individuals report. She felt a sense of peace and reassurance following the event, as though the friend had come to say goodbye. For Kübler-Ross, the experience was transformative, not only deepening her spiritual perspective but also reinforcing her belief in the possibility of life after death, which became a significant theme in her later work.

Another widely cited case is that of Mary Lincoln, wife of President Abraham Lincoln, who frequently reported feeling the presence of her deceased son, Willie, after his death at age 11 in 1862. Mary experienced vivid dreams where Willie appeared to her, conveying messages of love and comfort. She also claimed to feel his touch and hear his voice during quiet moments of reflection. These experiences brought her solace during a period of immense grief and personal turmoil. Cases like these are not uncommon and highlight how such encounters are deeply personal and often meaningful to those who experience them. Whether interpreted as psychological phenomena, spiritual visitations, or a combination of both, these experiences often serve as a powerful mechanism for coping with loss and processing grief.

Near-Death Experiences (NDEs)

Near-death experiences (NDEs) are frequently reported by individuals who survive life-threatening situations such as cardiac arrest, severe accidents, or surgeries. During these events, people describe phenomena like leaving their bodies, traveling through tunnels of light, encountering deceased loved ones, or experiencing profound feelings of peace and unity. These experiences are life-altering and often viewed as deeply spiritual, challenging conventional understandings of consciousness and the mind. Additionally, experiencing a severe illness or injury not resulting in a NDE can also be a deeply traumatic event that pushes individuals to confront their own mortality. Some people report paranormal phenomena during these crises, such as seeing loved ones or spiritual figures, experiencing out-of-body sensations, or receiving intuitive knowledge about their condition. Such experiences are often interpreted as the mind's way of coping with physical and emotional stress or as spiritual awakenings.

Two studies, in particular, have concluded the actuality of paranormal awareness related to NDEs. Hashemi et al. (2023) identified several key facts related to NDEs and paranormal experiences: (1) the most common NDE are supernatural experiences such as a person having the sensation of leaving their own body; (2) these experiences are both common and diverse across cultures; and (3) the heightened senses and sensitive consciousness indicate these are not easily attributed to dreams, sleep, or mental health disorders. A contemporary study by Lindsay et al. (2024) looked at the connection between NDEs, trauma, and dreaming. It found that people who had NDEs were more likely to have unusual dreams, such as lucid dreams, dreams that predict the future, and out-of-body experiences (OBEs). These types of dreams are different from regular dreams because they are clearer, more vivid, and follow a logical story, unlike the strange, disconnected images found in typical dreams. These experiences also seem to involve greater self-awareness and control, which is not common in normal dreaming.

Childhood Trauma

Individuals who have experienced significant trauma during childhood, such as abuse, neglect, or abandonment, are sometimes more prone to reporting paranormal experiences later in life. This may be due to the way trauma shapes perception and coping mechanisms, as well as an increased sensitivity to their environment. Some suggest that children, due to their developing sense of reality, might be more open to anomalous phenomena, and childhood trauma could heighten this openness. Some theorize that while childhood trauma triggers the brain to engage survival strategies, often a door is opened to the paranormal as a coping mechanism. This door often remains open throughout one's adult life.

One study (Rabeyron & Watt, 2010) investigated the relationship between childhood trauma and paranormal experiences and found significant correlations between early adverse experiences and increased reporting of such phenomena. The Childhood Trauma Questionnaire (CATS) and other assessments revealed that participants with higher trauma scores were more likely to report paranormal encounters. This connection is hypothesized to stem from altered perception and coping mechanisms developed as a result of trauma. Some believe these mechanisms may enhance sensitivity to environmental stimuli and create interpretations that align with paranormal beliefs, while others believe it activates a spiritual connection and sensitivity to paranormal phenomena.

The Experiential Source Theory (as discussed in Marks, 2021) suggests that early traumatic experiences might activate universal psychological responses, leading to anomalous experiences like apparitions or extrasensory perceptions. This theory, supported by qualitative research and participant interviews, highlights how trauma could heighten sensory awareness or distort reality, fostering openness to the paranormal. Themes such as finding meaning in unusual events and the link between perception, belief, and coping are central to understanding how trauma shapes paranormal sensitivity. The Motivational Theory of Marks and Kammann (1980) suggests that paranormal beliefs fulfill a deep human desire for meaning and escape from life's difficulties, such as physical limitations, loneliness, and the inevitability of death. These beliefs provide comfort by offering a sense of control or alternative explanations for harsh realities. However, the theory does not fully explain why some individuals strongly adopt paranormal beliefs while others remain skeptical, despite facing similar challenges. Regardless of how one might interpret the "why" of increased paranormal awareness from childhood trauma, the fact remains there is an established correlation between the two.

Surviving Natural Disasters or War

The intense fear, loss, and chaos associated with surviving natural disasters (e.g., earthquakes, hurricanes) or war can elicit reports of paranormal phenomena. Witnesses or survivors often describe sensing protective presences, such as guardian angels or the spirits of lost loved ones. In some cases, they report heightened intuition or precognitive dreams, which they perceive as warnings or guidance during their ordeal. After traumatic events such as war or natural disasters, many individuals report turning to spirituality or perceiving transcendent connections. Survivors often describe feeling accompanied by a protective presence, such as a guardian angel or loved one's spirit, which provides emotional resilience. These experiences are linked to a coping mechanism that reduces the isolation of trauma and fosters a sense of safety and connection. This can occur in various forms, including prayer, meditative practices, or a personal sense of the divine, helping survivors regain stability and process their experiences.

After the devastating 2011 Japanese tsunami, an unusual rise in reports of paranormal activity was observed in the affected regions. Many survivors and witnesses shared experiences such as sensing protective presences, seeing spirits of deceased loved ones, and even encountering "ghost passengers," especially among taxi drivers in heavily impacted areas like Ishinomaki. These phenomena are often attributed to the immense grief and unresolved trauma stemming from the disaster. For example, cab drivers recounted picking up passengers who would vanish during the ride, with some figures asking existential questions such as, "Have I died?" before disappearing. Others reported seeing spectral figures covered in mud walking through neighborhoods or receiving mysterious phone calls traced back to areas destroyed by the tsunami. These occurrences reflect Japan's cultural framework, which integrates Shinto beliefs about restless spirits and the importance of rituals to help the dead find peace. The surge in these accounts is interpreted as both a psychological response to the collective trauma and as an expression of traditional beliefs about the spirit world. Communities worked with priests and mediums to conduct rituals, aiming to calm these lingering spirits and bring closure to the living.

Traumatic Loss of a Home or Sense of Place

People who lose their homes due to fire, eviction, or displacement (e.g., refugees) may report paranormal experiences connected to their former residences or surroundings. These can include feelings of being watched, hearing phantom sounds, or perceiving the lingering energy of the past.

Sudden, Violent Deaths in the Environment

Individuals who live in places where sudden, violent deaths have occurred—such as accidents, murders, or suicides—often report paranormal phenomena. This might include unexplained noises, feelings of unease, or visual sightings, which are sometimes attributed to residual energies or the spirits of those who died tragically. Many paranormal experiences are reported in locations where violent death has occurred such as battlefields, wrecks, natural disasters, and mass shootings. The authors of this book (Drs. Bain and Garza) visited a site of a mass shooting in Texas (the name of which is intentionally withheld) in mid-2024. Upon approaching the building where the killings occurred, we suddenly heard what at first appeared to sound like loud banging against the walls as if someone was using a large sledgehammer. But as we crept closer, we realized it sounded more like the loud, muffled sounds of gunshots. What makes this a mystery indeed is that the building itself was no longer used and was locked, boarded, chained, and empty.

Many people have reported ghostly encounters at the Gettysburg Battlefield, which is known for being the site of a major Civil War battle in 1863. Visitors often describe seeing apparitions of soldiers in period uniforms, hearing unexplained footsteps or voices, and experiencing sudden cold spots. Some have claimed to see figures of soldiers marching or standing guard, and others report hearing the sounds of cannons and battle noises, despite the battlefield being peaceful today. These experiences are thought to be linked to the intense and tragic history of the battle, leading many to believe the site is haunted by those who met their end through violent death.

Experiencing or Witnessing Acts of Violence

Victims or witnesses of violent crimes, such as assaults or shootings, sometimes report paranormal experiences afterward. These experiences may manifest as seeing apparitions, sensing presences, or having precognitive warnings. Such phenomena may arise from heightened states of vigilance and emotional distress during or after the event. As professional counselors, we are also fully aware of the effect of media coverage and violent events. Often, people are traumatized by graphic displays of violence, death, and injury resulting in post traumatic stress disorder (PTSD)-type of fear and apprehension from internet or life television exposure.

In each of these cases, trauma appears to act as a catalyst, opening individuals to altered states of consciousness and heightened sensitivity to their environment. While some view these experiences as psychological responses to trauma, others interpret them as genuine encounters with a paranormal or spiritual dimension. Regardless of the explanation, these experiences often play a significant role in how individuals process and make sense of their traumatic events.

PARANORMAL PTSD: COULD IT BE?

As a personal story (Dr. Bain), I remember during the late night of September 10, 2001, I was awakened out of a sound sleep with a very fearful dream that a passenger jet had crashed in the field in front of my in-laws' house. I can remember how terrified I was and was crying out for people to come to the rescue of the victims as I could see them trying to flee the burning wreckage. The next morning, I literally witnessed (while watching live television) the second passenger plane crash into the World Trade Center tower. I have often wondered if this was synchronicity or something trying to warn me of an upcoming event. I did notice a rise in paranormal activity in my life for weeks and months following that. Watching that horrific scene live as it unfolded created a sense of fear and trepidation that resonates with me to this day. From that perspective, I could say with a high level of certainty that paranormal PTSD is very likely for those who experience anomalous experiences.

Paranormal PTSD is a very real and often overlooked phenomenon. Individuals who experience paranormal events can endure emotional and psychological trauma similar to that suffered by victims of child molestation or rape. In many cases, they face the same type of disbelief, invalidation, and even ridicule when they attempt to share their experiences. This lack of understanding and support only serves to deepen the trauma, leaving victims feeling isolated and vulnerable. The stigma surrounding these experiences often prevents people from seeking help, forcing them to suffer in silence. However, everyone deserves to be heard, believed, and supported, regardless of how unusual their story may seem.

One of the significant challenges of paranormal PTSD is the lack of tangible evidence or memory surrounding the event. Paranormal experiences often defy conventional understanding, leaving no physical traces or logical explanations. Victims may struggle to piece together fragmented memories or doubt their own perceptions, which can lead to feelings of confusion and self-doubt. This absence of validation can exacerbate their trauma, as they may feel that they have no proof to justify their pain. In a world that values empirical evidence, the intangible nature of paranormal encounters can make victims feel dismissed and invalidated by others, including friends, family, and mental health professionals.

Another layer of complexity arises when the experience challenges the victim's existing belief systems or faith. A paranormal encounter often shatters preconceived notions of reality, forcing individuals to question their understanding of the world and their place within it. For those with strong religious or scientific beliefs, such experiences can create a profound internal conflict. The event may feel like a betrayal of their faith or an unsettling contradiction to their worldview, leaving them feeling untethered and uncertain. This existential crisis can compound the emotional turmoil, making it even harder for victims to process and move past the trauma.

The societal stigma surrounding paranormal experiences further isolates victims. When individuals muster the courage to share their stories, they are often met with skepticism or outright ridicule. The fear of being labeled as delusional or attention-seeking discourages many from speaking out, even to close confidants. This silence can perpetuate feelings of shame and loneliness, deepening the psychological scars. In some cases, victims may even begin to doubt their own sanity, leading to a cycle of self-blame and emotional distress.

To address paranormal PTSD, it is essential to create an environment where victims feel safe to share their experiences without fear of judgment or ridicule. Throughout our book, we encourage mental health and life support professionals to seek training so they can approach these cases with sensitivity and an open mind, recognizing the profound impact that such events can have on an individual's psyche. Peer support groups can also provide a valuable space for individuals to connect with others who have had similar experiences, fostering a sense of understanding and community. Ultimately, validating the experiences of those suffering from paranormal PTSD is crucial to their healing journey. Everyone deserves compassion and support, regardless of how unconventional their story may seem. By fostering empathy and acceptance, we can help victims reclaim their sense of security, rebuild their trust in themselves, and begin the process of healing from their trauma.

THE W.H.O.L.E. STRATEGY

The W.H.O.L.E. strategy consists of five key components: Writing, Holism, Openness, Learning, and Embracing. Each component offers distinct methods and insights that counselors can use to assist clients in their recovery. In the following pages, we will explore each element in detail, providing counselors with practical tools and approaches to help clients navigate the complexities of trauma, particularly when it involves anomalous or paranormal experiences.

Traumatic experiences, especially those that involve anomalous or paranormal events, often leave individuals with a sense of confusion, fear, and vulnerability. These experiences can be difficult to process, as they challenge deeply held beliefs about reality and the self. For mental health professionals working with individuals who have experienced trauma, understanding how to help clients make sense of these events is essential for promoting healing and growth. The W.H.O.L.E. strategy is a multifaceted approach that can guide counselors in helping clients process and make sense of their trauma, ultimately fostering positive self-awareness and personal development.

(W) Writing: A Tool for Making Sense of Trauma

Writing can be a powerful therapeutic tool for processing trauma. When clients experience a traumatic event, their emotions and thoughts may be disorganized, leading to confusion and difficulty in making sense of the experience. Writing offers a structured way for clients to articulate their feelings, thoughts, and experiences, helping to clarify the meaning of the trauma.

One of the first steps in using writing as a therapeutic strategy is to encourage clients to write soon after the traumatic event occurs. This immediate response allows the client to capture their raw emotions and thoughts while they are still fresh. Writing can act as a "release valve," giving clients a safe and controlled outlet for expressing intense emotions such as fear, anger, or sadness. The act of writing itself can also be cathartic, providing relief from emotional tension.

Key Themes and Emotional Awareness

As clients begin to write, it is important to guide them in identifying key themes that emerge from their writing. These themes may relate to their emotional responses, their perceptions of the traumatic event, or their beliefs about themselves and the world. Counselors should encourage clients to reflect on these recurring themes, as they can offer valuable insights into how the client is processing the trauma. For example, a client who has experienced a paranormal event might write about feelings of fear, helplessness, or confusion. However, over time, they may begin to identify other themes such as curiosity, empowerment, or a desire for answers. These emerging themes can indicate shifts in the client's perception of the event and can serve as important markers of progress in the therapeutic process.

In addition to identifying themes, counselors should help clients explore the emotions they experience as they journal. Trauma often results in a wide range of emotions, some of which may be difficult to understand or articulate. Writing allows clients to externalize these emotions and observe them from a distance, which can foster greater emotional clarity and regulation. It also allows clients to process emotions at their own pace, without the pressure of having to explain themselves to others.

Writing as a Tangible Record

Another benefit of writing is that it provides clients with a tangible record of their experiences. For those who have experienced a traumatic event, particularly one that involves paranormal elements, it can be difficult to find others who understand or believe their experiences. Writing creates an objective record that the client can refer back to, offering a sense of validation and confirmation. This can be especially important in cases where the client feels isolated or dismissed due to the nature of their experience.

Paranormal Experience Writing Template

The following template might be used to help clients record and sort through their own stories:

1. Detailed Description of the Experience
    - Date and Time: When did this occur? (e.g., exact day, approximate time of day, season)
    - Location: Where were you? Describe the setting (indoors, outdoors, familiar/unfamiliar place).
    - What Happened: Record the sequence of events as you recall them.
    - Sensory Impressions: What did you see, hear, feel, smell, or even taste?
    - Other Witnesses: Were others present? If yes, what did they report or notice?
2. Personal Reactions and Emotions
    - Immediate Response: What did you feel at the moment? (fear, awe, peace, confusion, excitement)
    - Physical Reactions: Did you notice bodily changes (goosebumps, racing heartbeat, warmth, dizziness)?
    - Aftereffects: How did you feel minutes, hours, or days afterward?
    - Lingering Emotions: Are there feelings that persist even now when recalling the event?

3. Interpretation and Meaning-Making
   - Personal Beliefs: How does this align or conflict with your current beliefs or worldview?
   - Cultural/Spiritual Context: Does your background (religious, cultural, or personal) give a framework for interpreting the event?
   - Impact on Identity: Did this experience change how you see yourself or your place in the world?
   - Unanswered Questions: What aspects remain mysterious or unresolved for you?

By revisiting their written accounts, clients can track their emotional progress over time and notice patterns in their thoughts and feelings. This can offer a sense of control and agency in a situation that might have otherwise felt chaotic or overwhelming. Additionally, re-reading past entries can help clients gain new insights or perspectives as they continue their healing journey.

(H) Holism: A Comprehensive Approach to Healing

The holistic approach emphasizes the importance of considering the whole person—body, mind, and spirit—when addressing trauma. This is particularly relevant in the context of anomalous experiences, which can affect not only the individual's mental state but also their physical and spiritual well-being. Trauma is not a singular, isolated event; it touches every aspect of the person's life, and healing must similarly be comprehensive.

Counselors should engage with clients as physical, psychological, and spiritual beings, recognizing the interconnectedness of these dimensions. A holistic approach recognizes that trauma can manifest not only in psychological distress but also in physical symptoms (such as tension, sleep disturbances, or illness) and spiritual crises (such as existential questions or a loss of meaning). By addressing all of these dimensions, counselors can help clients process their trauma in a way that promotes overall healing and well-being.

Physical Well-Being: The Foundation of Emotional Resilience

Physical health is often the first aspect of well-being to suffer when a counselor is overburdened by the emotional demands of their work. Long hours, emotional exhaustion, and the physical toll of managing complex client stories can negatively affect a counselor's physical state. Therefore, it is important for counselors to engage in regular exercise, eat a balanced diet, and get adequate rest. Physical activity, for example, can help alleviate stress, improve mood, and enhance overall well-being. Counselors should also be mindful of the physical toll that prolonged stress can have on the body, such as headaches, digestive issues, or trouble sleeping. By engaging in self-care practices like yoga, walking, or even regular breaks throughout the workday, counselors can mitigate these physical symptoms and maintain a higher level of energy and clarity. Taking care of one's body is foundational to maintaining the stamina needed to hold space for clients, especially in emotionally taxing sessions involving trauma or paranormal experiences.

Psychological Well-Being: Coping with the Emotional Toll of Trauma Work

The emotional demands of working with trauma can be overwhelming. Clients who have experienced paranormal or anomalous events may share deeply unsettling or confusing stories that evoke strong emotional reactions in the counselor. Counselors who absorb these emotional burdens without proper self-care risk developing vicarious trauma, which occurs when the therapist becomes emotionally affected by the trauma stories of their clients. Symptoms can include feelings of sadness, anxiety, numbness, or intrusive thoughts related to the client's experience.

To avoid vicarious trauma, counselors should engage in regular supervision or peer support. Supervision provides an opportunity for counselors to process their own emotional responses to client stories, receive feedback, and explore difficult cases in a supportive environment. Peer support groups can also be valuable for counselors to connect with colleagues who understand the unique challenges of trauma work. These spaces offer emotional validation and a sense of shared experience, which is crucial for reducing isolation and maintaining emotional resilience.

Additionally, seeking personal therapy is an important self-care practice for counselors. Having a space to process their own emotions and experiences can help therapists avoid becoming emotionally overwhelmed by the stories they hear in their practice. Personal therapy allows counselors to address any unresolved feelings or traumas of their own, which might otherwise surface during work with clients.

Spiritual Well-Being: Finding Balance and Meaning

Trauma work, particularly with paranormal or anomalous experiences, often prompts profound existential questions, both for clients and counselors. For counselors, engaging in spiritual practices or philosophy can provide a sense of grounding, purpose, and clarity. Whether through religious faith, meditation, or mindfulness, counselors can cultivate a deeper understanding of the human experience and their role within it. Mindfulness and meditation practices can help counselors maintain emotional balance and mental clarity, allowing them to stay present with clients without becoming overwhelmed by the intensity of the emotions involved.

Incorporating spiritual practices into one's routine can also provide counselors with a sense of connection to something larger than themselves, which is especially important in trauma work. It fosters resilience and a sense of peace amidst the chaotic and often unsettling nature of the work. By maintaining their spiritual health, counselors are better equipped to manage their emotional reactions to clients' traumatic experiences and can approach their work with a sense of purpose and compassion.

Work–Life Balance: Preventing Burnout and Compassion Fatigue

A critical aspect of self-care for counselors is maintaining a healthy work–life balance. Trauma work can be emotionally and mentally exhausting, and without sufficient downtime, counselors risk experiencing burnout. Burnout is characterized by emotional exhaustion, reduced personal accomplishment, and a sense of detachment from clients. Counselors who do not take regular breaks or make time for personal activities are at risk of becoming disengaged from their work and may begin to feel ineffective or disconnected from their clients.

Establishing boundaries between work and personal life is essential. Counselors should be mindful of how many hours they are working each week and ensure they take time for personal activities that replenish their energy and help them decompress. This might include hobbies, spending time with family and friends, or engaging in creative outlets. Having a fulfilling personal life outside of work allows counselors to recharge emotionally and mentally, making them better equipped to support their clients in the long term.

Modeling Self-Care for Clients

By actively practicing self-care, counselors not only safeguard their own well-being but also model healthy coping strategies for their clients. Clients, particularly those who have experienced trauma, often struggle with self-care and may feel overwhelmed by the demands of processing their experiences. Counselors who practice self-care can offer tangible examples of how to integrate self-compassion, emotional regulation, and stress management into daily life. For example, a counselor who regularly engages in mindfulness or relaxation techniques can encourage their clients to do the same. By sharing self-care strategies—such as journaling, engaging in physical activity, or practicing deep breathing—the counselor can empower clients to adopt similar practices in their own lives. This not only helps clients to manage their emotions but also fosters a deeper sense of self-awareness and self-compassion, which is key to long-term healing.

The well-being of the counselor is integral to the effectiveness of trauma therapy, particularly when working with clients who have experienced anomalous or paranormal events. Counselors must prioritize their own physical, psychological, and spiritual health in order to prevent burnout and maintain the emotional resilience required to support their clients effectively. Through regular supervision, peer support, mindfulness practices, personal therapy, and maintaining a healthy work–life balance, counselors can safeguard their well-being. Moreover, by modeling healthy coping strategies, counselors not only enhance their own self-care but also provide clients with the tools they need to prioritize their own healing and well-being.

(O) Openness: Building Trust and a Safe Therapeutic Environment

Openness is essential in trauma recovery. Traumatized individuals, particularly those who have experienced anomalous or paranormal events, often feel misunderstood, ridiculed, or isolated. They may fear judgment or disbelief from others, which can make it difficult for them to share their experiences and feelings surrounding those events. As a counselor, creating an environment of trust and openness is crucial for helping clients process their experiences. Counselors must be open to the client's unique experiences, even if they challenge the counselor's own beliefs or understanding of reality. This requires setting aside personal biases and adopting a nonjudgmental stance. Counselors should validate the client's feelings and experiences, regardless of whether they conform to conventional or mainstream understandings.

At the same time, counselors must encourage clients to be open with themselves. This may involve helping the client confront uncomfortable emotions or memories that they have been avoiding. It may also involve helping the client examine aspects of their experience that they may find difficult to discuss, particularly when those experiences involve the paranormal or unexplained. One strategy may involve a conversation such as:

Counselor: Can you tell me a little more about your experience and why it has impacted you as it has?
Client: I'm not sure how to tell you this. I really haven't shared this with many people.
Counselor: Are you aware of how hesitant you are to discuss your experience with me? I want to assure you this is a "no judgement zone." I am here to listen to you. I believe what you have experienced is very real to you or you wouldn't be discussing this as we sit here.
Client: Well, it's just that when I've tried to talk to my family or friends, they always tell me that is was a figment of my imagination or that I am confused or that I am making it up to hide from the pain I endured.
Counselor: As your counseling professional, I'm not interested in what other people think about your experience. They didn't experience it. I want to know what *you* think about your experience. Why is it real to you?

So what are we hearing in this exchange? In the conversation between the counselor and client, several key themes emerge that are crucial for understanding the dynamics of trauma, the difficulty of sharing personal experiences, and the counselor's role in creating a safe and supportive environment for the client. The four key themes are:

1. *Hesitation and Difficulty in Sharing Trauma:* Clients often express clear hesitation and difficulty in sharing their experience, highlighting the emotional and psychological barriers that often accompany trauma. The phrase, "I'm not sure how to tell you this. I really haven't shared this with many people," reveals the client's sense of vulnerability and fear of judgment. This theme is critical as it underscores the shame or fear of being misunderstood that individuals may feel when attempting to disclose traumatic experiences, particularly those that are difficult for others to believe or understand. It indicates a deep-seated anxiety about being ridiculed, dismissed, or not believed, which can prevent individuals from seeking help or fully processing their trauma.
2. *Fear of Judgment and Invalidating Responses from Others:* The second theme is the client's past experiences with invalidation from their family and friends, who have dismissed the client's trauma as either imagined or a defense mechanism. The client shares, "When I've tried to talk to my family or friends, they always tell me that it was a figment of my imagination or that I am confused or that I am

making it up to hide from the pain I endured." This reflects the painful reality of being met with skepticism or outright denial by those they trust the most, a common experience for individuals who have undergone anomalous or paranormal trauma. The invalidation from others has compounded the client's sense of isolation, and likely contributes to their hesitation to discuss the experience openly. This theme speaks to the broader issue of how individuals who face experiences that fall outside the "norm," such as paranormal or unexplained events, may be met with disbelief or minimization. The lack of validation from others can deepen feelings of shame, confusion, and alienation, making it even harder for the individual to process their experience and move toward healing.

3. *The Counselor's Role in Creating a Non-Judgmental, Safe Space:* The third theme is the counselor's role in providing a safe, supportive, and non-judgmental space for the client. The counselor explicitly states, "I want to assure you this is a 'no judgement zone.' I am here to listen to you. I believe what you have experienced is very real to you or you wouldn't be discussing this as we sit here." This is crucial for the client's healing process. The counselor's response serves to normalize the client's feelings and experiences, signaling that the counselor will not dismiss or invalidate what the client has gone through. By emphasizing a "no judgment zone," the counselor is actively fostering a space where the client can feel heard and accepted, which is vital for trauma recovery. It is in this safe environment that the client can begin to confront and process their experience.
4. *Empowering the Client to Own Their Experience and Define Their Truth:* The fourth theme is the counselor's encouragement for the client to reclaim ownership of their experience and define its meaning for themselves. The counselor's question, "Why is it real to you?" encourages the client to explore their personal truth and self-validation. This question is pivotal in the therapeutic process, as it helps the client shift from seeking external validation (from family and friends) to finding internal validation for their experience. By asking this question, the counselor empowers the client to reflect on the significance and reality of the experience from their own perspective, which can be a transformative step in processing trauma. In this context, the counselor is not attempting to explain away or minimize the trauma but instead is encouraging the client to honor their subjective reality. This approach is important for people who have experienced anomalous events, as their experiences may be difficult to articulate or justify to others. The counselor's focus on *why* the experience is real to the client helps them reclaim a sense of agency and autonomy in their healing process.

The Power of Vulnerability

Openness in the therapeutic relationship is not only about being transparent or communicative—it also involves a willingness to be vulnerable. Vulnerability is an essential aspect of emotional healing because it requires individuals to expose their deepest fears, uncertainties, and truths. For true healing to take place, both the counselor and the client must be willing to open themselves up, creating a reciprocal dynamic of trust and emotional safety. When both parties engage in vulnerability, it fosters a deeper connection and allows for authentic, meaningful conversations about the trauma and its impact.

For the client, the process of being vulnerable often involves confronting painful or confusing aspects of their experience, particularly when dealing with trauma related to anomalous or paranormal events. These types of events are often outside the realm of normal understanding, and clients may feel deeply afraid of being judged, ridiculed, or misunderstood. For them to heal, they must feel safe enough to share these experiences without fear of dismissal or invalidation. When counselors create a nonjudgmental space, free from skepticism or disbelief, it encourages the client to be open about their fears and uncertainties. This level of openness is necessary for exploring the full scope of their trauma and moving towards healing.

Counselors, too, must be willing to be vulnerable, but in a way that supports and enriches the client's process. This might involve sharing relevant personal experiences or insights, particularly when they can help normalize the client's feelings. For example, a counselor might share that they, too, have faced difficult or inexplicable moments in their lives, which can help the client feel less isolated. However, this sharing must always remain client-centered, ensuring that the focus remains on the client's healing journey and does not detract from their process. By modeling vulnerability, the counselor sets an example of openness and emotional courage, reinforcing the message that it's safe to express difficult emotions and thoughts.

Ultimately, this mutual vulnerability cultivates trust within the therapeutic relationship. When both the counselor and the client show a willingness to be open and vulnerable, they create a dynamic where healing can truly take root. It is within this safe, open space that clients feel empowered to confront their pain, process their trauma, and begin to reclaim their sense of self.

(L) Learning: Personal Growth through Trauma

Trauma, though painful, can also serve as an opportunity for profound personal growth. As clients process their experiences, they may gain new insights into themselves, their beliefs, and their place in the world. This process of learning can help clients develop resilience, increase their sense of self-awareness, and cultivate a deeper understanding of life and spirituality. Counselors can guide clients in exploring what they have learned from their traumatic experiences. This might involve reflecting on how the trauma has changed their views of themselves, their relationships, or their values. It might also involve learning new coping strategies or gaining new skills for managing stress and anxiety. In some cases, clients may come to see their traumatic experience as a catalyst for positive change. They may find a new sense of purpose, a stronger sense of self, or a deeper connection to their spiritual or philosophical beliefs.

(E) Embracing: Acceptance and Integration

The final component of the W.H.O.L.E. strategy—embracing—is crucial for long-term healing, especially when dealing with trauma related to paranormal or anomalous experiences. Such events often challenge an individual's understanding of reality and can evoke intense feelings of confusion, fear, or isolation. For many clients, the experience may seem inexplicable, disturbing, or even shameful, leading them to deny or suppress it. However, true healing is not achieved by rejecting or avoiding the trauma but by fully embracing it as a part of the individual's personal narrative. Embracing trauma involves shifting from a place of fear or resistance to one of acceptance and integration. When working with a client who is dealing with paranormal or anomalous events we have discovered this process may initially feel counterintuitive. These events are often outside the bounds of normal experience, and society may dismiss or ridicule them. As a result, clients may internalize feelings of alienation, believing that no one will understand or validate what they have gone through. They may fear judgment or feel that they are "damaged" by their experiences.

We have discovered that as counselors, we have a vital role in helping clients reframe their trauma, especially in the context of experiences that are hard to explain. Rather than seeing the trauma as something that happened *to* them, counselors can guide clients to see it as something that happened *for* them—an opportunity for growth and self-discovery. This reframe allows those who have had these anomalous experiences to view the traumatic event not as a curse, but as a pivotal moment in their lives that holds valuable lessons or insights. By reframing the trauma, clients may begin to find meaning in their experience, even if they cannot fully understand it resulting in a healthy integration of the various components of the experience to achieve a state of internal balance, acceptance, and growth.

This process of embracing can be empowering. When clients accept their trauma as part of their life story, they regain a sense of deep healing. They reclaim control over how they interpret and respond to their experiences. Embracing the trauma allows clients to move beyond the victim mindset, replacing feelings of helplessness with a sense of ownership over their healing journey. It provides the emotional space for them to grow stronger, develop resilience, and find purpose in the aftermath of their experiences. Ultimately, embracing trauma is a pathway to transformation. It enables clients to incorporate their experiences into a more authentic version of themselves, one that is capable of facing future challenges with confidence and resilience. Through this acceptance, clients can turn their pain into a source of personal strength, moving forward with a renewed sense of self and hope for the future.

CONCLUSION

In conclusion, the relationship between trauma and anomalous experiences presents a unique challenge for mental health professionals, requiring approaches that honor both the psychological and spiritual dimensions of human experience. This chapter highlights the W.H.O.L.E. strategy as a comprehensive framework designed to equip counselors with the skills needed to help clients integrate these often-disruptive events into their broader life narratives. *Writing* serves as a foundational tool by encouraging clients to articulate their experiences and emotions in a structured way, creating both a therapeutic outlet and a record for future reflection. *Holism* emphasizes the importance of viewing clients as multifaceted beings, whose healing must address body, mind, and spirit, while also reminding counselors to practice self-care to prevent burnout. *Openness* fosters an atmosphere of trust, enabling clients to share details that may otherwise remain hidden due to fear of stigma or invalidation. Through *Learning*, clients are guided toward developing resilience, self-discovery, and spiritual growth, reframing trauma and anomalous experiences as opportunities for empowerment. Finally, *Embracing* invites clients to accept their experiences as meaningful, even if they remain partially unexplained, reinforcing the importance of personal integration and identity formation. Taken together, these five elements provide counselors with a roadmap to help clients move beyond fragmentation and toward wholeness. The W.H.O.L.E. strategy affirms that the counselor's role is not to resolve the objective reality of anomalous events but to support clients in their meaning-making process, thereby facilitating healing and growth. By integrating trauma-informed care with cultural and spiritual sensitivity, counselors can empower clients to transform their experiences into sources of resilience, insight, and renewed purpose.

Personal Reflection Questions for Chapter 8

Reflect on how you, as a counselor or helping professional, might differentiate between trauma-related symptoms (such as flashbacks or dissociation) and experiences that a client perceives as genuinely paranormal. How can you balance clinical discernment with empathy and openness?

The W.H.O.L.E. strategy encourages Writing, Holism, Openness, Learning, and Embracing as pathways to healing. Which of these elements resonates most with your personal counseling philosophy, and how might you incorporate it into your work with clients processing trauma and anomalous experiences?

Consider a time when you or someone you know found meaning or comfort in an unusual or unexplained experience following loss or trauma. What insights from that reflection can help you better support clients navigating the intersection between pain, mystery, and meaning-making?

REFERENCES

Hashemi, A., Oroojan, A. A., Rassouli, M., & Ashrafizadeh, H. (2023). Explanation of near-death experiences: A systematic analysis of case reports and qualitative research. *Frontiers in Psychology*, *14*, 1048929. https://doi.org/10.3389/fpsyg.2023.1048929

Lindsay, N., Tassell-Matamua, N., O'Sullivan, L., & Gibson, R. (2024). Trauma or transcendence? The relationship between near-death experiences and dreaming. *Dreaming. Advance Online Publication.* https://doi.org/10.1037/drm0000278

Marks, D. F. (2021). "God Spoke to me": Subjective paranormal experience and the homeostatic response to early trauma. *Imagination, Cognition and Personality: Consciousness in Theory, Research, and Clinical Practice*, *40*(3) 223–272. https://doi.org/10.1177/0276236620934003

Marks, D. F., & Kammann, R. (1980). *The psychology of the psychic.* Prometheus Books.

Rabeyron, T., & Watt, C. (2010). Paranormal experiences, mental health and mental boundaries, and psi. *Personality and Individual Differences*, *48*(4), 487–492. https://doi.org/10.1016/j.paid.2009.11.029

Chapter 9

Soothing the Sinister Spookiness of Grief and Loss

INTRODUCTION

We live in a day of unprecedented and immeasurable loss and sadness. Whether it be war, global pandemics, natural disasters, tragic accidents, or the natural consequences of illnesses and aging, humanity suffers losses at a regular and unrelenting frequency. Yet we as a contemporary society seem to misunderstand and misrepresent the importance of the grief process. In reality, grief is a profound and complex emotional experience that plays a pivotal role in personal and spiritual growth. However, in many societies, particularly in the United States, grief is viewed with discomfort and treated as something to be overcome as quickly as possible. Chapter 9 will offer important perspectives and strategies to assist counselors in making the connection to paranormal experiences and one's understanding of grief.

THE ROLES OF GRIEF IN HUMAN EXPERIENCE

Far from being the monstrous and sinister enemy of the mind and soul that it is often portrayed as being, grief is actually a natural and necessary part of the human experience. Sometimes, grief is seen as a form of illness that, with the proper medication and therapy, can and should be expunged. This perspective often leads to the suppression of grief through avoidance, distraction, or even medical intervention. While these methods may provide temporary relief, they fail to acknowledge the deeper purpose of grief. Grieving is not simply an unfortunate

DOI: 10.4324/9781003529477-9

consequence of loss; it is a process that helps individuals confront and integrate the reality of their experiences. It is not an ailment, a malady, or a state of being that needs to be fixed, medicated, or eradicated. Instead, grief is an essential component of our well-being. It validates our losses, underscores our humanity, and provides us with the opportunity to break down emotional barriers that may hinder our growth, healing, and progress. By embracing grief, individuals allow themselves to fully process the emotions that accompany loss, which is a necessary step toward healing and transformation.

Grief Validates Loss

Grief acknowledges the significance of what has been experienced. Whether it is the death of a loved one, the end of a meaningful relationship, or another type of significant change, grief serves as a testament to the depth of connections and the value placed on what has been lost. It reminds individuals that their emotions are real and meaningful and that it is okay to feel pain in the face of loss. In this way, grief affirms humanity and connects individuals to the universal experience of being human.

Grief Breaks Down Emotional Barriers

Grief has the potential to dismantle the emotional walls that individuals build to protect themselves from vulnerability. These walls may provide a sense of security, but they can also isolate and limit one's capacity for growth. When individuals experience grief, these walls are often shattered, leaving them exposed and raw. While this can be an incredibly painful experience, it is also an opportunity for profound personal growth. In the aftermath of this emotional shattering, individuals have the chance to rebuild themselves in a way that is more authentic, open, and resilient. Beyond the emotional transformation that grief initiates, it may also open the door to experiences that transcend the physical world. Many individuals report encounters with the paranormal during periods of deep mourning. Whether through dreams, visions, synchronicities, or an unexplained sense of presence, these occurrences suggest that the emotional upheaval of grief may create a heightened state of awareness, making individuals more receptive to experiences they might otherwise dismiss. One possible explanation for this phenomenon is that grief disrupts an individual's normal psychological and emotional state, allowing them to perceive realities beyond their typical awareness. When a person is emotionally raw, they are more sensitive to subtle energies and emotions, which can create the perfect conditions for paranormal experiences. Some people believe that this heightened sensitivity makes communication with deceased loved ones more possible, as the grieving individual becomes more attuned to signs, messages, and phenomena that might be easily ignored under ordinary circumstances.

Dream visitations are one of the most common ways that grieving individuals report encounters with the deceased. Unlike ordinary dreams, these experiences often feel intensely real, carrying messages of comfort, love, or closure. Many who experience these dreams describe them as vivid, peaceful, and transformative, leading to a sense of reassurance that their loved one continues to exist in some form. While skeptics may argue that these experiences are simply the brain's way of processing loss, those who have had such encounters often are strongly convinced that they are more than just subconscious projections.

Similarly, signs and synchronicities frequently emerge in the wake of loss. Objects moving without explanation, familiar scents appearing out of nowhere, or electronic disturbances occurring in significant moments are all commonly reported by grieving individuals. Some interpret these events as direct communication from the deceased, while others view them as coincidences made meaningful by the emotional state of the mourner. Regardless of interpretation, these experiences highlight the powerful connection between grief and altered perceptions of reality.

Grief's ability to break down emotional barriers does not just foster personal growth but also invites individuals to question the nature of existence and consciousness. Whether or not paranormal experiences during grief are genuine glimpses into another realm, they undeniably provide comfort and meaning to those who are suffering. In this way, the breakdown of emotional walls does not only leaves individuals vulnerable—it may also leave them open to new possibilities, deeper understandings, and a profound sense of connection beyond the material world.

Grief Serves as a Catalyst for Transformation

In the context of personal and spiritual growth, grief can be seen as a catalyst for transformation. It challenges individuals to confront the impermanence of life and the inevitability of change, leading to a deeper understanding of themselves and their place in the world. By working through grief, individuals can develop greater emotional depth, empathy, and wisdom. This process often requires confronting difficult truths about oneself and relationships, but it is through this confrontation that true healing and growth can be achieved.

WHY ARE WE SO RETICENT AND RESISTANT TO THIS NATURAL, INNATE HUMAN EMOTION?

Discomfort in Addressing Grief

One of the primary reasons for society's reluctance to openly engage with grief is the discomfort it elicits. Many individuals feel uncertain about how to support someone who is mourning, fearing that they might say the wrong thing or exacerbate the person's pain. This hesitation often results in the use of clichés and platitudes, such as "everything happens for a reason" or "time heals all wounds." While these statements may be well-intentioned, they often come across as dismissive and invalidate the depth of sorrow the grieving person is experiencing. Rather than providing meaningful support, such responses can create emotional distance and reinforce the idea that grief should be endured privately rather than shared openly. This avoidance of deep emotional conversations contributes to a cultural landscape where grief is perceived as an inconvenience rather than an essential human experience that requires communal acknowledgment and support.

The Cultural Emphasis on Productivity

Another significant factor in the resistance to grief is the societal prioritization of productivity. In many Western cultures, efficiency, work ethic, and maintaining a functional daily routine are highly valued. The grieving process, however, is inherently disruptive and unpredictable, often requiring an extended period of emotional processing. Despite this reality, bereavement leave in most workplaces is minimal, usually amounting to only a few days. Employees are expected to return to work and resume their responsibilities as though their world has not been irrevocably altered. This expectation not only suppresses the natural grieving process but also places undue stress on individuals who must compartmentalize their emotions in order to meet professional obligations. Consequently, grief becomes something to be managed swiftly and discreetly, rather than honored and navigated at a pace that reflects its profound impact on human well-being.

The Prioritization of Positivity and Emotional Control

Modern culture places a high value on positivity, resilience, and emotional regulation. Self-help movements, social media, and motivational discourses frequently promote personal success and happiness as the ultimate goals. Within this framework, emotions that do not align with these ideals, such as grief, are often marginalized or stigmatized. Individuals who openly express sadness, despair, or vulnerability may be perceived as burdensome or as failing to maintain control over their emotions. This pressure to remain composed and "strong" discourages people from fully engaging with their grief or seeking the support they need. Instead, many feel compelled to internalize their sorrow, leading to feelings of isolation and prolonged emotional distress. The absence of societal permission to grieve openly deprives individuals of the validation and empathy necessary for healing.

The Decline of Public Mourning Rituals

Historically, societies had established rituals and traditions that provided structured ways for individuals and communities to acknowledge loss. Public mourning customs, such as wearing black, participating in extended funeral ceremonies, and engaging in communal grief practices, served as tangible expressions of sorrow. These rituals not only honored the deceased but also allowed mourners to process their emotions within a supportive social framework. In contemporary society, however, such public mourning traditions have diminished significantly. Funerals are often brief, and the expectation to quickly "move on" discourages prolonged acknowledgment of grief. Without these shared rituals, grieving individuals may feel isolated in their sorrow, lacking both societal recognition and the communal support systems that once facilitated emotional healing.

The Medicalization of Grief

In addition to cultural influences, the medicalization of grief has further contributed to its marginalization. Increasingly, profound grief is pathologized as a condition requiring treatment, rather than being recognized as a natural and necessary response to loss. Terms such as "complicated grief" or "prolonged grief disorder" suggest that mourning beyond a certain timeframe is abnormal or unhealthy. While it is true that some individuals may require therapeutic support to navigate their grief, the broader tendency to categorize extended mourning as a disorder risks invalidating the complex, individualized nature of the grieving process. This medicalized perspective reinforces the idea that grief should be "treated" and resolved as quickly as possible, rather than acknowledged as an intrinsic part of the human experience that unfolds in its own time.

IMPACT ON MENTAL HEALTH AND WELL-BEING

The societal resistance to grief has profound implications for mental health and overall well-being. When individuals are discouraged from expressing their sorrow or seeking support, they may experience prolonged emotional distress, anxiety, or depression. The suppression of grief can manifest physical symptoms, including fatigue, headaches, and a weakened immune system. Additionally, the lack of open discourse around grief can prevent individuals from developing healthy coping mechanisms, leading to maladaptive behaviors such as substance abuse or emotional withdrawal. Recognizing and addressing grief as a legitimate and necessary process is crucial for fostering emotional resilience and long-term psychological well-being.

THE NEED FOR A CULTURAL SHIFT IN GRIEVING PRACTICES

To create a more compassionate society, there must be a shift in how grief is perceived and addressed. This involves fostering environments where open conversations about loss are normalized and encouraged. Educational initiatives can play a key role in increasing awareness about the importance of grief support, both in workplaces and social settings. Employers can implement more flexible bereavement policies that allow individuals the time and space to process their loss without fear of professional repercussions. Mental health professionals and community leaders can advocate for the reintegration of public mourning rituals that validate and honor the grieving process. Additionally, social media platforms and public discourse can be leveraged to challenge the stigma surrounding grief, promoting narratives that recognize its significance as a fundamental aspect of human life.

Grief is a natural, innate human emotion that has been systematically marginalized due to societal discomfort, cultural values surrounding productivity, and an overarching emphasis on positivity and emotional control. The decline of public mourning rituals and the medicalization of grief further contribute to its suppression, leaving many individuals without the necessary support to navigate their loss. However, by fostering a cultural shift that acknowledges and honors grief as a shared human experience, society can create more compassionate spaces where individuals feel validated in their mourning. Recognizing grief as an essential part of emotional well-being is crucial for breaking the cycle of silence and fostering a healthier, more empathetic approach to loss and healing. One way to harness the transformative power of grief is through the exploration of paranormal experiences.

While this may seem unconventional, the paranormal can provide a unique lens through which to understand and address grief. Paranormal experiences, such as sensing the presence of a deceased loved one or experiencing inexplicable phenomena, are not uncommon among those who are grieving. These experiences can serve as a bridge between the physical and emotional realms, providing comfort, validation, and insight.

FOUNDATIONAL PRINCIPLES FOR PROFESSIONALS

Sensitivity and Open-Mindedness in Counseling

As a counseling professional, it is crucial to approach the work of grief counseling with sensitivity and an open mind. Grieving individuals may experience a range of emotions, thoughts, and even perceived supernatural encounters as they process their loss. While not everyone who is grieving will report paranormal experiences, those who do often find them to be deeply meaningful. Dismissing or minimizing these experiences can invalidate a client's feelings and hinder their healing process. Instead, counselors should foster an environment in which clients feel comfortable exploring the personal and spiritual significance of these encounters. By providing a nonjudgmental space for discussion, counselors help clients find comfort and meaning in their grief, which can be an integral part of the healing journey.

Individualized Nature of Grief

Grief is a deeply personal experience, and there is no "one-size-fits-all" approach to navigating it. Each person's grief journey is unique and is shaped by factors such as personality, relationships, cultural background, and spiritual beliefs. Some individuals may experience grief as a quiet, introspective process, while others may express their emotions more outwardly. Recognizing and honoring these differences is essential in providing effective support. Counselors should adopt a flexible approach, tailoring their interventions to meet the individual needs of each client. Understanding that grief manifests in various ways allows professionals to validate and normalize their clients' experiences, fostering a sense of acceptance and understanding.

The Role of Cultural and Spiritual Beliefs in Grief

Cultural and spiritual beliefs play a significant role in shaping how individuals experience and process grief. In many cultures, grief is a communal experience, often marked by rituals and ceremonies that bring people together to mourn and honor the deceased. These traditions can provide a sense of support and solidarity, helping individuals navigate their loss with the backing of their community. In contrast, other cultures may emphasize a more private and introspective approach to grief, encouraging personal reflection and internal processing. Understanding and respecting these cultural differences is crucial for any professional working with grieving individuals. Counselors should take the time to educate themselves about diverse cultural practices surrounding death and mourning, ensuring they provide culturally competent care that aligns with their clients' values and traditions.

Spirituality and the Grief Process

Spiritual beliefs can offer a powerful framework for understanding and navigating grief. For many individuals, the belief in an afterlife or the possibility of continued connection with loved ones provides comfort and hope during times of loss. These beliefs can shape how people interpret their grief experiences, particularly if they encounter what they perceive as signs or messages from the deceased. Paranormal experiences, such as dreams, visions, or unexplained sensations, may be viewed as meaningful connections rather than mere coincidences. By acknowledging and validating these beliefs, counselors and therapists can help clients find solace and meaning in their grief. Rather than dismissing such experiences, professionals should encourage open conversations, allowing clients to explore how these encounters contribute to their healing process.

The Importance of Active Listening and Validation

One of the most essential skills a counselor can develop when working with grieving individuals is active listening. Actively listening to clients involves more than just hearing their words; it requires full engagement, empathy, and validation of their emotions. Clients who feel heard and understood are more likely to open up about their grief experiences, including any spiritual or paranormal encounters they may have had. Counselors should use reflective listening techniques, such as paraphrasing and summarizing, to demonstrate understanding and reinforce the client's feelings. Validating a client's experiences, rather than judging or dismissing them, fosters a therapeutic alliance that can significantly contribute to their healing process.

ETHICAL CONSIDERATIONS IN GRIEF COUNSELING

Ethical considerations are a fundamental aspect of grief counseling, especially when addressing spiritual or paranormal experiences. Professionals must balance respect for a client's personal beliefs with evidence-based practices and ethical guidelines. It is essential for counselors to avoid imposing their own spiritual or religious perspectives on clients while also refraining from dismissing or invalidating the client's experiences. Maintaining a client-centered approach ensures that individuals feel supported in exploring their grief in ways that are meaningful to them. Additionally, counselors should remain aware of ethical boundaries and refer clients to appropriate spiritual advisors or specialists when necessary, ensuring that their needs are met holistically.

THE ROLE OF SUPPORT SYSTEMS IN GRIEF RECOVERY

A strong support system can significantly impact the grieving process, providing comfort and stability during a difficult time. Family, friends, religious or spiritual communities, and professional counselors all play a role in helping individuals navigate their grief. Helping professionals should assess the support networks available to their clients and encourage them to seek and utilize these resources. For some individuals, engaging in grief support groups can be particularly beneficial, as it allows them to connect with others who have had similar experiences. These groups provide a sense of belonging and validation, reinforcing the idea that grief is a shared human experience. Grief is a profoundly personal and often overwhelming experience, characterized by a range of emotional, psychological, and physical responses to loss. While the grieving process is unique to each individual, one of the most influential factors in shaping how a person moves through grief is the presence—or absence—of a supportive network. Support systems serve as emotional anchors, offering comfort, stability, understanding, and a safe environment for expressing sorrow. These systems may include family, friends, religious or spiritual communities, professional counselors, and peer support groups. The presence of a strong support system can make a considerable difference in the trajectory of grief recovery, helping individuals process their emotions, find meaning in their experiences, and ultimately, reintegrate into life with a renewed sense of purpose and connection.

Family and Friends as Primary Support

At the core of most support systems are family members and close friends. These individuals often form the immediate circle of care, offering not only physical presence but also emotional solace during times of intense sadness. Family and friends who are able to listen without judgment, provide consistent companionship, and validate the mourner's feelings can create a healing environment. They help normalize the expression of grief, reducing the stigma often associated with talking openly about loss. Furthermore, the shared nature of familial grief—for example, when multiple members are mourning the same loss—can foster a sense of unity, reinforcing emotional bonds and mutual support. However, not all family systems are functional or equipped to support someone through grief. In some cases, family members may be experiencing their own overwhelming grief, making them less available or emotionally distant. At other times, cultural or familial norms may discourage open emotional expression, inadvertently causing the grieving individual to suppress their feelings. This is where the broader support network becomes crucial.

Religious and Spiritual Communities

For many individuals, especially those with strong religious or spiritual beliefs, their community of faith plays a central role in grief recovery. Places of worship and spiritual leaders often provide both existential comfort and practical support. Religious rituals, such as funerals, memorial services, and prayer gatherings, help mourners honor the deceased and find spiritual meaning in their loss. These practices offer continuity and tradition, which can be deeply comforting during times of emotional upheaval. Spiritual support also extends to the teachings and doctrines that give mourners a framework for understanding death and the afterlife. Belief in a higher power, reincarnation, or the reunion of souls in an afterlife can provide hope and lessen the sting of finality. Religious communities can also offer structured pastoral counseling, regular check-ins, and volunteer assistance, all of which reinforce a sense of being cared for and not alone in one's suffering.

The Role of Professional Counselors

Mental health professionals, especially those trained in grief counseling or thanatology (the study of death and dying), are an essential component of many support systems. Counselors provide a confidential, nonjudgmental space for clients to explore their feelings, thoughts, and behaviors surrounding the loss. Unlike well-meaning friends or relatives who may offer advice or unintentionally minimize grief, professional counselors are trained to facilitate healing by helping individuals identify unresolved issues, set goals for recovery, and learn coping strategies.

Counselors also play a vital role in identifying complicated or prolonged grief, which may require specialized therapeutic interventions. They can assess whether a client's grief is within the expected range of reactions or if it is leading to more severe mental health conditions such as depression, anxiety, or post-traumatic stress. In addition, therapists may help clients navigate secondary losses (e.g., financial hardship, loss of identity, or strained relationships) that often accompany the primary loss. A key task for counselors is to assess the support networks available to their clients. This includes inquiring about the presence and effectiveness of personal relationships, faith communities, and participation in grief-related activities. If clients are socially isolated or disconnected, counselors can encourage the intentional development of support systems, whether through community programs, therapeutic groups, or volunteer opportunities.

Grief Support Groups: Healing Through Shared Experience

Grief support groups offer a unique form of communal healing. These groups—often facilitated by trained professionals or volunteers—bring together individuals who have experienced similar losses. Whether it's the death of a spouse, child, parent, or friend, sharing one's story with others who understand firsthand can be profoundly validating. Grief support groups help individuals realize that their emotions are not only normal but also shared by others. This reduces feelings of isolation, shame, and abnormality. Participants often report that group settings allow them to give and receive empathy in ways that feel reciprocal and empowering. Hearing how others are coping can offer practical ideas for self-care, rituals, and meaning-making, while also building a sense of resilience. Some groups are short-term and structured around specific themes, while others are open-ended and ongoing, providing long-term community for those who need continued support. For certain populations, such as children, teens, or individuals grieving specific types of losses (e.g., suicide, overdose, or miscarriage), specialized support groups can be especially effective. These groups cater to the particular developmental or situational needs of their members, often incorporating activities, art, or storytelling as part of the healing process.

Social Media and Online Communities

In the digital age, online support systems have become increasingly prevalent and important. Social media groups, grief forums, and virtual counseling platforms allow people to connect with others across geographical boundaries. For individuals in rural areas or those with limited mobility, online grief communities can be a lifeline. These platforms allow for flexible and immediate support, sometimes available 24/7, which can be especially helpful during moments of acute distress. However, while online communities can be beneficial, they should not replace real-life connections or professional care when needed. Counselors should guide clients in discerning reputable online support resources from less helpful or potentially harmful spaces.

Cultural Considerations and Barriers

It is important to recognize that cultural beliefs and norms heavily influence how individuals seek and receive support. In some cultures, public mourning and emotional expression are encouraged, while in others, grief is seen as a private matter. Stigma around mental health, counseling, or vulnerability can act as a barrier to accessing support. Counselors must approach each client with cultural humility, ensuring that their guidance respects the individual's values, traditions, and identity. Some individuals may also encounter systemic barriers such as language, financial constraints, or lack of access to services. Community-based organizations, bilingual counselors, and sliding-scale or pro bono services can help bridge these gaps. Creating inclusive, accessible, and culturally sensitive support systems is vital for ensuring equitable grief care.

THE EVOLUTION OF GRIEF OVER TIME

Grief is not a static process; it evolves over time. While some individuals may experience acute grief in the immediate aftermath of a loss, others may find that their grief resurfaces in waves, triggered by anniversaries, life changes, or reminders of their loved ones. It is important for counselors to educate clients about the non-linear nature of grief and to help them develop coping strategies that support their ongoing healing. Encouraging clients to engage in activities that promote emotional well-being, such as journaling, meditation, or creative expression, can provide constructive outlets for their grief. By recognizing that grief is an ongoing journey, counselors can help clients cultivate resilience and a sense of hope for the future.

Grief counseling requires sensitivity, open-mindedness, and a deep understanding of the diverse ways individuals process loss. By acknowledging the significance of spiritual and cultural beliefs, validating personal experiences, and employing active listening techniques, counselors can create a supportive environment for clients navigating grief. Ethical considerations and respect for individual perspectives are essential in ensuring that counseling remains a client-centered practice. Additionally, recognizing the evolving nature of grief and the importance of support systems can aid in fostering long-term healing. Ultimately, by approaching grief counseling with empathy and cultural competence, professionals can help clients find meaning, comfort, and resilience in their journey toward healing.

CONCLUSION

In conclusion, grief is a powerful force that has the potential to shape and transform us in profound ways. It is not a disease to be cured or a weakness to be overcome, but a vital aspect of the human experience. By validating our losses, breaking down emotional barriers, and fostering personal and spiritual growth, grief helps us heal and progress. Through the exploration of paranormal experiences and the acknowledgment of individual and cultural differences, we can support ourselves and others in navigating the complexities of grief. In doing so, we honor not only our losses but also the resilience and depth of the human spirit. Grief is not a burden that should be carried alone. Support systems—whether they are familial, spiritual, professional, or communal—play an essential role in helping individuals navigate the complex emotional terrain of loss. These systems offer validation, connection, and guidance, transforming grief from an isolating experience into a shared human journey. Counselors and other professionals working with the bereaved should actively assess and encourage the development of support networks, tailoring recommendations to each person's unique needs and cultural context. By fostering connection and compassion, support systems become the scaffolding that helps individuals not only survive grief, but eventually thrive in its aftermath.

Personal Reflection Questions for Chapter 9

Reflect on how your personal beliefs or cultural background have shaped your understanding of grief. Do you tend to view grief as something to "get over" or as a natural process that can lead to growth and transformation?

Consider how you might help a client reframe grief—not as an illness or weakness, but as a necessary and sacred part of the healing journey. What counseling approaches or techniques could support this shift in perspective?

When clients' grief is connected to paranormal or anomalous experiences—such as sensing the presence of a deceased loved one—how might you validate their experiences while helping them find meaning, peace, and integration within their grief process?

Chapter 10

True Stories from Counselors, Their Clients, and Others

Sharing actual stories from counselors and clients related to the paranormal (while protecting the identity of those involved) will be critical in sharing the commonality of paranormal experiences, the impact of these experiences upon the mental health professional, and the challenges the mental health professional often has to help a client come to peace with their anomaly. The stories within this chapter seek to provide a comforting realization to counselors working with paranormally impacted clients that they are not alone. This is especially important as there is often a significant lack of professional development, openness of discussion, and peer support available to those counselors who are seeking to provide therapy to this type of client base. As mental health professionals increasingly encounter clients whose lives have been shaped by extraordinary, anomalous, or paranormal experiences, the need for open, grounded, and professionally oriented discourse becomes more urgent. The narratives—drawn from counselors, clients, and others—will serve as powerful illustrations of the lived reality of working with and through paranormal experiences. The shared paranormal experiences presented in this chapter are not for the purpose of entertainment, shock value, or literary intrigue. The stories presented are shared with a very different purpose. They are not meant to sensationalize the unexplainable or provide speculative theories about the supernatural. Instead, they aim to normalize what is still considered by many as marginal or rare, revealing how widespread these experiences are across diverse populations and professional settings.

The inclusion of these stories is more than just illustrative—it is also therapeutic. They serve as a bridge between theory and practice, helping to validate the counselor's role as both a professional and a fellow human being navigating the unknown. These narratives offer readers a chance to

DOI: 10.4324/9781003529477-10

reflect on the emotional labor involved in this work and to realize that others have walked similar paths. This can be particularly comforting for counselors working in environments where professional development opportunities related to the paranormal are scarce, where open dialogue about anomalous experiences is limited, or where colleagues may be dismissive or skeptical. By offering these stories, this chapter invites readers into a community of reflection and support. It extends a hand to those who are walking alongside clients into unfamiliar and often spiritually charged territory, assuring them that they are not navigating this path alone. What follows is a series of real-life encounters that demonstrate the experiences, feelings, and meaning behind these individual paranormal or unexplained happenings. While protecting the privacy and confidentiality of those involved, these accounts will illustrate the often-unspoken emotional and psychological dimensions of this unique therapeutic environment. Those wishing to tell their stories anonymously or under a pseudonym will be marked with an asterisk (*).

THE STORY OF A COUNSELOR'S EXPERIENCE*

As I was preparing for my session with a young client, I had no idea what I was about to encounter. Based on the information she provided in her intake form, I anticipated a fairly typical session. However, what unfolded was something entirely different. The session began with the client expressing that she had been feeling down and constantly burdened by a heavy sensation within herself. As I began asking questions to gather more insight, she suddenly mentioned that there were two individuals with her in the room. I gently asked her to clarify who these individuals were. She explained that they followed her everywhere she went. Initially, I considered the possibility of a mental health concern, such as schizophrenia. I continued to ask follow-up questions to better understand her experience. Then, quite unexpectedly, she stopped speaking and began staring intensely at both my left and right shoulders. Concerned, I asked if everything was okay. She calmly responded that the two individuals were standing behind me—one next to each shoulder. She went on to describe the figure beside my right shoulder as a woman who "didn't like" me. When I asked how she knew this, the client replied, "Because she's looking at you very ugly and is reaching out to try and grab you." At this point, I gently shifted the conversation to gather more context by asking a series of clarifying questions. I inquired when she first began seeing these two individuals and asked her to describe what they looked like. I also asked whether they spoke to her and whether their presence frightened her or made her feel uncomfortable.

As I asked these questions, I noticed her demeanor change. She appeared frightened and uncertain. She then shared that ever since moving into a new home with her parents, she had felt increasingly depressed and angry. That's when the experiences began. She told me that for the first few months, everything felt fine, but after about three months, things began to shift. She said, "My house doesn't feel the same anymore." She explained that the ghosts didn't speak to her but instead communicated through sad or angry expressions. When I asked again for a description of these individuals, she said, "I can see them, but I can also see through them." She then told me she believed her house was haunted. Wanting to ensure a thorough understanding, I revisited her intake form and medical history. There were no indications of mental health issues, either personal or familial. I had hoped to explore her experience further in subsequent sessions, but I never had the opportunity. Her mother later called to inform me they were moving out of state and thanked me for meeting with their daughter. Although our time together was brief, this case had a lasting impact on me. It opened my mind to the possibility that some individuals may genuinely be experiencing phenomena that fall outside the conventional boundaries of mental health.

THE STORY OF AIMEE

It was springtime in Maryland, and my relatives on my mother's side were starting to show up to my childhood home. The house was full of noises from my cousins running around, dishes being tossed about in the kitchen, and animated discussions in both Tagalog and English. I was probably 11 or 12 at the time, and I remember sitting on my parents' windowsill in their bathroom on the second floor watching everyone pull up to the house. I remember feeling sad, alone, and I had this overwhelming sense that I did not want to be of this world anymore. I love my cousins and spending time with them but on this day, I felt forgotten. The next memory I have is of my cousins and I crammed into my bedroom. They were all playing and rustling through my belongings, and I just remember this surge of anger erupting. I remember lighting a bathroom towel I had in my room on fire which ultimately frightened everyone…so they left me alone. Why was I so angry? I felt like I was a ghost in the room. No one saw me nor were they respecting my space. This is where it begins, and I wish I could fill in the gaps, but no one has been able to. I recall crying—the kind of crying where you can't control the sounds, snot, or shaking. I felt overwhelmingly alone and sad like I did not matter. I know I'm in the corner of my room balled up with my head on my knees. For a moment, I stopped and lifted my head to face my closed bedroom door. Time seemed to have passed quickly because now it was dark outside. I recall seeing the brightest light outlining my door frame instead of the yellowish hue that normally comes through from the hallway light. I'm immediately scared, tuck my head back into my hands and knees and scream for help. I'm calling my mom and my dad, but no one comes.

In the next blink of an eye, I find myself just outside my bedroom door lying in the hallway as if I crawled from the corner of my room to the hallway, but I don't remember doing so. I'm crying and I feel so weak that I can't stand up. I cry out for help again. Next, I wake up in my father's arms at the OTHER end of the hallway, and he's asking, "Who are you?" My mom and one of my brothers are also hovering over me. Confused and weak, I just look back up to him. They carried me down a flight of stairs to the sofa where all my relatives were gathered. The reason we were having a family celebration was to honor the death of my maternal grandfather. It is known in the Philippines as babang luksa which marks the end of a one-year mourning period. My mother wore only black and white clothes for the entire year after she lost her father. This weekend marked the one-year anniversary of his passing, and there was an altar set up for continuous prayers and rosary. As a child, I did not really know anything about this. To me it was another weekend with my cousins, which I always looked forward to. I was in and out of consciousness that day. I screamed for help or thought I did. My brother later told me that he was in my parents' bedroom which was adjacent to mine, and he claimed he heard nothing. He only realized I was in the hallway when he heard sniffling and the shuffling of me crawling in the hallway. When I was "in the dark," I was aware, and everything was shadows. Before me there was an infinite wall or barrier that had no end on either side or above and below. I could not see it, but I knew it was there. I remember "seeing" three figures approach from the right, two remained in the distance and one approached me at the wall. No words were spoken but I heard in my mind that I could not pass through, that I was meant to stay on my side because there are bigger things meant for me in life. Now that I was on the sofa, closer to the family that was praying and watching over me, I shared what I was experiencing when I lost consciousness. My mother stepped in and made the connection that all this time they had been praying for my grandfather and his soul, and they did not include her brother (my uncle) who had also recently passed away. She encouraged everyone to start including him in the prayers and rosaries that were being said. I have this feeling that the two other figures were of my grandfather and my dog who had recently been put down. Shortly after that, I regained strength and vitality wanting to spend time with my cousins. The feelings of sadness, anger, and loneliness dissipated.

As a side note, I was in my uncle's home at the time of his passing helping to watch and care for my younger cousins while the adults were at the hospital. I am the one that received the phone call. It was that night as I lay sleeping next to these cousins, his children, that I dreamed of him. He is smiling, steps onto an up escalator, and disappears. I have had similar dreams of family members that have passed. I wasn't particularly close to any of them, but I know they are visitations. That spring day was a shared experience with my extended family, but it was never spoken about afterward. My cousins remember it, but we joke about it out of discomfort. I once shared this with my ex-husband and after I saw the look on his face, I understood that it wasn't a safe place to do so. Since that experience, I feel a connection to something I cannot see and wish I could gain access to. There have been moments in my life where I feel I am at my lowest, or loneliest, and I remember the wall.

CLINT ARENDALL'S STORY

It was the summer between my junior and senior year of high school. It would have been June 2003. I live in a very rural area in Hardin County. It is known as the Burnt Church Community. My family has lived in the area since the early 1800s and still has remnants of the old homestead by my parents' house. My grandmother was still alive during this time and living by herself. So sometimes on my way home I would take the backway, so I could drive by her house and just make sure everything was fine. It was around 10:30 at night, my curfew wasn't till 11:30 but nothing was going on and I headed home early. I had my windows down, and keep in mind it is a rural road, so I was not going fast. I had slowed down to look at my grandmother's house, and everything seemed to be in order. When I passed her house and topped a small hill, I noticed a lady standing on the side of the road. She was on my side, and I thought something had happened and she needed help. In a small community, that late at night I just knew something was wrong. So, as I eased up to check on her and, to my shock, the closer I got the more I could see she wasn't real. I could see through her, but I could tell what she was wearing. She had a tall beehive hairdo, cat rimmed glasses, and a long dress on. I never came to a complete stop. We made eye contact through the open passenger side window, and she followed me with her head as I slowly kept going. It was like I was in a trance. I punched the gas pedal and flew home. It's less than 2 miles. As soon as I got home, I ran inside and I had tears in my eyes. I was crying and yelling that I had seen a ghost. My parents asked if I had been drinking (lol). I had not been on this night, that's why I came home early...nothing was going on in town.

Since that experience, I have done a little research and found nothing about a wreck or any tragic thing that had happened in the past. However, my uncles have told me that when they would ride horses in that area, odd things would happen. There is an old well, between where my grandmother lives and where I witnessed the lady. The distance between the two is about 150 yards. My uncles said that horses would always jump and be skittish in that area even though there was nothing to jump at. I still get goosebumps when I drive that way and pass. In fact, I'm getting goosebumps as I type this story. I do know I saw a ghost that night and have yet to see one since. The eyes scared me, and I will never forget that night as long as I live.

DAVID FLORES'S STORIES

The Soldier in the Lake

I was younger than five years old when it happened, but I can still see it clearly in my mind. My family was having a reunion at a local park in South Texas near a small lake. I was about five years old and enjoying the time with my family. Everyone was laughing, talking, and enjoying the day when I noticed something unusual. Suddenly, a man in a dark military uniform walked right past me. He moved stiffly, almost like he was marching. His clothes were dark and shadowed, and I couldn't make out the color of his eyes. For a moment, I thought he was just another person at the park. But then he walked straight into the lake. He didn't stop or look around. He just kept going until it seemed he stepped into a dropoff and disappeared beneath the water. This small lake is not but a few feet deep. I remember standing there, waiting for him to come back up. When he didn't, I panicked. I ran to my mother, yelling about what I had seen. I tugged at her, trying to get her attention, but she brushed it off. I was so little; she probably thought I was imagining things. Years later, when I was in junior high, I came across a story that stopped me cold. It told of a soldier who had drowned in that very lake. The report said he'd been drinking, passed out, and slipped under the water. It had been ruled an accident. When I read that, everything came rushing back—the uniform, the way he walked, the moment he vanished. Ever since then, I haven't been able to forget it. I've shared the story with a few people over the years, and most have been understanding. Some find it hard to believe, but I know what I saw.

Lovie and the Shadow

That wasn't the only strange thing I've experienced. When I was in high school, we lived in the small county seat town and we were in a house that was nice, but where we had a lot of strange things that happened. We had a little dog named Lovie—a small, scrappy thing that a family member had found and given to us. She got attached to my mom right away and was fiercely protective of her. If anyone got too close, she'd bark, run in circles, and nip at their ankles. She never hurt anyone, but she always made her presence known. One night, everyone was gone except me and Lovie. I was turning off the lights and getting ready for bed when she started growling. At first, I thought she'd heard something outside, but then I saw her focus on a spot in the dining area. Her body was tense, her eyes fixed. Suddenly, she lunged forward—barking, circling, and snapping at the air like someone was standing there. But no one was. It was the exact same way she acted when she was defending us from a real person. I'd seen her do it plenty of times, so I knew that behavior well. This time, though, it was directed at nothing I could see. Only a couple of days before this happened, I read that animals can sense things we cannot. And that thought still sends chills through me even as I tell this story. I grabbed Lovie, hurried to my room, and held my rosary while I prayed. Eventually, she calmed down, and the strange energy in the house seemed to fade. Still, I'll never forget how she circled that empty spot on the floor—barking and growling, as if someone unseen was standing right there.

The Haunted House

A couple of years later, we moved a few blocks to another house. I always had strange dreams in that house, and others felt a creepy vibe too. They were not just the kind that fade by morning, but the ones that cling to your mind and haunt your memories. I had repeatedly dreamed about me dying, probably because I knew the man who had lived there before had committed suicide. One night, I dreamed I woke up in my dream, and the fitted sheet was tucked tightly all around me. It was soaked in blood, and I couldn't breathe. I felt like I was suffocating. When I realized what was happening, I completely freaked out—and then I actually woke up for real. I was shaking but realized I was fine. It felt like I had woken up *inside* the dream before waking up for real. It was so vivid and terrifying—just a crazy experience.

Then there was another time—I was in the bathroom, sitting down to use the toilet. The door was shut and locked, and the window was closed. I remember I was reading a skateboard magazine. Suddenly, this cool breeze came through, even though everything was closed. The thin curtain by the window didn't move, but the pages of my magazine started flipping on their own, like someone had just brushed past. Then, out of nowhere, the locked bathroom door slowly opened by itself. I was completely freaked out. I got up and went to close it—and the lock was still engaged, just like before. There was no way anyone could have come in or out. It made no sense. That whole experience still gives me chills—there's just no explanation for it. I wonder if it was just because of these houses or if something was following me. Maybe I attract these things.

ANGELA FLORES'S STORY

I am David Flores's sister, Angela, and I remember the house we grew up in all too well. It looked ordinary from the outside—a quiet little home on a quiet little street—but something about it was always off. The air was heavy there; the kind of stillness that made you whisper without knowing why. Strange things happened all the time. The lights would flicker or turn on and off without anyone touching the switches. The ceiling fan would stop mid-spin, pause for a few heartbeats, then start again on its own. Sometimes the sound of footsteps echoed down the hallway when everyone was in bed. We got used to pretending it was "just the house settling," but deep down, none of us believed that. One night, when I was about ten, my best friend Diana came over for a sleepover. We stayed up late, giggling and playing in my room. I remember my mother poking her head in and telling me, "Angela, make sure you put your roller skates away before you go to sleep." Of course, I didn't. I was a kid—tired, distracted, and more interested in visiting with my friend than cleaning up. My skates stayed right where I'd left them, out in the open on the floor beside my bed. We finally drifted off sometime after midnight. I don't remember waking up, or hearing anything unusual—no footsteps, no movement. But when morning came, everything was different. My mother came into the room smiling. "Thank you, Angela," she said. "I saw that you picked up your roller skates and put them away." Diana and I exchanged a look—one of those wide-eyed, silent looks that says something's not right. I sat up and said, "Mom, I didn't do that." She laughed, thinking I was teasing her. But I wasn't. I got out of bed, opened my closet door, and there they were—my roller skates, neatly placed side by side, right where they should have been. Diana had a very scared look on her face and I could see she was terrified. "That's it," she said, backing toward the door. "I'm going home." And she did. She refused to sleep over ever again. To this day, I don't know who or what put those skates away that night. No one in the house claimed to do it. Maybe it was something trying to help. Or maybe it was just making sure we knew it was there, watching, waiting, moving quietly in the dark when we thought we were safe.

STORIES OF UNIDENTIFIED AERIAL PHENOMENA OF JESSE AND ANTONIA SUAREZ*

***Antonia's story*:** The only reason this incident grabbed my attention and has always been so meaningful to me is because my mother was so interested. She passed about three years ago and this incident happened about six years ago. She was very spiritual, a devout Catholic, and I never imagined she would believe something like this was happening. I would pick her up after work at my school several nights a week and she would come home to stay with me and my husband, Jesse. One evening, as we were driving home from the small rural south Texas town, I noticed a bright light in the sky. "Mom, look at that light. It's so bright," I said. We couldn't figure out what it was, and she immediately became curious. We stopped at a stop sign for a few minutes, watching it. When we finally turned onto the main road, the light began moving with us—sometimes beside us, sometimes behind us, always up in the sky. It was around 5:30 or 6:00 p.m., getting dark, but not completely. As we drove through a big curve in the road, the light made the curve with us, almost as if it intentionally turned to follow our car. I told my mom, "It's following us." She kept asking what it was, but I had no idea. We stopped at a church along the road to see what it would do. The light stopped directly above us and hovered there. It looked like a bright glowing ball—no sound, no shape that we could make out. We watched it for what felt like 20 minutes, though it was probably only five. Suddenly, it shot off to the west.

To my surprise, my mom said, "Let's follow it." That was unusual for her, but I agreed. We followed the light, stopping at a few intersections where it seemed to slow down and wait, as if checking to see if we were still behind it. Eventually, the road turned into an unpaved path through a field. I told my mom I wasn't going any farther. The light kept moving slowly ahead, almost urging us on, but I refused and we turned back. As we headed toward the main highway, I checked my rearview mirror and saw the light coming back toward us—fast. It stayed behind us until we reached the city where we live, then continued above us along the highway. When I finally turned off toward our neighborhood, it turned also. By then, I was terrified. We pulled into the driveway, and my husband Jesse was already outside. I got out of the car and said, "Jesse, there is something following us." But he had already seen it and was standing there shocked. The light hovered above us for a moment longer and suddenly left at an astonishing rate of speed. This was nothing like any of us had ever seen or experienced. Later, the few people I shared this with suggested it might have been a helicopter, but there was no sound—not when it hovered, not when it left. It moved too fast and too smoothly. My mom never called it a UFO. Because of her faith, she thought it might have been something from God bringing her comfort as she had been a widow for over 30 years. All she kept saying was, "Una luz, una luz"—"a light, a light." She was never afraid and to this day, I don't know what we saw. But I know it was not anything ordinary.

Jesse's Story:

Little did I know that the experience Antonia and her mother had would be only the beginning of a long line of events none of us can fully explain. I've had a deer lease for years now, a place I return to every season like clockwork. It's familiar land—quiet, steady, dependable. But over time, it's also become the setting for some of the strangest moments of my life. Across the ranch, I've placed game cameras in different spots, and more times than I can count, they've picked up things I can't explain—odd shapes, strange lights, and movements that don't match any animal I know. And when I'm out there in the early morning, just before daylight, I see things with my own eyes: glowing orbs drifting in the darkness, lights that seem to appear out of nowhere, even faint humanoid shapes made entirely of light. None of it fits into anything I've ever understood.

One morning in 2024 stands out above the rest. A light appeared in the distance, moving slowly toward me. I kept trying to take a picture, adjusting the focus again and again, but it was as if the camera itself didn't want to cooperate. Eventually, I managed to capture something I could enlarge—and what I saw stunned me. It looked like there was a window or some kind of portal on the outside of this bright round object. What surprises people when I tell this story is that I've never once felt afraid. Not for a moment. Whatever these things are, they've never seemed threatening. In fact, it often feels like they're seeking me out, as strange as that sounds. I try to stay open-minded, to consider every possibility, but I can't help wondering: Why me? Why do these objects keep appearing in my presence? What are they trying to show me or tell me? Those questions follow me long after I've left the ranch, and I'm still searching for the answers.

IRMA DELEON'S STORY: WHO'S LAUGHING?*

I was teaching at the old high school I was a teacher there for about 7 or 8 years. On a particular day, I was getting ready to pack up for the year. It was the last day of school but there were several kids wandering in the hallway saying their goodbyes. There were also several parents wandering around helping their kids get their stuff on the last day of the year. I had a teacher's desk in a lab station in my room, and my computer was sitting on top of my lab station which has an opening in the back where the chair fits in. I was cleaning around the room when I heard the laughter of small children from my lab station area. Remember I teach high school students not small children. I thought someone's younger brother or sister had come into the room when I wasn't looking and so I went and looked in the area where my chair fits which was large enough for someone to hide but there was no one there. I thought I was hearing things, so I went back to cleaning, and I heard the laughter again. I said it must be my computer, but I had already turned it off for the year. I normally wander around for many hours after school dismisses for the day but on this day, I got my stuff and left immediately. I did return the next day and looked around some more but no one was around my room. I never did find out who or what I heard nor do I really want to know. The next year the old school was torn down and the new and was built.

GABRIELLA CASTANADO'S STORY: THE THREE KNOCKS*

In mid-May 2012, my husband was bedridden at home and was on Hospice due to stage 4 colon cancer. One day at dawn, I was awakened by three loud knocks that were clearly made on wood. That continued to happen for the next 15 or 20 days. Each time, I would get up and peek through the front windows, but I saw no one or anything moving. I always went to my bed mystified and doubted my hearing and whether the knocks were real. The following week and the third week I had the same experience. By then I had shared the unexplainable experiences with my children who lived out of town. My adult son was visiting over the weekend to help care for his father when, in the middle of the night, the same three knocks came. He was in the front room and before I could get to the living room, he had gotten up and opened the front door. Just as I expected, nobody was there, but this episode confirmed to my children what I had been experiencing. That was the last time the mystifying and untimely knocks came. My husband died about a week later. I have not talked to anyone who could help me understand these mysterious knocks. I'm not sure they would believe me even if I tried.

CONCLUSION

In closing, this chapter reminds us that counselors and people professionals, much like the clients they serve, are often transformed by encounters with the unexplained. These stories reveal not only the profound impact paranormal experiences can have on clients, but also the subtle, often unspoken ways they shape the inner world of the professional sitting across from them. By acknowledging the emotional, spiritual, and cognitive weight carried by counselors, we begin to normalize the very human reactions that arise when the familiar boundaries of practice are stretched. The hope is that through shared narratives, thoughtful reflection, and a willingness to explore what lies beyond traditional clinical frameworks, counselors can find reassurance, community, and renewed confidence in their work. Ultimately, these accounts serve as a reminder that the therapeutic journey—especially when touched by the extraordinary—is one shared between client and counselor, each navigating the unknown together.

Personal Reflection Questions for Chapter 10

How have my own beliefs, biases, or past experiences with the paranormal—whether skeptical or accepting—shaped the way I respond to clients who share anomalous events?

In what ways do the emotional or cognitive reactions described by counselors in this chapter mirror challenges I've faced in my own professional work, and how might acknowledging these parallels strengthen my therapeutic presence?

What strategies or approaches discussed in the chapter could help me create a more supportive, nonjudgmental space for clients navigating paranormal experiences, and how might I integrate these into my existing counseling practice?

Chapter 11

Consulting the Sages

Future Implications for Mental Health Professionals

EMBRACING THE FULL SPECTRUM OF HUMAN EXPERIENCE

Understanding and appreciating the rich tapestry of human experience, including those that are paranormal in nature, enhances a therapist's ability to provide comprehensive care. When clients present with unusual experiences, it is often not the experience itself that causes distress, but the reaction of others—especially authority figures like counselors—who may dismiss, pathologize, or minimize the client's reality. Research has shown that invalidating a client's anomalous experience can lead to feelings of shame, isolation, and even trauma (Grof & Grof, 1989; Hastings, 1991). In contrast, a therapeutic approach that affirms the client's narrative and explores its meaning—without necessarily confirming its objective reality—can foster psychological healing, resilience, and personal growth.

DEVELOPING THE DEFINITION OF CLIENT REALITY

Mental health professionals are increasingly confronted with the challenge and opportunity of expanding their clinical lens to include client experiences that defy conventional understanding. These may include near-death experiences (NDEs), visitations, intuitive insights, or unexplained sensory phenomena. Rather than treating these accounts as symptoms of delusion or hallucination, clinicians must consider that such narratives may be deeply rooted in cultural, spiritual, or existential meaning systems. Clients who report anomalous events often not seek confirmation of scientific

DOI: 10.4324/9781003529477-11

validity but, instead, compassionate support and a space to explore their emotional and psychological implications.

By broadening the definition of what constitutes reality in the therapeutic encounter, clinicians can create an environment where clients feel seen, respected, and safe. This approach does not require the therapist to adopt the client's belief system but rather to remain open to the client's worldview as a valid framework for meaning-making. Culturally responsive therapy teaches us that client beliefs, regardless of whether they are empirically verifiable are part of the therapeutic material and should be approached with curiosity rather than correction (Sue et al., 2019). In doing so, clinicians model a form of relational empathy that strengthens the therapeutic alliance and supports deeper exploration.

VALIDATING WITHOUT PATHOLOGIZING

One of the most vital competencies a mental health practitioner can develop when working with clients who report paranormal or anomalous experiences is the ability to validate the significance of those experiences without reducing them to psychopathology. This nuanced skillset requires counselors to engage in empathetic listening, cultural humility, and clinical neutrality. Validation, in this context, does not equate to agreement or belief in the literal truth of the event. Instead, it involves affirming the emotional reality and psychological impact that the experience holds for the client. When a person describes seeing a deceased loved one, sensing energies, or encountering a spiritual presence, they are often conveying something deeply meaningful, regardless of its objective verifiability.

Unfortunately, clients who disclose such phenomena frequently encounter disbelief, ridicule, or dismissal—especially from authority figures or mental health professionals. Such reactions can retraumatize clients, making them feel silenced, judged, or emotionally unsafe. As Braud and Anderson (1998) emphasize, the therapeutic relationship must offer sanctuary—a place where a client's subjective reality is honored without the clinician imposing their worldview. Dismissing or pathologizing these experiences can inadvertently reinforce stigma, discourage disclosure, and disrupt the healing process.

Differentiating Experience from Disorder

A primary challenge for clinicians lies in distinguishing between spiritually transformative experiences and genuine psychopathology. Experiences that involve visions, voices, or altered states of consciousness may superficially resemble symptoms of psychosis or dissociation. However, context matters. Research has demonstrated that misdiagnosis of anomalous experiences remains a persistent issue, particularly when practitioners lack training in cultural, spiritual, or transpersonal frameworks (Menezes Júnior & Moreira-Almeida, 2009; Moreira-Almeida et al., 2021). The *Diagnostic and Statistical Manual of Mental Disorders* (5th ed., text rev.; DSM-5-TR; American Psychiatric Association [APA], 2022) explicitly warns against diagnosing hallucinations or delusions without adequate consideration of cultural and religious context. For example, in many Indigenous or spiritual traditions, visions and spirit encounters are normalized and even celebrated. Misinterpreting these experiences as clinical symptoms rather than cultural expressions may lead to incorrect diagnoses, inappropriate interventions, and erosion of the therapeutic alliance. According to Gone (2021), this intentional misrepresentation is often a result of colonized knowledge. As mental health professionals, we must make sure that culture is interpreted in the light of the people themselves rather than the perspective of a cultural outsider.

Therapists must be vigilant in conducting comprehensive biopsychosocial-spiritual assessments that explore the meaning, onset, frequency, and emotional impact of the reported experience. Questions like, "How did this experience affect your life?" or "What meaning do you make of this event?" can open a dialogue grounded in curiosity rather than correction. This approach encourages clients to integrate the experience into their life narrative, a process that often reduces emotional distress and promotes psychological coherence.

The Psychological Function of Paranormal Experiences

Paranormal experiences often emerge during periods of emotional upheaval, loss, trauma, or spiritual awakening. Rather than signs of dysfunction, these experiences may serve as mechanisms for coping, transformation, or existential insight. For instance, individuals grieving the loss of a loved one may report sensing their presence or receiving messages in dreams. According to Devereux and Devereux (2011), in the altered state of lucid thinking, one can awaken within dreams to explore limitless inner realities, reconnect with loved ones, and experience mystical states beyond waking life. These experiences, while not empirically verifiable, can offer profound comfort, strengthen resilience, and catalyze emotional processing (Wahbeh et al., 2018). From a meaning-centered therapeutic perspective, such experiences function as narrative bridges between internal and external worlds. They may prompt clients to reevaluate their values, life goals, and spiritual beliefs. Clients often describe these encounters as "life-changing," reflecting newfound clarity, empowerment, or peace. In many cases, these transformative experiences are associated with improved mental health outcomes, including greater emotional regulation, a sense of purpose, and enhanced relational connectedness.

CHALLENGING HISTORICAL BIAS AND STIGMA

Historically, the field of psychology has treated paranormal belief and experience with skepticism, often equating such phenomena with irrationality, superstition, or mental instability. This bias is rooted in psychology's early efforts to distinguish itself from religion and pseudoscience, which led to a rigid adherence to materialist and empirical paradigms. Consequently, clients who held unconventional beliefs or reported extraordinary experiences were frequently pathologized or ignored.

However, contemporary research increasingly challenges the assumption that paranormal beliefs correlate with poor mental health or cognitive deficits. For example, Irwin (2009) and Lange et al. (2000) found that belief in the paranormal is both widespread and psychologically diverse. Many individuals who report paranormal experiences function effectively in society, possess strong coping mechanisms, and score within normal cognitive and emotional ranges. These findings suggest that anomalous experiences are not inherently pathological and must be interpreted within the client's cultural and personal framework.

It is therefore imperative for mental health professionals to suspend premature judgment and approach such disclosures with openness. By reframing paranormal experiences as meaningful—rather than deviant—therapists affirm the client's agency, promote narrative coherence, and avoid the harms of diagnostic overshadowing.

ETHICAL AND CULTURALLY RESPONSIVE COUNSELING

The ethical responsibilities of counselors are clearly articulated in the *ACA Code of Ethics* (American Counseling Association, 2014), which urges practitioners to honor clients' values, cultural backgrounds, and lived experiences. These ethical standards advocate for unconditional positive regard, nonmaleficence, and respect for client autonomy—all of which are critical when navigating anomalous content. Counselors are encouraged to reflect on their own biases, engage in continuous cultural competence training, and adopt trauma-informed practices that recognize the diversity of human experience.

This includes expanding one's awareness of non-Western and Indigenous belief systems. In many cultures, paranormal experiences are integral to cosmology, healing practices, and spiritual identity. For instance, ancestral communication, dreamwork, and shamanic visions are normalized components of community life in many African, Native American, and Asian traditions. Failure to understand or respect these frameworks may result in ethnocentric interpretations that marginalize clients and obscure the therapeutic potential of their experiences.

Therapists who are trained to incorporate spiritual and cultural worldviews into treatment can create more inclusive and effective interventions. This may involve collaborating with spiritual leaders, integrating symbolic and narrative therapies, or employing rituals that resonate with the client's tradition. Such culturally attuned counseling reinforces the client's sense of belonging, identity, and inner authority.

SYNCHRONISTIC THERAPY: A PARADIGM OF HOLISTIC ENGAGEMENT

In this chapter, we have introduced the concept of synchronistic therapy, a holistic approach that embraces Jung's idea of synchronicity—the meaningful coincidences that occur without apparent causal connection. Carl Jung (1973) proposed that such events could reflect underlying patterns or archetypes at work in the psyche and collective unconscious. In synchronistic therapy, counselors are trained to attend to these experiences and help clients interpret them in constructive, empowering ways.

Practicing synchronistic therapy does not require the counselor to adopt the client's metaphysical beliefs but rather to understand these experiences as potentially meaningful symbols in the individual's psychological and spiritual development. When integrated into therapeutic work, synchronistic events have been associated with improved health behaviors, emotional resilience, and cognitive balance (Main, 2007). Clients often report a greater sense of purpose, emotional regulation, and lifestyle changes that promote holistic well-being when their experiences are validated and explored, rather than dismissed or ignored.

By adopting this perspective, counselors help foster a form of cognitive homeostasis, where clients can reconcile seemingly contradictory internal experiences and external realities. Clients who integrate their anomalous experiences in a healthy manner frequently report enhanced coping skills, spiritual growth, and more authentic interpersonal relationships (Roxburgh & Evenden, 2004).

BRIDGING RESEARCH AND CLINICAL PRACTICE

Although the field lacks a comprehensive evidence-based model for paranormal-focused counseling, a growing body of emerging research supports the development of informed clinical guidelines. Instruments such as the Paranormal Belief Scale (PBS) and Revised Paranormal Belief Scale (RPBS) (Lange et al., 2000; Tobacyk & Milford, 1983) have been used to assess beliefs across dimensions such as traditional religious belief, superstition, psi phenomena, and precognition. These tools can assist clinicians in understanding the scope and structure of clients' paranormal worldviews.

Another important area of research relates to haunted people syndrome (HPS), a term used to describe individuals who report recurrent paranormal experiences throughout their lives. Investigations into HPS suggest that these individuals may possess certain personality traits—such as high sensitivity, dissociation tendencies, or trauma histories—that predispose them to interpret experiences through a paranormal lens (Houran et al., 2019). Therapists who are aware of these frameworks can better differentiate between healthy belief systems and potential indicators of psychological distress.

There is also considerable overlap between trauma-informed care and the needs of individuals with anomalous experiences. For example, near-death experiencers often report symptoms similar to post-traumatic growth, such as increased spiritual awareness and life purpose (Greyson, 2003). By applying evidence-based trauma recovery models such as Eye Movement Desensitization and Reprocessing (EMDR), narrative therapy, or somatic experiencing, counselors can support clients in integrating intense or transformative encounters without further traumatization.

ETHICAL MARKETING FOR SPECIALIZED PRACTICE

As interest in the paranormal continues to grow in popular culture and academic circles, counselors who specialize in this area may choose to market their services to reach underserved clients. Ethical marketing in this context requires clarity, transparency, and adherence to professional codes of conduct. Counselors should avoid sensationalism, refrain from making unverifiable claims, and clearly state their credentials and areas of expertise. Potential titles for practitioners may include "spiritually integrated counselor," "paranormal-informed therapist," or "transpersonal psychotherapist," depending on licensure, training, and personal philosophy. Counselors should also be careful not to present themselves as psychics, mediums, or spiritual healers unless they hold distinct credentials in those fields and clearly separate such work from clinical services.

Moreover, professionals must be aware of and comply with state licensing board requirements regarding scope of practice and advertising. A best practice approach includes listing specific areas of competence (e.g., grief and loss, existential crisis, spiritual trauma, or anomalous experiences) rather than directly advertising belief in the paranormal. Counselors are encouraged to develop informed consent documentation that addresses the use of nontraditional therapeutic discussions or approaches, ensuring clients understand the counselor's intent to respect but not necessarily affirm metaphysical claims.

FUTURE DIRECTIONS IN RESEARCH AND PRACTICE

The next frontier in counseling research may well involve the rigorous exploration of anomalous and paranormal experiences, which remain underexamined despite their prevalence in clinical and cultural narratives. As more clients openly discuss encounters that defy conventional explanation—such as NDEs, apparitions, synchronicities, or telepathic episodes—counselors and researchers alike must adapt to address these phenomena with clinical relevance, cultural humility, and scientific rigor. These types of experiences, often laden with existential or spiritual significance, challenge traditional mental health paradigms and demand innovative methodologies for study and treatment. A multifaceted research approach that includes mixed-methods studies, clinical trials, and qualitative inquiry will be essential to comprehensively understand the phenomenology, psychological impact, and therapeutic implications of paranormal experiences.

Mixed-methods designs offer the advantage of capturing both the measurable outcomes and the deeply subjective nature of anomalous experiences. Quantitative data can assess symptom reduction, physiological responses, or neurological changes, while qualitative methods—such as phenomenological interviews or narrative analysis—can uncover themes of meaning-making, identity transformation, and spiritual insight. Clinical trials may explore the efficacy of interventions tailored to individuals reporting paranormal experiences, including trauma-informed approaches or spiritually integrative therapies. These methodologies are well-suited to evaluate not only the credibility and impact of such experiences but also the effectiveness of clinical responses that honor the client's subjective reality.

Given these developments, counseling programs and professional organizations should seriously consider the incorporation of formal coursework, clinical supervision models, and continuing education focused on anomalous and paranormal phenomena. These curricular additions would prepare future practitioners to engage with such experiences ethically and skillfully. Supervision, in particular, can help counselors-in-training reflect on their own biases, bracketing assumptions that might otherwise lead to the pathologization or dismissal of client reports. Continuing education modules can offer seasoned clinicians the tools to remain current with emerging theories and empirical findings in this evolving area of practice.

Emerging therapeutic approaches already offer frameworks for the clinical integration of spiritual and paranormal content. Transpersonal counseling, spiritually integrated therapy, and eco-psychology are among the most promising models. These modalities emphasize human potential, the capacity for transcendence, and the therapeutic value of symbolic and mystical experiences. As Friedman and Hartelius (2015) note, these frameworks allow for a deeper exploration of meaning-making and transformation that goes beyond conventional symptom relief. Transpersonal approaches, for instance, regard spiritual emergencies not as signs of pathology but as processes of psychological and spiritual growth. Similarly, eco-psychology situates paranormal phenomena such as animal communication or nature-based visions within a relational worldview that reconnects humans with the Earth.

Interdisciplinary collaboration will also be essential to fully understand the dimensions of anomalous experiences. Psychologists, anthropologists, and neuroscientists can jointly investigate the physiological, cognitive, and cultural underpinnings of paranormal phenomena. For instance, research by Newberg and Waldman (2009) has used neuroimaging to study the brains of individuals in deep meditative and spiritual states, providing insights into the neurological correlates of mystical and anomalous perceptions. Continued research in this area could help delineate the difference between pathological and non-pathological altered states of consciousness, providing clarity for both clinicians and clients.

Furthermore, any advancement in this field must be rooted in multicultural competence and a strong social justice framework. For many cultures—particularly Indigenous, Eastern, and African diasporic traditions—paranormal experiences are not anomalies but integral components of spiritual practice, cosmology, and healing. Dreams, visions, spirit communication, and ancestral guidance are often considered normative and even sacred. To pathologize these experiences is to impose a Western psychological framework that risks invalidating the client's worldview. Instead, validating these experiences not only enhances therapeutic rapport but also serves as an act of cultural respect and advocacy.

The field of counseling stands at the cusp of a paradigm shift. Embracing the study and clinical integration of anomalous and paranormal experiences will not only expand the horizons of counseling research and practice but also empower clients who have long been marginalized or misunderstood. Through rigorous research, culturally sensitive education, and interdisciplinary collaboration, counseling professionals can develop a more inclusive, ethical, and transformative approach to mental health care—one that honors the full spectrum of human experience.

SUGGESTED AREAS OF RESEARCH

As research advocates, we have given considerable thought to what particular areas that would benefit from academic exploration. These areas are connected across disciplines such as psychology, counseling, neuroscience, anthropology, sociology, religious studies, and parapsychology. Each topic could contribute to a growing body of evidence-based understanding of anomalous experiences and their implications for individual and collective human functioning. Our hope is that you, the reader, will identify an area of interest that ignites a deep and enduring curiosity—one that compels you to delve further into the mysteries that continue to perplex and inspire both scholars and seekers alike. Here are some of our suggestions:

1. ***Neurobiological Correlates of Paranormal Experiences***
   - Research Focus: Use neuroimaging (e.g., fMRI, EEG) to study altered states of consciousness during reported paranormal events (e.g., NDEs, mediumship, OBEs).
   - Key Question: What parts of the brain activate during anomalous perceptions, and how do these states compare to meditative, dream, or trauma-induced states?
   - Rationale: Clarifying whether experiences originate from endogenous brain activity or reflect something beyond neurobiology.
2. ***Therapeutic Outcomes of Validating Paranormal Experiences***
   - *Research Focus:* Investigate how validating, rather than pathologizing, a client's paranormal or spiritual experience affects treatment outcomes.
   - *Key Question:* Does acceptance of these narratives increase psychological well-being, resilience, or therapeutic rapport?
   - *Rationale:* Supports trauma-informed, client-centered, and culturally sensitive practices.
3. ***Cultural and Indigenous Interpretations of Anomalous Phenomena***
   - *Research Focus:* Cross-cultural comparisons of how paranormal experiences are interpreted, integrated, or ritualized in Indigenous, African diasporic, Eastern, and Western contexts.

- *Key Question:* How do belief systems and cultural cosmologies influence whether experiences are seen as gifts, symptoms, or delusions?
- *Rationale:* Deconstructs colonial and medicalized frameworks around "hallucinations" and spiritual phenomena.

4. ***Psychological Traits and Personality Factors Associated with Paranormal Belief and Experience***
   - *Research Focus:* Correlate traits such as absorption, openness to experience, trauma history, and dissociation with frequency or intensity of anomalous experiences.
   - *Key Question:* Are some individuals more "tuned" to nonordinary experiences due to cognitive or affective profiles?
   - *Rationale:* Informs psychological screening, resilience studies, and therapeutic matching.
5. ***Longitudinal Studies on Individuals with Recurrent Paranormal Phenomena***
   - *Research Focus:* Follow people who report frequent psi events (e.g., telepathy, precognition, poltergeists) over time.
   - *Key Question:* What are the mental health, social, and occupational impacts across the lifespan?
   - *Rationale:* Establishes patterns of functioning, trauma, adaptation, or spiritual development.
6. ***Near-Death Experiences (NDEs) and Post-Traumatic Growth***
   - *Research Focus:* Study the aftereffects of NDEs on life meaning, existential orientation, death anxiety, and personality change.
   - *Key Question:* Do NDEs lead to measurable personal transformation, and how can counselors harness this in therapy?
   - *Rationale:* Connects spiritual experience with recovery, resilience, and meaning-making.
7. ***The Role of Environment in Paranormal Hotspots***
   - *Research Focus:* Examine geomagnetic, electromagnetic, and environmental anomalies in places where paranormal activity is frequently reported.
   - *Key Question:* Are there measurable environmental variables that correlate with increased anomalous reports?
   - *Rationale:* Bridges parapsychology, geology, and consciousness studies.
8. ***Impact of Anomalous Experiences on Grief and Bereavement***
   - *Research Focus:* Explore how after-death communication (ADC), dreams, or sensed presence experiences impact the grieving process.

- *Key Question:* Do paranormal experiences facilitate or complicate grieving?
- *Rationale:* Informs grief counseling strategies, especially for bereaved clients reporting spontaneous spiritual contact.

9. ***Ethical and Clinical Training Implications***
   - *Research Focus:* Design and evaluate training models for mental health professionals working with clients reporting paranormal phenomena.
   - *Key Question:* How can clinicians be educated to address these experiences without inducing harm or disbelief?
   - *Rationale:* Reduces stigma, improves care, and enhances professional competency.
10. ***Role of Technology and Media in Paranormal Perception***
    - *Research Focus:* Study how ghost hunting equipment, EMF meters, EVP recordings, and social media influence belief in and the reporting of paranormal events.
    - *Key Question:* Are anomalous experiences increasing due to technological mediation and digital storytelling?
    - *Rationale:* Intersects with media studies and modern myth-making.

Additional Niche Topics for Consideration

- Sleep paralysis and entity encounters
- Psychedelics and paranormal phenomenology
- AI and consciousness anomalies (machine-interpreted hauntings or spiritual messages)
- Dream ESP and precognitive dreams
- Poltergeist phenomena and adolescent psychodynamics
- Reconciling paranormal experiences from a religious/spiritual perspective
- Connecting the Bible and other ancient texts to the paranormal

Whether your fascination lies in the neurobiology of NDEs, the cultural interpretations of spirit visitations, or the therapeutic potential of validating anomalous phenomena, your inquiry holds the potential to shape new paradigms of understanding. The field of paranormal and anomalous studies is still emerging within mainstream academic and clinical circles, yet it touches a universal human experience—those moments of awe, fear, or transcendence that defy explanation and linger in memory. Rather than dismissing such experiences as delusional or irrelevant, we encourage a rigorous yet open-minded approach, one that is grounded in empathy, scientific inquiry, and respect for the personal and cultural significance of these events. Your research may not only contribute to scholarly knowledge but also offer healing, affirmation, and insight to those who have struggled in silence with experiences they cannot easily name or explain. In doing so, you become a pioneer—bridging the worlds of academia and the unexplained, of science and spirit, of data and meaning. By following the thread of your own interest, you may find yourself illuminating paths not only for your own understanding but for others who are navigating the liminal spaces of human experience. The journey begins with a single question—what calls to you most deeply?

CONCLUSION

The future of mental health counseling lies in its willingness to embrace the full complexity of human experience, including the paranormal. Rather than dismissing anomalous encounters as pathology, mental health professionals are called to expand their frameworks, refine their clinical tools, and engage in ethical, culturally competent practice. Through synchronistic therapy, empirical openness, and affirming therapeutic relationships, counselors can help clients find meaning, integration, and empowerment in their experiences.

As research continues to evolve and societal attitudes shift, mental health professionals who position themselves as knowledgeable, respectful, and willing to engage with the unknown will be better equipped to serve a diverse and spiritually curious clientele. Indeed, consulting the sages—both ancient and modern—may be essential in guiding the next generation of therapeutic innovation.

Personal Reflection Questions for Chapter 11

How do your personal beliefs about paranormal or anomalous experiences influence the way you might respond to a client who shares such encounters?

In what ways can practicing cultural humility and openness create a safer, more supportive environment for clients reporting experiences that fall outside traditional psychological frameworks?

> What ethical responsibilities do you feel mental health professionals hold when working with clients who present paranormal or anomalous experiences, and how might this challenge or expand your current clinical approach?

REFERENCES

American Counseling Association. (2014). *ACA code of ethics.* https://www.counseling.org/resources/aca-code-of-ethics.pdf

American Psychiatric Association. (2022). *Diagnostic and statistical manual of mental disorders* (5th ed., text rev.; DSM-5-TR). https://doi.org/10.1176/appi.books.9780890425787

Braud, W., & Anderson, R. (1998). *Transpersonal research methods for the social sciences: Honoring human experience.* SAGE Publications.

Devereux, P., & Devereux, C. (2011). *Lucid dreaming: Accessing your inner virtual realities.* Daily Grail Publishing.

Friedman, H., & Hartelius, G. (Eds.). (2015). *The wiley-blackwell handbook of transpersonal psychology.* Wiley-Blackwell.

Gone, J. P. (2021). Decolonization as methodological innovation in counseling psychology: Method, power, and process in reclaiming American Indian therapeutic traditions. *Journal of Counseling Psychology, 68*(3), 259–270. https://doi.org/10.1037/cou0000500

Greyson, B. (2003). Incidence and correlates of near-death experiences in a cardiac care unit. *General Hospital Psychiatry, 25*(4), 269–276. https://doi.org/10.1016/s0163-8343(03)00042-2.

Grof, S., & Grof, C. (1989). *Spiritual emergency: When personal transformation becomes a crisis.* Tarcher.

Hastings, A. (1991). *With the tongues of men and angels: A study of channeling.* Holt Paperbacks.

Houran, J., Laythe, B., & Owen, C. (2019). Haunted people syndrome: Towards a transdiagnostic explanation. *Journal of the Society for Psychical Research, 83*(3), 129–147.

Irwin, H. J. (2009). *The psychology of paranormal belief: A researcher's handbook.* University of Hertfordshire Press.

Jung, C. G. (1973). *Synchronicity: An acausal connecting principle.* Princeton University Press. (Original work published 1952)

Lange, R., Irwin, H. J., & Houran, J. (2000). Top-down purification of Tobacyk's revised paranormal belief scale. *Personality and Individual Differences, 29*(1), 131–156.

Main, R. (2007). *Revelations of chance: Synchronicity as spiritual experience.* SUNY Press.

Menezes Júnior, A., & Moreira-Almeida, A. (2009). Differential diagnosis between spiritual experiences and mental disorders of religious content. *Archives of Clinical Psychiatry (São Paulo), 36*(2), 75–82. https://doi.org/10.1590/S0101-60832009000200006

Moreira-Almeida, A., Mosqueiro, B. P., & Bhugra, D. (Eds.). (2021). *Spirituality and mental health across cultures.* Oxford University Press. https://doi.org/10.1093/med/9780198846833.001.0001

Newberg, A., & Waldman, M. R. (2009). *How God changes your brain.* Ballantine Books.

Roxburgh, E. C., & Evenden, R. E. (2004). Experiencers' interpretations of anomalous experiences and the impact on well-being: A qualitative study. *Journal of Parapsychology, 68*(2), 245–263.

Sue, D. W., Sue, D., Neville, H. A., & Smith, L. (2019). *Counseling the culturally diverse: Theory and practice* (8th ed.). Wiley.

Tobacyk, J. J., & Milford, G. (1983). Belief in paranormal phenomena: Assessment instrument development and implications for personality functioning. *Journal of Personality and Social Psychology, 44*(5), 1029–1037. https://doi.org/10.1037/0022-3514.44.5.1029

Wahbeh, H., Radin, D., & Delorme, A. (2018). A pragmatic trial of mind-matter interaction training. *Explore, 14*(6), 389–395. https://doi.org/10.1016/j.explore.2018.05.002

Chapter 12

Safe Spaces

Developing Paranormal Support Groups

INTRODUCTION: UNACKNOWLEDGED NARRATIVES IN A RATIONAL WORLD

Across cultures and time, people have reported experiences that challenge conventional understandings of reality events involving apparitions, unexplained intuitions, near-death phenomena, or other encounters often categorized as paranormal. Despite their historical and cross-cultural prevalence, these experiences remain largely unacknowledged within mainstream psychological discourse. Rather than being welcomed as meaningful or transformative, such accounts are frequently dismissed, pathologized, or trivialized, leaving individuals who report them feeling isolated and misunderstood. The absence of structured, empathetic support systems for this population contributes to a deep sense of emotional and social alienation. Many individuals find themselves caught between the intensity of the experience and the fear of judgment from others. The result is often silence- an internalization of doubt, shame, or confusion that can hinder emotional integration and personal growth. While there is growing public interest in the paranormal across media and social platforms, this attention rarely translates into serious, trauma-informed, or culturally sensitive care for those navigating these deeply personal phenomena. Counselors and others in the helping professions are uniquely positioned to change this narrative by creating spaces grounded in empathy, meaning, cultural awareness, and professional understanding.

At the heart of this issue lies a mismatch between lived experience and societal response. People who undergo anomalous events frequently describe them as vivid, impactful, and emotionally real. Yet when they attempt to articulate these encounters, they often face ridicule, disbelief,

DOI: 10.4324/9781003529477-12

or clinical suspicion. Without access to safe, inclusive spaces where their stories are heard and honored, many individuals retreat from seeking support altogether. The lack of affirmation can lead to long-term psychological consequences, including loneliness, existential confusion, or spiritual crisis. Several emerging and community-based avenues offer promise in bridging this support gap. Peer-led virtual spaces, online affinity groups, and faith communities may serve as alternative environments where individuals find connection, validation, and meaning. In addition, mental health professionals and community leaders are increasingly called to explore more inclusive models of care that neither romanticize nor pathologize, but rather accompany individuals through the complexity of their experiences. The development of appropriate resources begins with understanding the needs and perspectives of those directly impacted. Needs assessments, narrative inquiry, and culturally attuned listening practices offer critical entry points into this work. By centering the voices and values of those with lived experience, new frameworks for care can emerge frameworks grounded in empathy, respect, and the recognition that human experience cannot always be reduced to what is measurable or explainable.

BARRIERS TO DISCLOSURE: STIGMA, SILENCE, AND THE WEIGHT OF EXPERIENCE

Disclosing a paranormal experience often carries a far greater emotional cost than many realize. While such events may hold deep personal significance, offering comfort, insight, or even transformation to those who attempt to share them frequently encounter social, cultural, or clinical roadblocks. Fear of being misunderstood, disbelieved, or pathologized creates a climate in which silence becomes a form of self-protection. I (Garza) have worked with clients, students, and Licensed Professional Counselor Associates who have shared with me their fear of talking about their paranormal experiences due to being judged or looked at differently. This hesitance often brings a great deal of stress and anxiety, as they carry the weight of experiences, they feel they cannot voice. Many have said that all they want is a safe place to talk openly, somewhere they can begin to make sense of what happened without fear of ridicule. For them, the ability to speak freely is not only about understanding their own experience but also about helping others who may be struggling with the same silence. This pattern of hesitation reveals something deeper about the social and professional climate that surrounds such disclosures. It is not simply a personal fear, but a learned response shaped by how society and even helping professionals define what is considered acceptable or real.

Much of this hesitancy also stems from the dominant cultural framework that privileges empirical evidence and rationalism. Within this context, narratives that cannot be verified through scientific means are often dismissed as fantasy, delusion, or attention-seeking. As a result, even close family members or trusted peers may react with discomfort, skepticism, or ridicule when someone attempts to disclose a paranormal event. The emotional impact of such responses can be profound, leading to feelings of shame, confusion, or disconnection from others.

In clinical settings, these disclosures present additional complexities. While mental health professionals are trained to differentiate between pathological symptoms and non-clinical phenomena, few receive education that prepares them to engage with paranormal narratives in a culturally competent, nonjudgmental way. A client who reports sensing a deceased relative's presence, for example, may be met with clinical concern rather than curiosity or respect for the client's meaning-making process. Misinterpretations of spiritual or anomalous experiences as psychotic symptoms can lead to inappropriate interventions, further reinforcing the individual's reluctance to share. Beyond interpersonal and professional dynamics, internal barriers also emerge. Individuals may begin to question the validity of their own perceptions, wondering whether what they experienced was "real" or simply imagined. This self-doubt can be compounded by the lack of language or conceptual frameworks available to describe what occurred. Without a safe outlet to process the event, individuals may suppress or compartmentalize it denying themselves the opportunity to explore its psychological, spiritual, or emotional significance (Rabeyron, 2022).

For counselors, understanding these barriers requires humility and patience. Many clients who carry the weight of unspoken experiences do so for years, uncertain whether anyone will listen without judgment. Creating a space where their story can unfold freely allows the counselor to witness not only the details of the event but the meaning beneath it. By honoring the courage it takes to speak about the unseen, counselors help transform silence into strength and isolation into connection. In this way, disclosure becomes an act of healing rather than risk.

EMERGING SOURCES OF SUPPORT: DIGITAL PATHWAYS AND PEER CONNECTION

In the absence of widespread institutional acknowledgment, many individuals who have experienced paranormal phenomena turn to alternative sources of support particularly those found in digital and peer-centered spaces. These emerging platforms offer both anonymity and community, allowing individuals to share their stories, seek validation, and connect with others who have undergone similar events. While these spaces are not without limitations, they often serve as the first point of contact for those seeking to make sense of an experience that traditional systems have yet to fully embrace. These online communities, forums, and social media groups often become modern-day support circles where participants find understanding without fear of judgment. Members can share detailed narratives about their experiences, offer interpretations grounded in empathy, and exchange coping strategies that reflect both spiritual and psychological perspectives. In many ways, these spaces recreate what traditional counseling aims to provide—a sense of validation and connection, especially for those who feel dismissed or misunderstood in conventional settings. Some participants describe these peer interactions as transformative, giving them the courage to reframe their experiences as meaningful rather than pathological. The immediacy of digital communication also helps people reach out during moments of distress, reducing feelings of isolation and despair that can accompany unexplained or stigmatized phenomena.

At the same time, the accessibility of digital and peer networks raises important considerations for mental health professionals. While these spaces can foster belonging, they can also circulate misinformation or reinforce unexamined beliefs that may deepen confusion. This dual nature calls for a more proactive response from the counseling field, one that acknowledges the value of these emerging pathways while promoting informed, ethical engagement. Counselors who recognize the influence of online support groups can help clients critically evaluate the information they encounter and encourage balanced exploration that integrates both experiential and psychological insight. Ultimately, these evolving digital and peer-based networks highlight the need for counselors to adapt their understanding of community and healing, recognizing that the search for meaning and connection is no longer confined to the therapy room.

Virtual Support Groups: Bridging Distance with Empathy

One of the most powerful developments in modern social connections is the emergence of virtual support groups. These online gatherings can transcend geographic boundaries, allowing people from all walks of life to find common ground in their shared experiences. For those who have encountered the paranormal, virtual groups provide an environment where honesty is welcomed and judgment is suspended. With platforms like Zoom, Discord, or even private Facebook groups, individuals can gather in real-time, listen, share, and validate each other's stories. Moderated spaces led by mental health professionals or experienced facilitators can further ensure that the environment remains respectful, safe, and productive. The anonymity afforded by virtual groups can be particularly important. Not everyone is ready to attach their name and face to something that may challenge societal norms. Online spaces offer a chance to dip a toe in the water, to test the waters of community before diving into more public engagement. For many, these groups are the first step toward healing, understanding, and reclaiming a sense of agency over their narratives.

In many cases, participants find that virtual meetings recreate the same sense of comfort that an in-person, face-to-face meeting might offer. Seeing familiar names on a screen, hearing empathetic voices, and recognizing shared emotions across distance builds an unexpected sense of belonging. When guided by an ethical and compassionate facilitator, these online spaces can model healthy dialogue, self-reflection, and mutual support. Participants learn to listen deeply, respond with care, and hold space for others in a way that mirrors the foundational skills of counseling. For counselors, virtual groups open new opportunities for outreach and advocacy. They provide a platform to connect with individuals in rural areas, those with mobility challenges, or anyone reluctant to seek help in traditional settings. Counselors can collaborate with community leaders, provide psychoeducation, and help develop guidelines that balance openness with psychological safety. When designed thoughtfully, virtual support groups can bridge isolation with empathy, transforming technology into a tool for healing and human connection. In addition, these spaces allow counselors to observe group dynamics, promote healthy communication, and introduce coping strategies that encourage resilience and self-awareness. Over time, these online connections can evolve into meaningful communities that extend beyond the screen, helping participants build confidence in sharing their experiences and translating the support they receive into personal growth and real-world relationships.

Social Media: A Double-Edged Sword for the Paranormal Community

Social media has revolutionized how we share our lives, and for experiences of the paranormal, it can serve as both a lifeline and a minefield. On one hand, platforms like Reddit, TikTok, and YouTube have created vibrant communities where paranormal stories can thrive. From amateur ghost hunters to survivors of near-death experiences, people are building digital archives of unexplained phenomena. These platforms allow experiencers to find others like them, fostering a sense of community and validation. However, social media also brings risks. The viral nature of content means personal stories can quickly spiral out of control. What starts as an honest attempt to share may be met with sarcasm or dismissal, misinformation, or sensationalism. Therefore, it's important that individuals seeking support through these channels be cautious and intentional. Creating closed or private groups, establishing clear rules of conduct, and assessing group leaders are all ways to ensure that social media is used responsibly and supportively. When curated well, these spaces can reduce stigma, spread awareness, and connect people across the globe.

For many, the digital world becomes both a mirror and a magnifier of their experiences. A single story shared online can spark meaningful dialogue, lead to new friendships, or inspire others to seek understanding of their own encounters. Yet the same environment can also amplify doubt and criticism, making it vital for users to ground themselves emotionally before engaging publicly. Counselors and mental health professionals can play an important role here by helping clients navigate these spaces with discernment, self-awareness, and healthy boundaries. In doing so, social media can shift from a potential source of harm to a modern tool for connection, healing, and collective growth. As these online interactions evolve, they often give rise to more intimate and personal exchanges, where stories move offline and into trusted circles of conversation, paving the way for the quiet but enduring power of word of mouth.

Word of Mouth: The Quiet Power of Personal Networks

Sometimes, the most profound support comes from the simplest source: a trusted friend, relative, or coworker. Word of mouth remains a powerful tool in the realm of paranormal support. Whether it is sharing your story with someone who has had a similar experience or being directed to a local resource through a friend of a friend, personal referrals often lead to the most meaningful connections. Connections such as these can also form a safe place for individuals to share their stories without judgment. In my own experience of sharing paranormal phenomena with others who I believed would understand, I found a sense of comfort and belonging that helped me move past fear. It was not always easy, and I had to be sure I felt at ease with those I confided in. Yet, hearing others describe similar encounters encouraged me to speak more openly, even with larger groups, in the hope that others would feel less alone in their own unexplained experiences.

This method can be particularly helpful for those who hesitate to join larger gatherings or public forums. When someone you trust recommends a group, a counselor, or a community circle, it eases the worry of being ridiculed and builds confidence in the process. Developing these connections naturally, through genuine human interaction, lays the foundation for small but meaningful networks of care. Over time, these circles can grow into community-based initiatives or simply remain close-knit groups where people listen, believe, and support one another. For many, this quiet exchange of trust becomes the first step toward healing and the first time they feel safe enough to give their experience a voice. One of the most remarkable things about these personal networks is how they continue to grow in ways that feel effortless. A single conversation shared in honesty can travel far beyond the people in the room, reaching others who are quietly searching for understanding. Stories move through families, workplaces, and communities, weaving invisible threads of empathy that connect those who might never meet otherwise. This kind of organic connection holds a power that no structured program can replace, because it emerges from real emotion and shared humanity.

For counselors, word of mouth serves as a reminder that healing often begins outside the therapy room. When clients come forward after hearing from a friend or colleague that they too were heard and respected, the counselor is stepping into a chain of trust already in motion. Recognizing and honoring this process can strengthen the counselor's relationship with both the client and the community. When handled with care, word of mouth becomes more than an informal exchange of advice; it becomes a living network of support, compassion, and understanding that continues to grow long after the initial story is told. As these personal connections deepen and communities begin to form, many individuals turn to spiritual or faith-based settings for further understanding and guidance. In these spaces, the search for meaning often finds a; sacred home, where shared belief and compassion help anchor experiences that feel beyond explanation.

Faith-Based Organizations: Spiritual Anchors in the Face of the Unknown

Throughout history, religious and spiritual communities have been sanctuaries for those grappling with life's great mysteries. In many traditions, the idea of supernatural or divine encounters is not only accepted but revered. Faith-based organizations can, therefore, be crucial allies in the development of paranormal support groups. Clergy, spiritual counselors, and congregation members may be more open to such experiences and better equipped to respond with compassion rather than skepticism. However, not all faith traditions view paranormal experiences the same way. Some may interpret them as signs of spiritual awakening, while others may view them with suspicion or concern. For this reason, it's vital to approach faith-based spaces with sensitivity and awareness of doctrinal boundaries. Still, for those who find resonance within their faith, these communities can offer not just support, but a framework for understanding experiences that defy explanation.

When approached with mutual respect, collaboration between mental health professionals and faith leaders can bring about powerful results. Counselors who engage with these organizations in an open and informed way can help bridge the gap between psychological understanding and spiritual meaning. Such partnerships create opportunities for education, shared dialogue, and referral pathways that honor both belief and well-being. In this shared space, individuals can find comfort in knowing that their experiences are not dismissed but instead explored with compassion and curiosity, allowing healing to take place on both emotional and spiritual levels.

Faith-based communities also have a unique ability to create a sense of belonging that extends beyond discussion or counseling. Rituals, prayer circles, and fellowship gatherings provide a rhythm of connection that grounds individuals who may otherwise feel isolated by their experiences. Within these spaces, people can express their encounters through familiar spiritual language, finding reassurance in shared symbols and collective faith. The support offered here is not limited to words; it becomes a lived expression of empathy, where acceptance is woven into the daily practices of the community. For counselors, working alongside faith leaders can open new pathways of care. By understanding the beliefs and values that shape a client's worldview, the counselor can integrate those elements into the healing process without imposing judgment or contradiction. This collaboration helps ensure that both the psychological and spiritual dimensions of a person's experience are acknowledged. When faith leaders and counselors work together with mutual understanding, clients can experience a deeper form of healing—one that honors both the mystery of their experiences and the humanity that seeks meaning within them.

Community Organizations and Agencies: Institutional Support for Marginalized Voices

While paranormal experiencers may not traditionally be seen as a demographic in need of community aid, there's growing recognition that support is warranted, especially when these events lead to emotional, psychological, or social distress. Community centers, nonprofit organizations, and even local mental health agencies can play a role in creating inclusive, nonjudgmental environments. These organizations are uniquely positioned to offer meeting spaces, resource referrals, and trained facilitators. Bringing paranormal support into the fold of community mental health initiatives also helps normalize the conversation. Rather than pushing these experiences into the shadows, we integrate them into broader dialogues about trauma, grief, perception, and belief. This institutional backing not only legitimizes the experiences of those affected but opens the door to long-term solutions, such as partnerships with universities, therapists, or even crisis response teams who are trained to handle unusual cases with empathy and discretion.

In many communities, local agencies already serve as the first line of outreach for individuals in crisis, making them a natural place to extend this type of support. When staff are trained to respond without judgment, they can offer a sense of safety that encourages disclosure rather than fear. Simple actions, such as including language about spiritual or unexplained experiences, intake materials, or providing contact information for supportive peer networks, can signal openness and acceptance. Even modest steps like these can shift public perception and remind individuals that their stories are worthy of being heard. Collaboration between agencies and counselors can also help bridge the gap between informal community care and professional mental health practice. Workshops, continuing education sessions, and interdisciplinary panels can help professionals better understand the cultural and emotional layers behind these experiences. This kind of education benefits not only the individuals seeking help but also strengthens the competency of the organizations that serve them. When community agencies work alongside counselors, they begin to build a shared language of care, one that recognizes the importance of belief, lived experience, and emotional safety. Over time, this kind of inclusion can help transform public understanding of what it means to experience the unexplained. When community institutions acknowledge and support these experiences, they send a powerful message that healing and understanding belong to everyone, not just those whose stories fit neatly into conventional categories. In this way, community organizations become more than service providers, they become partners in restoring dignity, belonging, and voice to those who have often been overlooked.

Needs Assessments: Listening Before Building

Before any support group can be effective, it must be built on a foundation of listening. A needs assessment tool often used in community planning and public health helps identify what people truly need before attempting to provide it. When applied to the paranormal community, needs assessments can uncover everything from preferred meeting styles (online versus in person) to what kinds of facilitation are most helpful, to what language feels safest. This step ensures that support groups are not created based on assumptions, but on real data collected from real people. Surveys, interviews, focus groups, and informal outreach efforts can all serve to inform this process. Just as important, the act of asking shows respect—it acknowledges the experiencers as experts in their own lives and gives them agency in shaping the very resources designed to support them.

Listening deeply during this phase can reveal more than logistical preferences; it can expose the emotional landscape that underlies people's experiences. Many who have encountered the unexplained carry layers of fear, confusion, or loneliness that extend far beyond the event itself. A thorough needs assessment allows facilitators to recognize these emotional needs early on, ensuring that group structures are built with sensitivity and awareness. It also helps identify the types of guidance or education that participants may find useful, whether that means trauma-informed practices, spiritual integration, or opportunities for creative expression. One structured method that can be especially valuable in this process is the Delphi method. Traditionally used in research and strategic planning, the Delphi approach gathers insight from a panel of informed individuals through multiple rounds of anonymous feedback. Each round builds on the last until a clear sense of consensus emerges. When applied to paranormal support initiatives, the Delphi method can help professionals, experiencers, and spiritual leaders collectively define what kind of support is most needed. Because responses are anonymous, participants feel free to share honest perspectives, leading to a deeper understanding of shared priorities without the pressure of group influence or judgment.

The Delphi method can also help bridge communication between diverse voices who might not otherwise interact directly. Mental health practitioners, clergy, community organizers, and experiencers each bring unique insight that, when synthesized through this process, can guide program development more effectively than any single viewpoint. In this way, the Delphi method not only strengthens the design of support groups but also models the very values those groups aim to uphold: collaboration, inclusion, and respect for multiple ways of knowing.

Finally, the information gathered through these combined approaches can guide both short-term and long-term planning. It can inform facilitator training, shape outreach efforts, and highlight the kinds of partnerships that may strengthen the group's mission. Needs assessments also create a record of community voice, an evolving reflection of what experiencers truly value and hope for. When counselors and facilitators use this information thoughtfully, they lay the groundwork for support systems that are not only responsive but genuinely transformative. By beginning with listening, and by using methods that honor every participant's contribution, we ensure that what is built grows from understanding, not assumption, and that the foundation of every support effort is respect.

CONCLUSION: TOWARD INCLUSIVE AND COMPASSIONATE SUPPORT SYSTEMS

The experiences described by individuals who encounter paranormal phenomena defy simple categorization, yet their emotional and psychological realities are undeniable. When these individuals are met with silence, disbelief, or pathologization, the effects can be profound, contributing to isolation, confusion, and self-doubt (Roxburgh & Evenden, 2021). As this chapter has shown, a diverse array of informal supports from digital platforms to faith-based networks are often filling the void left by formal mental health systems. These avenues provide a critical lifeline, offering understanding and validation in spaces where individuals feel safe enough to explore the meaning of their experiences (Greyson, 2021). However, without collaboration and intentional design, these supports remain fragmented and inconsistent. A shift toward inclusivity begins with reimagining how care is offered and whose stories are deemed worthy of attention. Needs assessments, peer-led initiatives, and spiritually integrated care models provide promising frameworks for addressing this population's unique needs (Braud & Anderson, 2022; Rabeyron, 2022). When counselors and support providers approach anomalous experiences with cultural humility and therapeutic neutrality, they not only affirm the dignity of their clients but also expand the boundaries of mental health practice itself.

Building a more compassionate system of care begins with listening. Counselors must be willing to suspend judgment and sit with the uncertainty that these experiences often bring. It requires shifting from a mindset of explanation to one of exploration, asking not "What happened?" but "What does this mean to you?" That single question invites the client into a space of agency and reflection, rather than fear or defensiveness. In doing so, the counselor becomes a partner in meaning-making rather than an evaluator of truth. This subtle change in stance allows for healing conversations to occur, where both client and counselor can hold the mystery without needing to solve it. Collaboration across disciplines is also essential. The counseling profession stands to benefit greatly from partnerships with anthropologists, theologians, medical professionals, and community leaders who approach human experience from different angles. Such dialogue can deepen understanding of how culture, spirituality, and psychology intersect within paranormal or anomalous events. Training programs and continuing education opportunities can help counselors develop competence in this area, not as a specialty for the few, but as an integral skill for those who wish to serve diverse populations. When counselors learn to recognize the cultural and spiritual layers that shape a client's experience, they become better equipped to respond with sensitivity, care, and ethical awareness.

At a community level, inclusive support systems should aim to create safe environments that honor differences. This could mean establishing specialized support groups within community centers, developing partnerships between universities and local agencies, or offering professional workshops that explore nontraditional experiences in a respectful way. When agencies and educational institutions validate these conversations, they help remove the stigma that often keeps individuals silent. Moreover, these efforts can contribute to a broader cultural shift, one that acknowledges the full spectrum of human experience as worthy of empathy, inquiry, and care. The future of counseling and community support lies in integration rather than separation. It is not about dividing the scientific from the spiritual or the rational from the experiential, but about finding a balance that allows both to coexist. Clients do not live in compartments; their experiences are whole, often spanning the psychological, emotional, and spiritual domains. When counselors recognize this, they are better able to help clients achieve genuine healing that encompasses all dimensions of their being. For practitioners, the challenge is to hold curiosity without fear, professionalism without rigidity, and compassion without overidentification. It is to meet each story with openness, acknowledging that mystery itself can be a teacher. The counselor's role is not to validate every claim of the supernatural, but to validate the human experience within it, the fear, the awe, the transformation, and the search for meaning. When we approach these moments with empathy and presence, we allow clients to find their own grounding and meaning in what may otherwise feel like chaos.

Ultimately, creating inclusive and compassionate systems of support is not about proving whether the paranormal is real. It is about recognizing that the people who experience it are real. Their pain, confusion, hope, and courage deserve the same respect and care as anyone facing grief, trauma, or loss. When mental health professionals, educators, and community leaders come together with this shared understanding, they build a foundation for healing that is both human and humane. For counselors and those in the helping profession, the work ahead is not easy, but it is necessary. By continuing to study, listen, and engage with humility, counselors can help shape a profession that honors the unseen dimensions of life without fear or dismissal. This does not mean abandoning science or reason. It means expanding them to include the depth and diversity of lived experiences. In doing so, the field of mental health becomes not only more inclusive but more authentically human. The goal is not to explain away the mystery but to make room for it, allowing both the professional and the experiencer to find meaning, healing, and peace within the shared story of being human.

Personal Reflection Questions for Chapter 12

What emotional and psychological risks might individuals face when disclosing paranormal experiences in environments that lack culturally sensitive or supportive frameworks?

In what ways can faith-based organizations, virtual communities, or grassroots networks serve as alternative support systems for those who feel marginalized by traditional mental health services?

Why is it important to conduct needs assessments for individuals who report anomalous experiences, and how might such assessments contribute to more inclusive and effective support models?

REFERENCES

Braud, W., & Anderson, R. (2022). *Transforming self and others through research* (2nd ed.). SUNY Press.

Rabeyron, T. (2022). When the truth is out there: Counseling people who report anomalous experiences. *Frontiers in Psychology, 12,* Article 693707. https://doi.org/10.3389/fpsyg.2021.693707

Greyson, B. (2021). *After: A doctor explores what near-death experiences reveal about life and beyond.* St. Martin's Press.

Roxburgh, E. C., & Evenden, R. E. (2021). 'They daren't tell people': Therapists' experiences of working with clients who report anomalous experiences. In D. Loewenthal, *What is paranormal?* (pp. 26–44). Routledge.

Chapter **13**

An Epitaph for the Telepath

INTRODUCTION

As we arrive at the final chapter of this book, it is important to clarify what this conclusion is—and what it is not. While we are not writing an epitaph for the reader, we are offering an epitaph for the material contained in the preceding chapters. This is the place where threads are woven together, where diverse perspectives find coherence, and where the challenge is set forth for the reader to carry the work forward. In these pages, we will summarize, synthesize, and issue a call to action, reminding the professional counselor—and anyone who works with those reporting anomalous or paranormal experiences—of the sacred trust inherent in the therapeutic relationship. Mental health professionals are not ghost investigators, nor are they charged with disproving or validating their clients' experiences. Instead, their task is far more significant: to provide support to individuals who have encountered what they themselves perceive as unexplained phenomena. To do this well requires humility, ethical grounding, and the practice of bracketing—intentionally setting aside personal biases and pre-conceived notions to make room for the authentic narratives of clients. Above all, we must remember that most individuals presenting with these concerns are not experiencing schizophrenic hallucinations or other psychotic disorders. Rather, they are often culturally and psychologically healthy individuals who find themselves grappling with meaning, stigma, and integration. As professionals, we are bound to honor the ethical principles of non-maleficence, beneficence, and veracity. In other words: do no harm, act in the client's best interest, and maintain honesty in the therapeutic process. When viewed through this ethical lens, paranormal beliefs and anomalous

DOI: 10.4324/9781003529477-13

experiences are not inherently pathological but are often culturally normal and usually nonharmful.

CORE REMINDERS FOR THE PRACTITIONER

Before reflecting on the whole of this book, it is worth pausing to underscore the core reminders that anchor the work of counseling individuals who report paranormal or anomalous experiences. These reminders are not abstract concepts but practical guidelines for maintaining professional integrity, ethical responsibility, and cultural humility in practice. They represent the attitudes and commitments that undergird the counseling relationship when clients bring experiences that may challenge the counselor's worldview, training, or comfort zone.

Leave pre-conceived notions at the door. The first and perhaps most critical reminder is that clients do not enter the counseling room to be ridiculed, dismissed, or trivialized. Nor do they come seeking skepticism disguised as curiosity. Rather, they come seeking understanding, empathy, and guidance from someone they hope can hold space for their experiences. When a counselor allows personal preconceptions to dominate the therapeutic encounter, the result is almost always harm: the client feels invalidated, shamed, or silenced. This is where the discipline of bracketing becomes indispensable. Bracketing, drawn from phenomenological traditions, is the intentional act of setting aside one's assumptions, theories, and biases in order to fully attend to the lived experience of the other. In practice, this means resisting the impulse to immediately categorize an experience as hallucination, delusion, fantasy, or fraud. Instead, the counselor acknowledges the reality of the experience *for the client* and seeks to understand what it means to them. Consider a client who shares that they have repeatedly heard the voice of a deceased loved one offering comfort during moments of grief. The counselor may not personally believe in the possibility of communication from the dead. Yet the task of the counselor is not to evaluate the metaphysical veracity of the experience. The task is to listen deeply, to empathize, and to explore how this experience shapes the client's grief, resilience, or meaning-making process. By bracketing personal disbelief, the counselor opens the door to genuine therapeutic engagement. Leaving pre-conceived notions at the door also means resisting the temptation to become a "debunker" or "investigator." Counselors are not called to explain paranormal phenomena; they are called to walk with people through the impact of these phenomena on their lives. A client who feels mocked or dismissed may never again risk bringing such vulnerable experiences into the therapeutic space. Thus, bracketing is not optional; it is a fundamental posture of respect.

Clients are not automatically disordered. The second reminder addresses the deeply ingrained professional reflex to pathologize. In the counseling and psychiatric traditions of the twentieth century, anomalous experiences were often collapsed into the categories of disorder—hallucinations, delusions, dissociations. While differential diagnosis remains an important responsibility, counselors must carefully avoid assuming that paranormal reports are *ipso facto* signs of illness. To be clear, this is not a call to abandon diagnostic rigor. If a client's experiences are accompanied by disorganized thinking, severe functional impairment, or other clinical indicators, then careful assessment is appropriate. However, what must be resisted is the automatic equation: "Paranormal experience equals disorder." Research demonstrates that paranormal experiences are common among otherwise psychologically healthy individuals. Studies indicate that more than half of Americans report at least one paranormal experience in their lifetime, ranging from sensing a presence to seeing an apparition or experiencing synchronicity. These experiences, though unusual, are often transient, benign, and integrated into the person's worldview without harm. By contrast, pathologizing such experiences can generate a "second wound." The first wound is the stigma the client feels in broader society; the second wound is inflicted when their counselor treats their experience as illness rather than as a meaningful part of their life. For example, an individual who reports seeing the spirit of their grandmother may interpret the event as comforting and affirming of their cultural heritage. If the counselor immediately interprets this as psychosis, the client may feel invalidated and misunderstood, leading to mistrust of the counseling process. The reminder here is simple but profound: resist premature pathologizing. Approach each report with curiosity and compassion, allowing space for meaning to emerge before rushing to clinical judgment. In doing so, counselors safeguard the dignity of the client while still fulfilling their professional responsibility to assess for risk and impairment when necessary.

Cultural and existential normalcy. Third, counselors must recognize that paranormal and anomalous experiences are not anomalies in the human story; they are woven deeply into cultural traditions, spiritual practices, and existential narratives across time and geography. What may appear bizarre or irrational in one cultural framework may be considered sacred, healing, or normative in another. For instance, Indigenous communities across the Americas have long traditions of visions, dreams, and spirit encounters that are central to their spiritual identity. In parts of Africa, communication with ancestors is understood as a vital dimension of community life. In Eastern traditions, mystical experiences during meditation or prayer are valued as signs of spiritual growth. To dismiss these experiences as pathological is to misunderstand their cultural significance and to risk perpetuating cultural oppression within the therapeutic encounter.

Counselors, therefore, must cultivate cultural humility—an openness to learn from the client's cultural framework rather than imposing their own. This requires asking respectful questions, such as:

What does this experience mean to you?
How is this experience understood in your community or tradition?
What role does this experience play in your sense of identity, purpose, or belonging?

Existential normalcy is equally important. Many paranormal experiences occur at times of transition, grief, or existential searching. A person may see an apparition following the death of a loved one, not as a sign of psychosis, but as a moment of comfort or meaning. Another may interpret a synchronistic event as confirmation that their life has purpose. These interpretations are part of the normal human struggle with meaning, mortality, and belonging. By recognizing cultural and existential normalcy, counselors affirm the client's humanity. They shift the focus away from "Is this real?" toward the more therapeutic question: "What does this mean for you?"

Ethical obligation. Finally, counselors are not simply passive listeners when it comes to reports of anomalous experiences. They are bound by an ethical obligation to model compassion, respect, and openness in every encounter. This obligation is grounded in the foundational principles of the counseling profession:

Non-maleficence (Do no harm). Counselors must ensure that their responses do not inflict additional harm through ridicule, dismissal, or careless pathologizing. Even subtle invalidation can deepen a client's sense of isolation.

Beneficence (Act for the good of the client). Counselors must consider how to respond in ways that promote the client's well-being, whether by fostering meaning, strengthening coping strategies, or affirming cultural identity. Beneficence requires active support, not mere tolerance.

Veracity (Commitment to truthfulness). Counselors must maintain honesty and integrity in their work. This does not mean affirming beliefs they do not hold; rather, it means being truthful about the limits of one's knowledge while remaining fully present and respectful of the client's truth.

Ethical obligation also extends to advocacy. Counselors who encounter clients with paranormal experiences should challenge the stigma that still surrounds these reports in professional and social contexts. This might involve educating colleagues about cultural frameworks for anomalous experiences, incorporating these topics into supervision, or advocating for curricula that prepare new counselors to work effectively with such clients. Ultimately, the counselor's ethical responsibility is not to solve the mystery of paranormal phenomena but to uphold the dignity of those who report them. By embodying compassion, respect, and openness, the counselor becomes a safe harbor in which clients can explore experiences that may feel too vulnerable to share elsewhere.

INTEGRATING THE PREVIOUS 12 CHAPTERS

The previous chapters were not isolated essays but interconnected parts of a larger whole. To bring them together, we must revisit and integrate their key insights.

Chapters 1–2 introduced the prevalence of paranormal experiences in modern society. We examined compelling statistics indicating that more than half of Americans report at least one paranormal encounter. These chapters normalized the discussion, affirming that such experiences are neither rare nor necessarily pathological.

Chapters 3–4 emphasized a person-centered counseling framework. Here, the importance of active listening, unconditional positive regard, and empathic engagement was made clear. Counselors were invited to set aside the impulse to explain and instead to validate.

Chapters 5–6 moved into the terrain of spirituality, grief, and meaning-making. We explored how anomalous experiences often occur in liminal moments—times of transition, loss, or trauma—and how they can serve as catalysts for new meaning.

Chapter 7 presented the essential technique of *bracketing*. This was perhaps one of the most crucial skills for counselors, reminding us that the counselor's role is not to interpret but to hold space, not to judge but to accompany.

Chapters 8–9 expanded the conversation into multicultural competence and ethical boundaries. Readers were challenged to recognize how anomalous experiences may be woven into the cultural fabric of Indigenous traditions, Eastern philosophies, and African diasporic practices, all of which provide frameworks of acceptance and integration.

Chapter 10 addressed emerging technologies and research frontiers, pointing to the exciting interdisciplinary opportunities between neuroscience, psychology, and anthropology. These fields provide fertile ground for investigating anomalous experiences without reducing them to pathology.

Chapter 11 brought in the wisdom of sages and forward-looking perspectives. This chapter emphasized that future counseling practice must be shaped by openness, humility, and innovation, particularly in how we train the next generation of professionals.

Chapter 12 concluded the main body of the book with systemic and institutional advocacy. Counselors were reminded that the stigma surrounding paranormal experiences is not merely individual but systemic, requiring advocacy, education, and leadership within the profession.

Taken together, these chapters create a holistic model of care: one that validates experience, integrates cultural knowledge, upholds ethical practice, and fosters innovation.

READER'S PERSONAL REFLECTION AND INTEGRATION

As you arrive at the conclusion of this book, it is important to pause and look inward. The material presented in the previous chapters is not meant to remain as abstract theory or distant analysis. Rather, it is intended to shape your professional identity, challenge your assumptions, and inspire you toward new levels of openness and compassion in your work. Reflection is the bridge between reading and transformation. By considering how the themes of this book intersect with your personal beliefs, cultural lens, and professional practice, you create space for genuine integration. The following questions are offered as guides for that process. Consider the following:

What assumptions have I carried? Every counselor, no matter how skilled, experienced, or self-aware, enters the counseling relationship carrying assumptions. These assumptions are often invisible, woven into personal worldviews, professional training, or cultural upbringing. Some stem from deeply held personal beliefs—whether a strong skepticism toward anything paranormal or an openness that borders on credulity. Others are inherited through professional norms that emphasize pathology or through cultural frameworks that determine what is "normal" and what is not. For the counselor, the challenge is not that assumptions exist—for assumptions are inevitable—but that they can unconsciously shape the therapeutic encounter. A counselor inclined toward skepticism might, without intending harm, dismiss a client's paranormal account as delusion, fantasy, or misperception. A raised eyebrow, a subtle shift in tone, or a too-quick suggestion of diagnosis can communicate to the client that their story is not welcome. On the other hand, a counselor who is overly credulous may risk affirming the literal truth of the client's experience too quickly, overlooking its symbolic, psychological, or cultural dimensions. Both extremes can limit the depth of exploration and inadvertently hinder the client's process of making meaning.

What chapter resonated most with me and why? Each chapter of this book offered a unique perspective, from cultural frameworks to ethical principles, from techniques of bracketing to systemic advocacy. While every reader may find value across the whole, certain chapters often strike a particularly deep chord. Perhaps the cultural insights resonated most, reminding you that paranormal experiences are woven into the traditions of countless communities worldwide. Perhaps the ethical reminders stood out, calling you back to the principles of non-maleficence, beneficence, and veracity as anchors in the midst of uncertainty. Or perhaps it was the encouragement to listen without judgment that spoke directly to your practice, offering a renewed vision of what empathy truly means. Whatever chapter most resonated with you, that resonance is a clue. It reveals where your professional growth is already stirring. If the cultural dimensions struck you, you may be called to deepen your cultural humility. If the ethical considerations inspired you, you may feel a stronger pull to examine how these principles play out in your day-to-day interactions. If the emphasis on bracketing touched you, you may recognize a need to practice greater intentionality in setting aside biases. Ask yourself: *Which chapter stayed with me after I closed the book? Why did it speak to me? What does this reveal about where I am on my own journey as a counselor or helping professional?*

How has this book reshaped my professional vision? Counseling is not merely a set of techniques; it is a vocation rooted in vision. How we see our role, our clients, and the communities we serve shapes every decision we make. For many, this book may have disrupted the assumption that paranormal experiences are marginal curiosities with little relevance to clinical work. Instead, it has underscored that these experiences are often central to identity, meaning, and healing. Has this book reshaped your vision of counseling? Perhaps you are leaving these pages with a renewed commitment to openness, determined never again to dismiss a client's story too quickly. Perhaps you are embracing humility, recognizing that no single worldview—including your own—can fully encompass the mystery of human experience. Perhaps you are inspired toward advocacy, aware that stigma around anomalous experiences does real harm and must be addressed within professional and academic settings. The reader is encouraged to take time to articulate this reshaped vision. A clear professional vision provides direction and sustains resilience. Ask yourself: *Am I leaving this book with a broader perspective? Do I feel more committed to openness, humility, and advocacy than before?*

What concrete steps will I take? Integration requires action. Perhaps you will begin by initiating discussions with colleagues, revising course syllabi to include anomalous experience, or simply practicing deeper empathy with clients who share these stories. One meaningful exercise is to write your own "professional epitaph" as it relates to this work. Imagine what you would want to write about you as a counselor who worked with clients reporting paranormal experiences. Perhaps it reads: "Here was a counselor who listened without judgment, who honored the mysteries of human experience, and who stood with those who felt unseen." Such an epitaph is not an ending, but a beginning—a vision to live into.

CALL TO ACTION

Knowledge without action risks becoming sterile, and insight without application quickly fades into memory. The true value of this book will not be found in the words themselves but in the ways you, the reader, choose to live out its message. As mental health professionals, educators, and helpers of all kinds, you are entrusted not only with theoretical knowledge but also with the ethical responsibility to put that knowledge into practice. Therefore, this final chapter issues a clear call to action—an invitation to move from understanding to application, from reflection to practice.

Practice with courage. Perhaps the greatest barrier to engaging with clients who report paranormal or anomalous experiences is fear of professional stigma. Many counselors worry that if they take these accounts seriously, they will be viewed by peers as unscientific, gullible, or unprofessional. This fear is not unfounded; stigma around paranormal belief remains strong in both academic and clinical circles. Yet courage is precisely what is needed in these moments. To practice with courage does not mean discarding clinical judgment or abandoning professional standards. Rather, it means being willing to listen, validate, and explore without immediately dismissing or ridiculing. It means setting aside the fear of what colleagues might say and choosing instead to honor the humanity of the client. For the person sitting across from you, the experience they share is not trivial—it may be among the most profound or frightening events of their life. Your openness may, quite literally, be life-changing. Think of the courage it takes for a client to disclose something so vulnerable. When you meet that courage with your own, you create the possibility of deep healing. Courage, then, is not simply a professional virtue but a relational gift you offer to those who entrust you with their stories.

Educate and advocate. Education and advocacy can best be accomplished by the mental health professional by intentionally creating spaces for open dialogue and awareness. By bringing these conversations into supervision groups, professional associations, and training programs, one can help future counselors and mental health professionals feel more comfortable addressing complex or unconventional client experiences. When these topics are discussed within academic, clinical, and professional settings, they begin to lose their stigma and become recognized as legitimate areas of exploration and care. Normalize the discussion within your own circles of influence by modeling curiosity, respect, and inclusivity in how you approach these subjects. By fostering understanding rather than skepticism, you not only contribute to professional growth but also help ensure that clients with diverse or anomalous experiences receive the empathy, validation, and ethical care they deserve.

Model openness and compassion. Whether or not you personally believe in the literal existence of ghosts, UFOs, or apparitions is ultimately irrelevant to your role as a counselor or helping professional. What truly matters is your ability to demonstrate empathy, respect, and nonjudgmental curiosity in every client encounter. Clients who share experiences that fall outside conventional understanding often do so with great vulnerability, and the counselor's response can significantly shape whether they feel validated or dismissed. By maintaining an open, compassionate stance, you create a therapeutic space where clients feel safe to explore the meaning of their experiences, reflect on their emotions, and move toward healing or integration. This approach communicates unconditional positive regard, reinforcing the counselor's commitment to honoring each client's truth while fostering trust and connection within the therapeutic relationship.

Commit to lifelong learning. Commit yourself to lifelong learning, especially within the field of anomalous experience, which continues to evolve as new discoveries, perspectives, and methodologies emerge. Counselors and researchers must remain attentive to the latest empirical findings, theoretical developments, and interdisciplinary collaborations that bridge psychology, neuroscience, spirituality, and cultural studies. Such openness not only enhances professional competence but also deepens the ability to serve clients whose experiences may transcend traditional frameworks of understanding. Staying informed about diverse cultural interpretations and the shifting landscape of paranormal and transpersonal research fosters both humility and adaptability. Above all, lifelong learning invites practitioners to keep their minds as open as their hearts—balancing intellectual curiosity with empathy and blending critical inquiry with compassionate understanding.

CONCLUSION: THE LIVING LEGACY

These four calls—to practice with courage, to educate and advocate, to model openness and compassion, and to commit to lifelong learning—are not optional add-ons to your professional life. They are the natural outflow of the insights you have gained through this book. Taken together, they form a path forward, ensuring that the knowledge you have acquired does not remain sterile but becomes a living force in your practice and in the lives of those you serve. The clients who bring you their most extraordinary stories are not asking you to solve mysteries. They are asking you to honor their humanity, to help them find meaning, and to walk with them through the unknown. When you live out this call to action, you affirm that counseling is not merely about resolving problems but about accompanying people in the deepest questions of what it means to be human. By engaging in this kind of reflection, you position yourself to respond with empathy, humility, and integrity. You become the kind of counselor who not only hears the extraordinary but honors the humanity within it.

The ultimate responsibility of the counselor is not to solve the mystery of anomalous experiences but to honor the mystery of the human experience itself. This means practicing humility, courage, and compassion. It means seeing the person before you as a whole being, worthy of respect, regardless of whether their story fits into scientific explanation or cultural expectation.

Paranormal experiences are not marginal curiosities to be dismissed or mocked. They are part of the tapestry of human life. These are experiences that shape identity, meaning, and community. As counselors, educators, and advocates, our task is to stand with those who share these experiences, offering support, validation, and dignity. Let this be your charge: to listen deeply, to practice ethically, to advocate boldly, and to engage compassionately. In so doing, you will carry forward not only the lessons of this book but also the living legacy of what it means to be human—an essence that shimmers with both the seen and unseen. Within each of us stirs a quiet, supernatural spark, a spiritual echo that reaches beyond reason and into the mystery of existence itself. To embrace this truth is to honor the light that moves through every soul, reminding us that our humanity is not merely a condition of flesh and thought, but a sacred continuum between the earthly and the eternal. How will your professional epitaph be written…?

Personal Reflection Question for Chapter 13

How might embracing the mystery of a client's anomalous or spiritual experience deepen your own understanding of what it means to be human, both as a counselor and as a fellow traveler in life's mysteries?

In what ways can you cultivate humility, courage, and compassion when encountering experiences that challenge your personal beliefs or defy conventional explanation?

Reflect on the "quiet, supernatural spark" within yourself—how does acknowledging this inner light influence the way you listen, validate, and honor the stories of those who seek your care?

Index

For Product Safety Concerns and Information please contact our EU
representative GPSR@taylorandfrancis.com
Taylor & Francis Verlag GmbH, Kaufingerstraße 24, 80331 München, Germany

www.ingramcontent.com/pod-product-compliance
Ingram Content Group UK Ltd.
Pitfield, Milton Keynes, MK11 3LW, UK
UKHW022353190926
475702UK00015B/2263
* 9 7 8 1 0 3 2 8 6 8 3 4 9 *